Eastern Europe 1914-191[7]

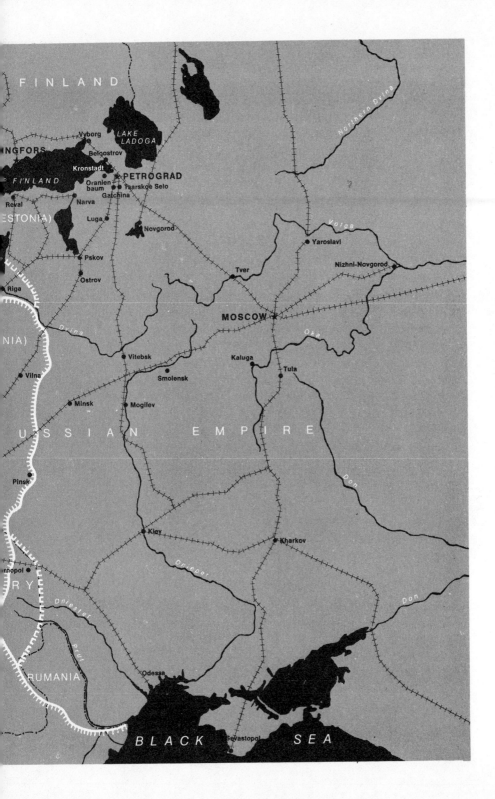

RED OCTOBER

BOOKS BY ROBERT V. DANIELS

Red October

The Bolshevik Revolution of 1917

ROBERT V. DANIELS

BEACON PRESS   BOSTON

Library of Congress Cataloging in Publication Data

Daniels, Robert Vincent.
  Red October.
  Reprint. Originally published: New York:
Scribner's, c1967.
  Bibliography: p.
  Includes index.
  1. Soviet Union—History—Revolution, 1917–1921.
I. Title.
DK265.D27   1984   947.084′1   84–45069
ISBN 0–8070–5645–6 (pbk.)

TO ALICE

Preface

This book is an attempt to describe and explain one of the decisive events of the twentieth century, the seizure of power by the founders of Communism in October, 1917. It is hardly necessary now to argue the historical importance of this "October Revolution," not only for Russia but for practically the whole world—the birth of Communist power and the international Communist movement; the Russian agony of violent self-experiment and terror; the fervent hopes, the frantic hatreds, the bleak disillusionment that the Revolution engendered; the bitter cleavages among and within nations that have proceeded inexorably from those fateful days. Two or three days of fighting, as Lenin predicted, decided the fate of the Russian Revolution, and recast the whole face of world politics.

Behind these events, to be sure, lay all the tumultuous experience of Russia's year of revolution, as well as centuries of oppression under the autocracy of the tsars. This background has been studied and recounted many times, but the immediate events preceding the uprising —the activities of the Bolsheviks in the Russian capital, and the actual history of the October insurrection, have not until recently been approached with the attention to detail that their importance warrants.

I began my own detailed inquiry into these events in 1961, when I was invited to give a paper on the Russian Revolution in a panel on "Communist Seizures of Power" at the annual meeting of the American Historical Association in Washington, D. C. At the time I felt there was nothing new to be said on the subject, but I undertook to restate the familiar story so that the speakers on Czechoslovakia in 1948 and on China in 1949 could compare their topics with mine. I needed, I thought, only to look up a few basic facts—the Bolshevik plan, the meeting when the Bolsheviks set the date for their uprising, etc. But neither the plan nor the setting of the date was easy to find—in fact, the plan never existed and the date was never set. As I pursued these questions, I found more and more puzzles and obscurities in the story of the Bolshevik takeover. Eventually I was forced to restudy the entire history of the Bolshevik Revolution. *Red October* is the result.

My aim in this book is to show how the Bolsheviks seized power. To do this I follow in detail the history of the Bolshevik Party in the revolutionary year 1917, especially its debates and preparations from the summer of 1917 until the capture of the Winter Palace and the overthrow of the Provisional Government. To set events in their historical context I have devoted Chapter One to an introductory discussion of the Russian Revolution and its background, and in Chapter Two I analyze the development and character of the Bolshevik Party. The six chapters following are the main body of the book, recounting chronologically the story of the Bolsheviks' rise to power in the fall of 1917. The two final chapters tell briefly how the Bolsheviks consolidated their victory of October, and appraise the meaning of the revolution in the perspective of half a century.

When *Red October* was originally published in 1967, the fiftieth anniversary of the Revolution, detailed Western study of the event and the forces that led to it was just beginning. Since then an impressive volume of research has appeared on all aspects of the revolutionary process of 1917—on political parties, social movements, the armed forces, various regions of the Empire. The "Study Group on the History of the Russian Revolution" in the United Kingdom has especially stimulated interest in that era. Serious Soviet study of the Revolution, in abeyance since the 1920s, resumed in the mid-1950s, and has resulted in many useful documentary and monographic publications. Nevertheless, the story in *Red October* of what the Bolshevik leadership actually did and did not do in 1917 has been neither refuted nor superseded.

In its original edition *Red October* was sharply criticized by Soviet reviewers, predictably distressed by the theory of accident in the Bolshevik Revolution which runs altogether counter to the Marxist-Leninist view of historical inevitability plus all-seeing leadership. American reviewers, reflecting the new interest in social history, found fault with the book's focus on political events. But as I pointed out in my original preface, my political emphasis did not mean that I denied the significance of social history or developments in the provinces or the debilitating politics of the Provisional Government. My focus was a necessary choice in order to clean up the most obfuscated aspect of the history of the Revolution. The central arguments of *Red October*—that the Bolshevik Revolution lacked a plan, that the violent takeover desired by Lenin was only triggered by accident, and that unplanned violence deeply affected the character of Russia's subsequent history—must still be reckoned with in any attempt to understand how the Revolution happened and what it meant.

The difficulties of establishing the historical truth about the October Revolution are vast. Much documentation is missing; many records were lost—or never kept; and Stalin purged the Soviet archives during the 1930's. Bias is everywhere in the sources and commentaries—Communist and anti-Communist, democratic and monarchist, Stalinist and Trotskyist. Eyewitness observations and recollections of the events, distorted by the confusion and anxiety of the moment, are often unreliable and sometimes contradictory. This is particularly the case with the "siege" of the Winter Palace. There are few real "documents" of the siege, and no photographs at all—only paintings done after the fact under the influence of wrong recollections and political biases. A narative of the October Revolution can only be the most probable reconciliation of the sources; the absolute truth will never be fully known.

The Russian Revolution is one of those complicated and controversial events that puts the historian's art most severely to the test, by accentuating its inherent tension. History aims to be objective and scientific in its aims and standards—to find the truth and explain it, to tell "what really happened," and why. But in its materials and methods history is more like the subjective arts, depending on fallible human observations and recollections, and on each historian's intuitive work of organization, selection, and judgment in accordance with his own perspective and values. Thanks to these limitations, final and complete historical knowledge can never be achieved.

＊ ＊ ＊

In any book on the history of Russia there are certain problems of usage that must be explained at the outset. First, the dates—"old style" and "new style." Until the revolution, Russia was officially on the old Julian Calendar which after 1900 was thirteen days behind the Gregorian Calendar of the West. Hence the revolution of March 12, "new style," was the "February Revolution," on February 27, "old style," and the revolution of November 7 was the "October Revolution," on October 25, as the Russians counted it. Russia shifted to the Western calendar in February, 1918.

Certain place-names in Russia were repeatedly changed. St. Petersburg (colloquially called Petersburg or "Peter") was changed to the more Russian-sounding Petrograd in 1914 and to Leningrad in 1924. In this and other cases I have used the form current in 1917. The same applies to political terminology: up to 1918 the Communists were the "Russian Social Democratic Workers' Party (of Bolsheviks)," and "Bolshevik" was their usual designation during the revolution.

Russian names raise the problem of transliterating from the Russian alphabet. I have used a modification of the Library of Congress system, to avoid phonetic complications and adhere to forms that are already familiar.

There are many individuals and institutions to whom I am indebted for valuable assistance at various stages of my work on this book. I am grateful to the University of Vermont for a sabbatical leave that permitted me to complete the writing of the book and to the Bibliothèque de Documentation Internationale Contemporaine of the University of Paris for the opportunity to research its unsurpassed collection of source materials. I am indebted to the Inter-University Committee on Travel Grants and to the Ministry of Higher Education of the USSR for the opportunity to do research and field study in the Soviet Union in 1966 as a participant in the American-Soviet Cultural Exchange. Many teachers, friends, and colleagues have helped me with their knowledge and suggestions; I would particularly like to mention Michael Karpovich (under whom I was first introduced to the study of the Russian Revolution), Geroid T. Robinson, Harold H. Fisher, Marc Ferro, Georges Haupt, and my colleagues in the Department of History of the University of Vermont. I am also grateful to the numerous Soviet historians and the staff of the Museum of the Revolution in Leningrad who brought to my attention many interesting points of detail.

R. V. D.

Burlington, Vermont
March, 1984

CONTENTS

LIST OF ILLUSTRATIONS

RED OCTOBER

"On s'engage, et puis on voit."
       —NAPOLEON

CHAPTER ONE

The Freest Country in the World

On the eighth of March, 1917, a hundred thousand striking factory workers, men and women, jammed the streets of Petrograd demanding bread and freedom. It was International Women's Day, February 23 in the old calendar. This was the day that marked the beginning of the February Revolution, the downfall of the Russian Emperor, and a train of consequences that has affected the life and destiny of the entire modern world. The next day and the day after, despite the absence of plan or leaders, the demonstrations snowballed. Crowds of workers surged across the ice on the Neva and into the center of the city. The Tsar's police could not contain the demonstrators, and the soldiers of the garrison had to be called out as the workers offered themselves to be shot at.

A government that cannot or will not shoot at the point of this ultimate test is finished. It was Saturday, February 25, old style, when Tsar Nikolai II decided that the situation had gotten out of hand, and from his military headquarters at Mogilev, on the central battle front, wired the Petrograd commander General Khabalov, "I command you to put an end as of tomorrow to all disorders in the streets of the capital." Khabalov ordered his troops to disperse the crowds and to shoot when necessary.

The next day, Sunday the 26th, several units opened fire on the crowds, and scores of demonstrators were killed, but at this point the troops rebelled at the further prospect of cutting down their own compatriots. The trouble started in the Pavlov Reserve Guards Regiment, quartered in their impressive colonnaded barracks on the Field of Mars. "At 3 P.M.," the troops reported to their counterpart unit at the front, "the fourth company, aroused by the government's harsh treatment of the people, in a noble burst of indignation, rushed almost unarmed in a spontaneous avalanche onto the streets of the capital, to die for the great cause of the people's freedom." Actually they were only arrested, but during the night another regiment, the Volynsky, reached the point of mutiny; the next morning someone shot one of their officers, and there was no turning back. The soldiers of the unit rushed to the other barracks to call the men to join the demonstrators. In a matter of hours virtually the entire garrison had merged with the mobs, and the populace went wild. Jails, courts, police stations—all the physical symbols of the old oppression—were invaded and burned. In the twenty-third year of his reign, the authority of Nikolai Romanov, Emperor of All the Russias, ceased to exist.

❖   ❖   ❖

The fall of the Tsar released all the strangled hopes and compressed rage that had eternally choked the Russian nation. Every sort of political and social question rose to demand an answer. Profound processes of emotional mobilization and social conflict began among the people of Russia, freed for the first time in their history from the heavy hand of imperial authority. The February Revolution had given them the chance or the hope of resolving all their grievances by democracy if possible and by force if necessary. February had released a tide of revolutionary emotion that reached its crest with the fateful climax of Red October.

Very little real power was salvaged by the Provisional Government, the self-appointed cabinet of well-meaning but conservative politicians who nominally succeeded the Tsar. Instead, power cascaded down like water from a broken dam, to every town and province, to every village and regiment, to every mob and every committee that would receive it. Hungry, clumsy, war-weary Russia became, as even Vladimir Ilyich Lenin acknowledged it, "the freest country in the world."

4

The Russian people were quick to show that no long tutelage is needed to make a nation understand democracy. They threw themselves into a veritable orgy of democracy, carrying it far beyond their Western mentors into practically every area of life. For politics they had their councils—the soviets—in every town and soon in every village. The rebellion against the old authoritarianism extended also into economic life and into the army. In the spirit of "Order Number One" proclaimed by the Petrograd Soviet, the soldiers elected committees to control their officers and defied any discipline that displeased them. Factory workers elected their "fabzavkomy"—factory and plant committees—and began to press toward the ideal of "workers' control of industry." The non-Russian minorities—Finns, Ukrainians, and many others—long victimized by the Russification policies of tsarism, began to claim the right of self-determination. Finally the great peasant mass began to stir with its own instinctive democracy—the democracy of the torch and the scythe that banished or killed the landlord and took his land for the tillers.

❁　❁　❁

None of Russia's political leaders, conservative or revolutionary, were prepared for the event of the February Revolution of 1917, but they were quick to improvise their respective answers to it. The well-intentioned leaders of the old Duma, representing the comfortable property-owners of Russia, joined the revolution with the hope of keeping it in the orderly channel of a constitutional monarchy. Since the Duma had just been officially dissolved, they met on the afternoon of the 27th as a "Temporary Committee" to maintain order and persuade the Tsar to abdicate in favor of his son.

Simultaneously the left wing of the revolution, represented by the handful of socialist Duma deputies and a number of Petrograd labor leaders, proclaimed themselves a "Temporary Executive Committee of the Petrograd Soviet of Workers' Deputies" and summoned the factories to elect deputies to a new soviet—Russian for "council"—on the model of the St. Petersburg Soviet of 1905. That very evening the soviet convened, in the Duma chamber in the Tauride Palace, a magnificent structure in the eastern quarter of Petrograd (originally built by Catherine the Great for her lover Potëmkin). The two hundred-odd deputies voted to make the Executive Committee a permanent body, and chose as their chairman one of the cautious Marxists of the Menshevik faction of Social Democrats, Nikolai Chkheidze, a Georgian who had come from the Caucasus to win his political spurs in the small Socialist contingent of the Duma. The members of the Petrograd Soviet, as of the similar councils that sprang up all over the country, were mostly Mensheviks or members of the peasant-oriented Party of Socialist Revolutionaries ("SRs"). Only a few among them belonged to the group of radical Marxists, the Bolsheviks, whose prospects for making themselves masters of the country at first seemed remote indeed.

The prospective competition of the soviet and the bloodless spread of the revolution to Moscow and other centers hastened the decision of the Duma Committee to form a new government without waiting to settle the future of Nikolai II and the monarchy. The Committee appointed men to oversee the government ministries and began to negotiate with the Executive Committee of the soviet about the composition of a provisional cabinet. The soviet, for its part, was turning to the army; the Executive Committee invited the regiments of the Petrograd garrison to send deputies to a "Soldiers' Section" of the soviet and insisted that any new government promise not to transfer the revolutionary troops out of the city.

Representatives of the soldiers crowded into the Tauride Palace the evening of March 1 to help compose a statement of their demands. As published the next day by Bonch-Bruevich, the Bolshevik editor of the soviet's new newspaper *Izvestiya* (*The News*), this "Order Number One" became a charter of revolution in the army—no more deference to rank off duty, elected committees to issue the arms and supervise the officers in each unit, authority for the soviet to cancel orders of the government. The foundation was being quickly laid for the "dual power" that plagued the Provisional Government throughout its history.

On March 2 the Duma Committee and the Petrograd Soviet announced the provisional cabinet, after the soviet leaders expressed their reluctance to take part personally in a supposedly "bourgeois" government. The Prime Minister was a liberal but ineffective nobleman, Prince Georgi Lvov, head of the union of provincial councils. Professor Pavel Milyukov, eminent historian and leader of the Constitutional Democratic Party ("Kadets" for short), was the Foreign Minister and strong man of this first provisional cabinet. Alexander Guchkov, chairman of the War Industries Committee, took the post of Minister of War. Mikhail Tereshchenko, a beet-sugar magnate from the Ukraine, became Finance Minister. Alexander Konovalov, a munitions maker, received the portfolio of Trade and Industry. The cabinet was leavened with one representative of "the democracy"—a thirty-five year old Petrograd lawyer and Duma deputy by the name of Alexander Kerensky, Minister of Justice. The soviet promised to support this government "insofar as" it did not violate the hopes of the revolution—a rather skeptical endorsement.

Late that night, on his private train in the town of Pskov, Tsar Nikolai was finally prevailed upon by the new government's representatives and his own generals to abdicate his throne, but he surprised the whole entourage by stepping aside in favor of his brother, Grand Duke Mikhail, instead of his son. Mikhail was forthwith visited by a delegation from the Provisional Government, openly divided between Milyukov's monarchism and Kerensky's republicanism. Under the circumstances the Grand Duke decided to refuse the throne and declared it vacant. So perished the Russian monarchy, for lack of takers.

*　*　*

The Russian Revolution of February, 1917, had been consciously awaited longer than any other in history. For a hundred years before, the Tsar's police state was the target of conspiracy and agitation, of plots and assassinations. From the time of the abortive "Decembrist" uprising of liberal officers in 1825 the socially-conscious best of Russia's educated class was attracted to the cause of revolutionary opposition, and the boldest among them periodically sacrificed themselves in the little organizations of the revolutionary underground. A tradition was established of terroristic conspiracy by dedicated and disciplined intellectuals who would seize power in the name of the masses. But not even the murder of the Emperor—it was, most ironically, the reforming Tsar Alexander II who was killed by the "People's Will" organization in 1881—could shake the power of the Russian autocracy until the stirrings of industrialization and modernization began to reshape the fabric of Russian society. Finally, in the 1890's, after generations of crying in the wilderness, the revolutionaries began to get a response from the masses. The reason was simple: Russia was experiencing all the change, dislocation, hope and frustration of the early industrial revolution. This, and not overripe capitalism, seems to be the stage at which any country is most vulnerable to a movement of revolutionary socialism. The intelligentsia was alienated both from the rulers of the old order and the builders of the new. The working class in the new industrial agglomerations was raw, ill-treated, and volatile. The peasants were poor, backward, and land-hungry; they were beginning to feel the whip of commercialization at the same time that their young men were learning to read the pamphlets of the revolutionaries.

There was a party and a philosophy for each awakening social class. The business class and many professionals were attracted by the advocates of Western liberalism, who created the Constitutional Democratic Party in 1905. The rapidly growing working class responded to the Marxists, who, inspired by their *émigré* mentor Georgi Plekhanov, founded the Russian Social Democratic Workers Party in 1898. The peasants—scarcely a generation out of serfdom—rallied to one or another of the groups representing the native Russian socialist tradition of "Populism," especially the Party of Socialist Revolutionaries organized in 1900. Besides all these there was a vigorous current of anarchism among the spiritual heirs of Mikhail Bakunin who repudiated all forms of constituted authority; this attitude was particularly strong among the sailors of the Imperial Navy.

In the year 1905, when defeat in the Far East by the Empire of the Rising Sun had thrown the regime of Tsar Nikolai II temporarily off balance, all these aggrieved social forces combined in a spontaneous outburst of revolutionary protest, the so-called Revolution of 1905. Actually this movement never came near to overthrowing the government, but at least it wrung from the authorities a significant concession—the granting of a constitution and the creation of a representative legislative body of limited powers, the Duma. Neither Lenin nor any of his Bolsheviks played any leading part in these events, but there was one future Bolshevik who made his reputation as the chief leader of the St. Petersburg Soviet of Workers' Deputies—a brilliant twenty-six-year-old Menshevik orator named Leon Trotsky.

There has been much speculation that the political gains of 1905 might have served as the foundation for Russia to evolve gradually into a modern democracy. But progress in this direction was quickly checked by the Tsar's ministers, who reduced the Duma to an impotent and largely conservative sounding board. The government became the plaything of a series of increasingly reactionary and incompetent bureaucrats, under the influence of the hysterical Empress Alexandra and the sinister faith healer Rasputin. With this sickness at the top and the strains of a half-developed society below, the Imperial Russian government let its imperialist aspirations in the Balkans draw it into the holocaust of the First World War.

Russia was economically and logistically unprepared for a long war, though numbers alone—some fifteen million men were mobilized— might make the Tsar's army overwhelming. Germany crushed the Russians' 1914 offensive at the battle of Tannenberg and struck back in 1915 to drive the Russians out of Russian Poland and part of the Baltic provinces in a series of bloody battles. Russian successes against the Austrians and Turks were not enough to redress the balance. Russian morale sagged, the railroad system faltered, and the enemy blockade cut off vital imports. Deficits mounted because wartime prohibition eliminated the vodka revenues. Agriculture slipped back because too many peasant men were drafted, and the cities began to get hungry. Surplus soldiers in reserve regiments were crowded into city barracks, where their morale atrophied. The Tsar went to the front to take personal command of the army, with the only effect that his wife and ministers were the less inclined to heed the advice or take the help of the nation's moderate elements.

By the end of 1916 the whole nation was sunk again in the desperate frustrated feeling that had foreshadowed revolution in 1905, and the assassination of Rasputin by a conspiracy of patriotic nobles did little to restore confidence in the government. In retrospect, it is easy to see that Russia was ripe for revolt, though no one realized it at the time, not even the Bolsheviks. Lenin, spinning theories of world revolution against imperialism while he fretted in his Swiss exile, said as late as January, 1917, "We of the older generation may not live to see the decisive battles of this revolution."

*   *   *

The mounting series of revolutionary crises that convulsed Russia in 1917 was not altogether unique. With the fall of the Tsar the country had entered upon the tumultuous and irresistible process of a great social revolution, distinguished by the breakdown of most institutions of authority and property such as occurred in the English Revolution of the seventeenth century and the French Revolution of the eighteenth. In each case long pent-up grievances, frustrations, and social conflicts were released when the old authority faltered at a moment of military or financial embarrassment. The ensuing strife shredded what remained of the social order, until at a point of near-anarchy some party appeared with the will and the way to begin rebuilding a new and more modern authority. Each revolution saw a series of more and more radical leaders or governments attempt to install their philosophy, culminating in a dictatorship of revolutionary fanatics more oppressive and bloody than anything the old regime had perpetrated. Ultimately such extremism could not be sustained, and yielded to some more pragmatic form of rule, of the Left or of the Right, utilizing the foundations of new authority laid by the terrorists themselves. In their particular policies and consequences these revolutions diverged according to the circumstances of time, place, and leadership, but the process and problems of breakdown, social struggle, and rebuilding are essentially common to all of them. In this perspective it is hardly surprising that Russian society in 1917 yielded to galloping chaos and violent political struggle, even if the ultimate victor was not foreordained.

All of Russia's moderate men were fearful of the forces that the revolution had unleashed. They feared the disintegration of the army that might open the front to the German enemy before an honorable and democratic peace could be negotiated. They feared the breakdown of respect for public order that might invite popular indulgence in "pogroms" of all sorts. They strove with much delay and dissension to work out the fundamentals of a new era of freedom with order, which absorbed their energies so much that they could not come to grips with the country's pressing problems. Wordy inadequacy in the face of unprecedented events was the sad story of the Provisional Government. Issues and movements unfolded that moderate legalism and even socialistic goodwill were impotent to handle.

Most active and articulate of the forces challenging the February leadership were the industrial workers, particularly the workers of Petrograd, no less radical because the wages of war industry had made them relatively well off. The national minorities were not far behind, with their growing defiance of the authority of the government in Petrograd. The great reserve force of the revolution was the peasantry, eagerly eyeing the land that remained in landlords' estates. Finally the crucial issue and the decisive force that spelled the undoing of the Provisional Government were the war and the army respectively. Notably absent from the ranks of extremism, despite their revolutionary traditions, were the students and the intellectuals, except for some whose main specialty was political oratory. Even the revolutionary novelist Maxim Gorky went no further than the Mensheviks.

The industrial workers of Petrograd—in the arms and machine plants along the lesser Neva in the "Vyborg" district (named after the city then part of Finland, not to be confused with it); in the shipyards like the great Franco-Russian Yard; in the vast Putilov works that turned out most of Russia's railroad rolling stock—the industrial workers were one group under considerable Bolshevik influence since before the war. They answered to all the classic requirements of the revolutionary proletariat—energetic, literate, disciplined, class-conscious. Time and again they had gone on strike during the war years, and the February Revolution was initially their doing. Their instincts were profoundly socialistic and collectivist, and they were ready to strike and fight again at a moment's notice to defend what the revolution had won and move ahead to the goal of workers' control of industry. They were a very different species from the working class of the rest of Russia, which was marked still by peasant crudeness. Even the Moscow worker was much less westernized and sophisticated.

Exceptional as they were in the vast human sea of Russia, the Petrograd workers played a decisive role in the flow of events because they were the strongest social force in the deciding center of the country, the capital city. From the start, they were the mainstay of the Petrograd Soviet, where at first they gave the Mensheviks a strong lead. The shooting was hardly over in February when they began organizing their workers' militia, a sort of police, followed in April by the creation of "Red Guard" units, who drilled after working hours. As the months passed, the mood of the Petrograd workers became increasingly radical. By summer they were sending a Bolshevik majority to their section of the Petrograd Soviet. They gave the Bolsheviks control of the Factory Committees. The Vyborg section became practically an autonomous Bolshevik commune. Strikes mounted in number and magnitude, with an increasingly political direction. Frustrated in their anti-capitalist aims and fearful of counterrevolution, the workers by fall were ready to go wherever their Bolshevik leaders pointed, the most militant with arms in their hands.

The revolutionary movement of democratic decentralization, when it reached the non-Russian areas of the Empire, immediately called into question the future unity of the Russian state. The conservatives in the Provisional Government held to the tradition of centralism, though they could hardly enforce it. The moderate socialists believed in federalism, while Lenin had boldly promised self-determination and independence to any nationality that wanted it. The Finns, who had enjoyed their separate law and parliamentry insitutions ever since Russia took the country from Sweden in 1809, were operating virtually as an independent republic by the middle of 1917. The most revolutionary force in Finland was the Russian garrison and the Baltic Fleet based on Helsingfors, which were to loom large as strategic support for the Bolsheviks in the fall. The most nationalistic region of all, Russian Poland, was entirely under German occupation in 1917, and hence no more than a theoretical issue. Less traditionally defined, and therefore more controversial, was the autonomist movement in the Ukraine, an area vital to the Russian economy. The Ukrainian nationalists set up a Central "Rada" (Council) in Kiev and assumed what amounted to powers of home rule. Later on in the year, autonomist stirrings began to be felt among the peoples of the Caucasus and even among the Moslem Tatars. The Empire, in its new freedom, was disintegrating.

To the peasants of Russia, the fall of the Tsar heralded the long-awaited day when the land would be theirs. Actually a good deal of the land was theirs already; at the time of their emancipation from outright serfdom in 1861, and by purchase thereafter, peasants had acquired about 85 per cent of the tillable land of the country. The remaining estates were still a temptation, however, especially in the provinces centering around Moscow where the peasants were poorer and had less land. Throughout European Russia rural population growth ran ahead of land acquisition, and the peasants' perennial land hunger remained unabated, even though the expropriation of the landlords would be an illusory solution.

The Provisional Government promised justice to the tillers of the soil and began work on a thorough-going land reform law. But on this question as on the other vital issues, the moderate politicians were reluctant to take binding action until another promise had been realized first—the election and convocation of a Constituent Assembly to write a formal constitution for the New Russia. Work began on an electoral law to give the country the first genuinely democratic choice in its history, but the election had not yet been held, and the land had not been released, when the whole moderate experiment was overturned by the exponents of a violent solution. The peasants, in fact, did not wait for the Bolshevik signal; by the summer, and especially after they completed the harvest in September, they began to put land reforms into effect by their own direct action. Their erstwhile leaders, the Party of Socialist Revolutionaries, decent men opposed to any violence except that directed against tsarism or Germany, were left behind, except for the rapidly growing left-wing faction that finally broke away as the Party of Left SRs on the eve of the October Revolution. By this time, rural Russia was in the throes of a rapidly spreading revolt and could give the Provisional Government no basis of support in its last days of agony.

The more direct role of the peasantry in the revolution was played by the peasants who made up the bulk of the army. Catalyzed by the February events in Petrograd, the multi-million man army, all up and down the front and in every provincial garrison, was permeated more profoundly than any other social group with the spirit of social revolution. The entire system of conventional military authority was repudiated as soon as the ultimate authority of the Tsar and the death penalty for disobedience were removed. The troops elected committees at every level of the military hierarchy, debated their orders, lynched unpopular officers, and fraternized with the enemy. In growing numbers they began to desert, to return to their villages to put in their claims for land seized from the landlords. The ties of the army and the soviets were often close; the troops in the garrison towns usually elected delegates to the local soviets along with the workers. The Petrograd Soviet (followed by the Central Executive Committee) dispatched political representatives to each regiment in the city and later on to each army group at the front. The name of these representatives was borrowed from revolutionary France—commissars. Through the commissars the soviet had considerably more military authority than the government or the regular military chain of command through General Headquarters at Mogilev on the Central Front. In Petrograd, crammed with reserve regiments who had been temporarily promised that they would not be transferred to the front, the loyalty of the troops to the soviet soon became almost unconditional.

Fortunately for revolutionary Russia the war on the Eastern Front in 1917 was practically dormant most of the time. The German General Staff preferred to withhold military pressure and let the political ferment of revolution corrode their adversary from within. To this end they did whatever they could to facilitate revolutionary agitation in Russia, from permitting *émigré* revolutionaries such as Lenin to pass back through German territory, to scattering considerable sums of money where it might advantage extremist groups in Russia. The Russians had time to debate the whole issue of war and peace without an immediate crisis on the battlefield.

At the outset of the Provisional Government the war was already a divisive question, and it turned Russians more bitterly against each other than any other single issue. When the Tsar went to war in 1914 the majority of the socialist leaders were opposed, but after the Tsar gave way to the incipient democracy most of the socialists reasoned that Russia must henceforth be defended, until the conclusion of a "democratic peace without annexations and without indemnities." This stance was challenged on both sides. It was resisted by the conservatives in control of the Provisional Government, who wanted to fight loyally with Russia's allies until Germany was crushed and Russia got the Turkish Straits, as promised in the secret treaties of 1915. On the other side there were a few Bolsheviks, and more after Lenin returned, who denounced the war in any guise as an imperialist crime as long as it was waged by a "bourgeois" government.

During the short life-span of the Provisional Government one political crisis followed another, as the country's pent-up tensions came to a head and the radical spirit of the populace mounted. Sharper voices rang out from the old-line leaders of the various socialist parties who swarmed back to Petrograd like homing bees from Siberia and abroad. At the end of April the nominal government had to be broadened to include the leaders of the Petrograd Soviet. They stepped in to share the powers and problems of the administration, at the risk of losing their popular support to the call of revolutionaries less constrained by belief in orderly legality.

Meanwhile the soviets were evolving an organization that made them much more nearly a national popular government than the actual cabinet, though they represented only the workers and the army. Each local soviet elected an Executive Committee to handle its day-to-day business. Peasant soviets began to extend the council idea to the rural areas. To supplement the symbolic leadership of the Petrograd Soviet, an All-Russian Congress of Soviets convened in Petrograd early in June, in the eighteenth-century Menshikov Palace on Vasilevsky Island. Numbering over a thousand delegates from the various local soviets, the Congress gave added authority to the Petrograd socialist leaders by sanctioning the formation of an "All-Russian Central Executive Committee of Soviets" and electing them to serve in it under the chairmanship of the Menshevik Fyodor Dan. Shortly afterwards a Congress of Peasant Soviets created a similar structure headed by the SR Avksentiev.

Despite all their apparatus of popular endorsement, the leaders of the soviets soon began to be overtaken by the tides of social revolution. The soviet structure had become a clumsy tangle of committee democracy, and it was easy to postpone unpleasant problems for more authoritative gatherings. The closer the moderate socialists of the soviets drew to the seats of power, the more cautious they became, lest the fragile unity of revolutionary Russia be broken. No one in authority was prepared to do what the nation needed or demanded—above all, decree the land to the peasants and end the war. In the face of such issues, revolutionary unity was a short-lived dream.

*   *   *

The date when revolutionary unity ended is easy to define—it was the third of April, the day (or evening) when Lenin arrived at the Finland Station after his memorable train trip from Switzerland across Germany in the so-called "sealed car." As befitted a celebrated revolutionary, like Plekhanov when he returned a week before, Lenin was met by a great crowd of workers and soldiers, and politicians of all the parties in the Petrograd Soviet. Alexander Shlyapnikov, who headed the Bolshevik welcoming committee, recalled the scene in his memoirs: "On the station platform sailors, workers' militia, and a group of Red Guards were drawn up in ranks. A band played the 'Marseillaise,' which was then in fashion." Alexandra Kollontai, the Bolsheviks' petite but flaming feminist, thrust a bouquet of flowers into Lenin's arms. Chkheidze delivered the soviet's official welcome in the name of the unity of the whole democracy. Lenin ignored this gesture, ridded himself of the bouquet, and climbed up on an armored car in front of the station to speak his fiery greetings to "the vanguard of the world proletarian army." He can still be seen there, in bronze, standing on a bronze turret with one hand characteristically grasping his overcoat lapel and the other extended to summon his listeners to civil combat.

From the station Lenin was paraded by his followers across the Sampsonievsky bridge over the lesser Neva to the island known as the "Petrograd Side," where the Bolsheviks had planted their headquarters in the mansion of the Tsar's ballerina. There was tea and *zakuski*—snacks—for all the party faithful, and then Lenin made a formal address. "I shall never forget that thunder-like speech," wrote the Menshevik journalist Sukhanov, "which startled and amazed not only me, a heretic who had accidentally dropped in, but all the true believers." Lenin spoke with singular power and impact, to drive his points home without reservation. The convictions he had brought from Switzerland and now proposed to make the guidelines for his party were startling in their uncompromising clarity: the real revolution had not begun; Down with the bourgeois imperialist Provisional Government! All power to the soviets! Long live the world revolution! These were the celebrated April Theses, that served as the guiding directives for the Bolshevik Party until it was itself ensconced in the seats of power.

There was no recorded text of this speech or the follow-up that Lenin delivered at the Tauride Palace the next day, but he put the substance of them into print in the Bolshevik official organ *Pravda* a few days later. First of all he condemned continuation of the war, at least under Provisional Government auspices. This was his most popular line of propaganda, and one with which practically no one in the other parties, government or soviet, was prepared to compete. Secondly Lenin announced, to the particular dismay of the Mensheviks, that the time was already ripe to overthrow the power of the bourgeoisie, as he characterized the Provisional Government, and "place the power in the hands of the proletariat and the poorest peasantry," i.e., the soviets. For his Bolshevik Party Lenin spoke only of an oppositionist role for the time being, to explain to the masses the "errors" of the soviet leaders who persisted in backing the Provisional Government. But it soon became clear that if no one else would join in a second revolution, Lenin was prepared to go it alone. At the Congress of Soviets in June the great Menshevik orator Tsereteli declared that there was no party prepared to assume the responsibilities of government all by itself. To this Lenin boldly replied, "There is such a party!"

CHAPTER TWO

The Professional Revolutionaries

THE Russian Social Democratic Workers Party (of Bolsheviks) had never known any leader but Lenin. It was his personal political creation, starting as a devoted little group of twenty-two Russian *émigrés* (counting Lenin, his wife, and his sister) who met in Geneva in 1904. Their aim was to keep alive his side of the controversy that had split the Russian Marxist movement the year before.

The Congress of the Russian Social Democrats, convened in Brussels in July, 1903, but soon forced to move to the freer atmosphere of London, was the first real assembly of the leaders of the movement, though the designation of First Congress goes to the meeting in Minsk in 1898 that officially founded the party. True to the traditions of Russian revolutionary politics, the movement split irreparably, first between the orthodox class-struggle Marxists and the "Economist" followers of Eduard Bernstein, the German "revisionist" who anticipated gradual and peaceful progress toward socialism. On top of this the orthodox Marxists split between the supporters of Lenin and the followers of Julius Martov, the most articulate Russian exponent of ideal democratic socialism. Lenin had been adroit enough to seize the label "Bolsheviks"—"Majority men"—for his faction, even though he won only one of the numerous votes that turned around the "hard" political philosophy that he represented. The others, the democratic Marxists, got the unexciting label "Mensheviks"—"men of the minority"—though they included Plekhanov and his older colleagues, and outnumbered the Leninists until 1917. Ostensibly the issue was only the definition of party membership—whether the whole body of like-minded followers, in the Western democratic custom, or an inner core of active party workers, on the lines of the Russian conspiratorial organizations that Lenin admired so much. Behind this disagreement lay fundamental philosophical assumptions about the nature of a political party, the relation of the party's leaders to their followers, the role of the party in revolution, the nature of history itself.

Lenin had worked out his personal version of Marxist revolutionary philosophy between 1897 and 1900 while serving a sentence of Siberian exile for his revolutionary agitation among the St. Petersburg workers. In 1902, soon after he had left Russia for Western Europe, he published his propositions in the celebrated book, *What Is To Be Done?* Like practically everything Lenin ever said or wrote, the book was couched in the form of a polemic—in this case against the "Economists" because they put the economic progress of the workers ahead of political revolution. "The history of all countries," Lenin insisted, "shows that the working class, exclusively by its own effort, is able to develop only trade union consciousness." What would make them revolutionary, then? "Socialist ideology" and "class political consciousness" that could be "brought to the workers *only from without,* that is, from outside of the economic struggle." By whom? By the Social Democratic Party, and more specifically, "a small compact core of the most reliable, experienced and hardened activists . . . , an organization . . . chiefly of people professionally engaged in revolutionary activity."

Unlike the Mensheviks, who kept to the Marxist doctrine that a bourgeois revolution and capitalism had to precede the proletarian revolution, Lenin took the position that the Russian middle class was too cowardly to revolt, and that the proletariat—led by Lenin—should seize power directly and rule with the peasantry as its "allies." But this revolution would never occur of its own accord. Contrary to Marx, and more in keeping with the tradition of Russian revolutionary conspiracy, Lenin insisted that the proletarian revolution had to be accomplished by the deliberate action of a tightly organized conspiratorial party. He did not trust spontaneous mass movements, and at several crucial moments—in 1905 and in July, 1917—opposed the "adventurism" of Bolsheviks who wanted to exploit a popular outburst. In the fall of 1917, when it seemed as though the proletarian revolution might roll to victory almost as spontaneously as the bourgeois revolution of February, Lenin was beside himself. He was desperate then to demand that his party impose itself by force, to prove its own necessity and keep alive for himself the chance of ruling alone.

The formula Lenin adopted for his philosophy of the party organization was "democratic centralism," which he defined as "freedom of criticism, complete and everywhere, as long as this does not disrupt the unity of action already decided upon." The Central Committee of the party, elected by the party congresses every year or two, would have absolute decision-making power in the interim. In practice, however, when the Central Committee went against Lenin's will, all the rules were suspended. "For God's sake, don't trust the Mensheviks and the Central Committee," Lenin wrote to one of his followers early in 1905, "and everywhere, unconditionally, and in the most determined way, force splits, splits, and more splits."

Between Lenin and the Mensheviks the basic difference was more temperamental than doctrinal. The Mensheviks, like many earlier critics of Russian injustice, were idealists driven by sympathy for the masses but disinclined to conspire and fight; they admired Western democratic socialism and hoped for a peaceful and legal path to social reform once the Russian autocracy was overthrown. They were appalled by Lenin's elastic political morality and the philosophy they termed "dictatorship over the proletariat."

It is impossible to escape the very strong suspicion that Lenin's deepest motive was the drive for personal power, however he might have rationalized it. Like practically every politician Lenin had a philosophy about the welfare of the people—in his case it was the entire world proletariat—but the philosophy also said or implied that power for him and him alone was the only way this goal could be achieved. Lenin had an inordinate dislike of any sort of political cooperation or compromise, not because it might fail, but because it might succeed, and leave him with less than the whole loaf of power. He never worked honestly under or alongside anyone else, but only as the sole and unquestioned leader of his own forces, even if they had to be whittled down to meet his conditions. He was fascinated by armed force, and did not believe that any revolution worthy of the name could come about without it. "Major questions in the life of nations are settled only by force," he wrote when he was a spectator to the Revolution of 1905. "The bayonet has really become the main point on the political agenda . . . , insurrection has proved to be imperative and urgent—constitutional illusions and school exercises in parliamentarism become only a screen for the bourgeois betrayal of the revolution. . . . It is therefore the slogan of the dictatorship of the proletariat that the genuinely revolutionary class must advance."

Many attempts, none very successful, have been made to explain Lenin's psychology. His childhood environment and youthful experiences, hardly exceptional for a family of the nineteenth-century Russian intelligentsia, offer only the sketchiest explanations of the demon that soon came to possess him. He was born in 1870 to a family of the lesser nobility—to be sure, the principal seedbed of the Russian revolutionary movement. His father, Ilya Ulyanov, was the Superintendent of Schools in the Volga city of Simbirsk, also the hometown, interestingly enough, of Alexander Kerensky. Lenin had some traumatic experiences —the untimely death of the father he esteemed; the execution of his older brother Alexander for complicity in an attempt on Tsar Alexander III; and his own expulsion from Kazan University because of a student demonstration. But the most abnormal thing about Lenin was his lack of abnormality among the typically eccentric and extremist Russians. He combined his natural brilliance and energy with an utterly un-Russian rigor and self-discipline which gave him an untold advantage in every political confrontation of his career. "Lenin is sheer intellect—he is absorbed, cold, unattractive, impatient at interruption," wrote John Reed's wife when she met the Bolshevik chief just after the Revolution. In another society Lenin would have risen to Grand Vizier or Corporation Counsel. In fact he did start a legal career in St. Petersburg, in 1893, before the encounter with a circle of Marxist agitators including his future wife Nadezhda Krupskaya finally committed him to the Marxist revolutionary movement.

Most people were either repelled or spellbound by Lenin. He was endowed with an extraordinary force of personality, along with an unbelievably vituperative vocabulary, that made most mortals helpless to oppose him within his own camp—they yielded or left. His extremism attracted many revolutionary romantics of independent mind but none of them were at ease in what Trotsky once called the "barrack regime" of the Bolshevik Party. Lenin hated liberalism and softness and the "circle spirit" of impractical discussion. "Nothing was so repugnant to Lenin," Trotsky recalled, "as the slightest suspicion of sentimentality and psychological weakness." Lenin hated the "spontaneity" of social movements without conscious leadership, and he hated the "opportunism" and "tail-end-ism" of people who went along with such movements. His life was consumed with hatred, and hatred of his rivals for the future of Russia almost more than the old regime. He wrote scarcely anything that was not aimed immediately to abuse an opponent, and usually a democratic and socialist opponent at that.

It is something of a puzzle that young Russian revolutionaries like Lenin embraced the philosophy of Marxism. Literally interpreted, Marx's doctrine of the change of society by deep-seated economic forces held out for an underdeveloped country such as Russia only the prospect of capitalism and middle-class rule for generations—the last thing that the radical intelligentsia wanted. Nor did they plump for Marxism for lack of an alternative philosophy, for the Russian revolutionaries since the 1850's had worked out a substantial body of socialist doctrine—"Populism," it was later termed—based on revolution by the peasants under the direction of the intelligentsia. The conspiratorial methods which so attracted the Russian extremists were an integral part of the Populist philosophy, whereas they were quite foreign to Western Marxism. In short, Marxism did not fit either the way the Russian revolutionaries wanted to work or the goals they wanted to work for, yet they flocked to its banner in ever-increasing numbers. They seem to have been attracted to Marxism because it gave them the secure sense of scientific inevitability and more especially because it stressed the role of the people who were obviously becoming the most vigorous, if small, revolutionary force in Russia, the industrial workers in the big cities.

*   *   *

In 1905 Lenin had to endure the frustration of a Russian Revolution that began without him and eluded his influence until it had run its course. The man of the year, both as leader in the events and Marxist interpreter of their meaning, was Trotsky. Nine years younger than Lenin—he was only twenty-six when he led the St. Petersburg Soviet—and a much more brilliant speaker and creative thinker, Trotsky is the one man in the history of the Bolshevik Revolution whose stature approaches that of Lenin himself.

Trotsky, born Lev Davydovich Bronstein, was the son of an illiterate but prosperous Jewish farmer—a "kulak"—in the southern Ukraine. Secondary school in Odessa and the relatives with whom he lived there gave him the background of a typical Russian intellectual. But his university was the revolutionary underground and the Tsar's prisons, where he was confirmed in the Marxist faith. He was a gifted writer and talker from boyhood, and as soon as he escaped abroad, he became a leading spokesman of Russian Social Democracy. He argued brilliantly for the Menshevik view at the 1903 Congress and in the polemics that followed. In his Van Dyke and pince-nez Trotsky always looked slightly sinister, and his abrasive temperament made it hard for him to work with equals both before and after the revolution. But his lifelong reputation was assured when he returned to Russia in 1905 and became vice-chairman and real leader of the St. Petersburg Soviet. Jail was his reward again, after Prime Minister Count Witte appeased the liberals with the constitution and cracked down on the socialists. But like countless Russian revolutionaries, Trotsky profited from the relative comfort of the Tsar's prisons to work out his theory of revolution.

The book Trotsky wrote in 1906, called *Results and Prospects,* was exceedingly important in the thinking of the Bolsheviks a decade later. It was the one sophisticated attempt to square Marxist theory with the aim of immediate proletarian revolution in Russia, and explicitly or implicitly it gave Lenin and his most ardent followers the theoretical rationale they needed to call for insurrection in 1917. Trotsky's idea, somewhat confusingly called the "theory of permanent revolution," was this: The Russian Revolution, when it resumed, could not rest at the "bourgeois" stage as most of the Mensheviks preferred to believe. The working class, strong and militant in the key cities, could not be prevented from taking over temporarily, and thus the revolutionary situation would be continuous or "permanent" while the bourgeois phase gave way to the proletarian. But with most of Russia a nation of backward peasants, the workers' government could not hold out alone. It would be saved by a second, international aspect of the permanent revolutionary situation—spread of the revolutionary example from Russia to Germany, France, and England, supposedly ripe for the real proletarian revolution. "There is no doubt," wrote Trotsky, "that a socialist revolution in the West would allow us to turn the temporary supremacy of the working class directly into a socialist dictatorship." It may seem farfetched, but Trotsky was squarely in the spirit of Russian revolutionary messianism when he wrote, "the influence of the Russian Revolution on the proletariat of Europe is immense. . . . It imbues the minds and the souls of the European proletariat with revolutionary daring. . . . The Russian workingman will issue to all his brothers the world over his old battle cry which will now become the call for the last attack: Proletarians of all the world, unite!"

Trotsky's theory proved to be uncannily accurate as a forecast of the social dynamics that would lift the Bolsheviks to power in 1917. But what, then, if the international revolution failed to materialize? Trotsky warned, "The Russian working class must necessarily be crushed." Fearing this, the Bolsheviks had to believe in the world revolution.

        ❄   ❄   ❄

The years from 1905 to the outbreak of the First World War were bleak ones for the Russian revolutionaries, hounded by the police or quarrelling in exile, while capitalism and the cautious procedures of limited constitutionalism seemed to be getting rooted in Russia. The Bolshevik Party in Russia was virtually outlawed and honeycombed with police agents, while the devotion of its leaders was tested and hardened by repeated arrests and deportation to Siberia. Lenin went into exile again, to Paris, Krakow, then Berne and Zurich, but he never flagged in his determination to keep a pure and disciplined revolutionary organization intact and under his own exclusive control. He found that he had to fight most of his original followers, ultra-left utopian extremists whose impatient tactics of boycotting the Duma elections Lenin considered a case of "adventurism." While he continued to coexist with the Mensheviks in the nominally unified Social Democratic Party, Lenin insisted in 1909 on purging the undisciplined leftist deviation out of his Bolshevik organization. In their stead he began to build the leadership that ran the party in 1917.

The man who served as Lenin's second-in-command from this time until the revolution was Grigori Zinoviev, born in 1883 to a middle-class Jewish family (whose real name was Radomyslsky) in western Russia. Curly-haired and clean shaven, contrary to the fashion, Zinoviev was inclined to panic and sometimes gave the impression of a slight effeminacy, though he had great powers of endurance both in oratory and conspiracy. Lenin is supposed to have complained, "He copies my faults," but trusted him both before and after the revolution as the kind of lieutenant who would handle any unsavory task without question. Zinoviev lived and worked with Lenin almost without interruption from 1907 until 1917, spent the war years with him in Switzerland, and rode with him on the train across Germany to get back to Russia in April, 1917. Probably no one knew Lenin better—and none among the Bolsheviks was a more determined opponent when Lenin called for insurrection.

Another new figure in the recast Bolshevik faction was Lev Kamenev, the same age as Zinoviev and like him from a Jewish family (Rosenfeld). He was married to Trotsky's sister—a fact that did not prevent the two men from being political adversaries. Throughout his life Kamenev was a cautious and conservative personality, with a dignified beard, but he worked diligently for the cause. He was one of the few Bolsheviks elected to the Duma in 1912, along with Lenin's flamboyant favorite, Roman Malinovsky—who later turned out to be one of the numerous police agents planted in the party. Kamenev went to Siberia in 1914 when the Bolshevik Duma deputies were arrested for opposing the war, and remained in exile until the February Revolution liberated him.

Much like Kamenev in career and temperament was Alexei Rykov, born in 1881. He had been close to Lenin since 1904, but pushed hard for unity with the Mensheviks. He was arrested in 1910 when Malinovsky betrayed him: the police were eager to help Lenin split the Social Democratic movement and thus keep it weak.

Lenin made his final break with the Mensheviks in 1912, when he called a conference of his own faction in Prague and set up his own Central Committee. Lenin, Zinoviev—and Malinovsky—were the leaders. After the meeting a new man of future note was co-opted into the Central Committee—Joseph Vissarionovich Dzhugashvili, a professional revolutionary born in Georgia in the Caucasus in 1879. He was already calling himself the Man of Steel—Stalin. The Bolshevik Party led by these people had by now a fairly extensive underground network inside Russia, though the number of members remained relatively few—no more than twenty-five thousand when the February Revolution broke out. It was reaching the working class militants, though it had little of the leadership that could inspire insurrectionary fervor. The lieutenants who stuck with Lenin were passive and dependent men, or narrow functionaries. To excite the masses when the time came, the party would need new blood.

* * *

All the prospects for Russia's political future were altered by the outbreak of war in 1914, and the physiognomy of the Social Democratic movement was completely recast by the issue of national defense. Like the socialists in the other belligerent countries, the Russian Marxists split. A majority of the Mensheviks and almost all the Bolsheviks opposed the war effort, though few went as far as Lenin to advocate openly the defeat of the Tsar by Germany. In this coincidence of views lay the basis for a factional realignment that gave the Bolshevik movement its ultimate shape and direction of 1917. It was from the left-wing anti-war Mensheviks—from Trotsky on down, ardent but undisciplined theoreticians and agitators—that Lenin drew the supplementary leadership he needed.

The nucleus of the left-wing anti-war Mensheviks was among the Russian *émigrés* in Paris and the Russian-language newspaper they published called *Nashe Slovo* (*Our Word*). Trotsky and Martov were two of the editors, along with a former officer of the Imperial Army, Vladimir Alexandrovich Antonov-Ovseyenko. Himself the son of an officer, Antonov was born in 1884 and became a revolutionary of the Menshevik faction while he was in a St. Petersburg officer cadet school. He looked like a frenetic schoolteacher; a contemporary described him debating, "with his curls falling down his back, invoking thunderbolts, shaking his fist against the corrupters," i.e., the Leninists. Antonov was destined to figure very prominently in the October Revolution, but that was not his first such experience. He organized an uprising at the Sevastopol naval base in 1905—unsuccessfully to be sure, but he then escaped abroad and threw himself into the work of revolutionary journalism.

Around the editors of *Nashe Slovo* a galaxy of revolutionary talent gathered as contributors and commentators. One was Anatol Lunacharsky, a popular orator and amateur philosopher, friend of Gorky, expelled from the Bolshevik faction in 1909. There was also David Riazanov, a leading scholar of the history of Marxism. Alexandra Kollontai was famous as an aristocratic revolutionary and free-love exponent; she was the first of the group to join the Bolsheviks formally, in 1915. The patriarch of the group was Moisei Uritsky, born in 1873. In Petrograd there was a small organization of non-Bolshevik left-wingers who kept in touch with the *Nashe Slovo* people—the so-called "Interdistrict Committee of United Social Democratic Internationalists" (Mezhraionka), under an independent-minded labor leader, Konstantin Yurenev. This was the organization with which the Menshevik Left first affiliated when they returned to Russia in 1917, and through which most of them found their way into the ranks of the Bolshevik Party.

Lenin welcomed the war of 1914 as the death knell of world capitalism. He wrote a treatise, "Imperialism, the Highest Stage of Capitalism," purporting to prove that monopoly capitalism inevitably led to imperialist war and that war would lead with equal certainty to international revolution. "Change the international war into a civil war" was his slogan, and to this end he envisaged a special role for Russia: because Russia was the "weakest link" in the "chain" of capitalism, the Russian workers could start the international upheaval going. He was well on the way to assimilating Trotsky's argument.

Like every other Russian revolutionary at home or abroad, Lenin was taken completely by surprise by the events of February, 1917, but the opportunity electrified him. He wrote, "Only a special coincidence of historical conditions has made the proletariat of Russia, *for a certain, perhaps very short time*, the advance skirmishers of the revolutionary proletariat of the whole world." Trotsky, who had found refuge in the Bronx after the French expelled him, could not agree more; he wrote in the New York Russian-language paper: "An open conflict between the forces of revolution at whose head stands the urban proletariat, and the anti-revolutionary liberal bourgeoisie temporarily in power, is absolutely inevitable. . . . The international struggle against worldwide butchery and imperialism is now our task more than ever before."

❉   ❉   ❉

When the collapse of the Russian monarchy allowed the underground to emerge and the exiles to return, the Bolshevik movement was in a feeble state. Its top leaders, Lenin and Zinoviev, were abroad, facing the problem of transit across the territory of one or another of Russia's enemies or suspicious allies. The second-level leadership—Kamenev, Stalin, the future party secretary Yakov Sverdlov—had to make their way back to European Russia, a long, cold, and slow rail journey from Siberia. For a couple of weeks the leadership of the party and the control of its revived newspaper, *Pravda*, lay in the hands of three men who made up the underground "Bureau of the Central Committee": Shlyapnikov, a proletarian of anarchist proclivity and sometime lover of Alexandra Kollontai; a certain Zalutsky (never more than a minor figure); and Vyacheslav Skriabin, a methodical Bolshevik journalist born in 1890, nephew of the composer, but better known to history by his revolutionary pseudonym, Molotov, the Hammer.

Lacking any contact with the rest of the party leadership, Shlyapnikov and Molotov had to act on their own impulses—that a revolutionary, defeatist party should stand for revolution and oppose the war. The few dozen Bolsheviks elected to the Petrograd Soviet were a feeble voice of left-wing intransigence, though they found sympathizers—the Interdistrict Committee of left-wing Mensheviks, who were already getting a foothold among the rebellious troops of the Petrograd garrison. The two groups started to negotiate a merger.

At this juncture the leaders from Siberia arrived. Kamenev and Stalin, ranking as Central Committee members, quite naturally took over the party organization and the editorial control of *Pravda*. The surprising thing was the line of policy they demanded—reversal of the Shlyapnikov-Molotov revolutionary stance and support of national defense under the Provisional Government as long as it respected the interests of the masses. This position, essentially no different from the Menshevik and SR leadership of the soviets, was endorsed at the end of March at a conference of Bolsheviks from all over the country. The Bolsheviks of Moscow, led by Rykov and Victor Nogin, a thirty-eight-year-old veteran of the Tsar's prisons, were particularly strong for the moderate line of non-violent opposition. Against the hotheads who called the Provisional Government "a conspiracy against the people and the revolution," Stalin defended it as "the fortifier of the conquests of the revolutionary people."

In Switzerland Lenin was fuming impatiently as the papers brought word that his followers were declining to exploit their revolutionary opportunity. Ruling out transit via France or Italy because of his opposition to the war, Lenin decided to go through Germany whatever the political risks. He negotiated the trip through the Swiss socialists, and more importantly, through the mysterious figure Jacob Fürstenberg, alias Hanecki (or Ganetsky, in the Russian spelling), an Austrian-Polish socialist who ran a smuggling business in Scandinavia. Hanecki worked for the German socialist businessman Alexander Helphand-Parvus, who in turn served as a political warfare advisor to the German Foreign Office. Berlin gave permission for Lenin's group to go by train across Germany to the Baltic ferry and Sweden—not in a "sealed" car but in a transit status, without permission to stop. Not only this, but through the same intermediaries the German government began to send considerable amounts of money to facilitate anti-war political agitation in Russia. When Lenin arrived in Petrograd he had both the means and the opportunity to make his revolutionary dream a reality, provided he could weld his followers into the instrument to carry it out.

CHAPTER THREE

The Rising Tide

THE first revolution that Lenin accomplished in 1917 was in his own Bolshevik Party. He began the minute his train crossed from Finland to Russia proper at Beloostrov, when Kamenev got on to meet him. "What's this that's being written in *Pravda?* We saw several numbers and really swore at you!" Hardly any of the regular Bolsheviks in Petrograd, let alone the moderate Socialists, were prepared for the uncompromising revolutionism of Lenin's April Theses. Plekhanov called it "a fantasia of fever." "Hatchet socialism," exclaimed the SR theorist Chernov. "Lenin's speech produced on everyone a stupifying effect," one of the Bolshevik listeners recalled. "No one expected this. On the contrary, they expected Vladimir Ilyich to arrive and call Comrade Molotov to order . . . because he had taken a particularly irreconcilable position with respect to the Provisional Government. It appeared, however, that Molotov himself was closest of all to Ilyich."

Up to Lenin's return on April 3 most Bolsheviks followed Kamenev's thinking about their role as a peaceful opposition. They were not even keeping up with the growing revolutionary spirit among the workers and in the army. But in the short space of three weeks Lenin succeeded in "rearming the party," as Trotsky put it, and identified it with the most extreme revolutionary demands that welled up from the workshops and barracks during the months that followed. In another two months the Bolsheviks would be able to put themselves at the head of a serious revolutionary challenge to the Provisional Government.

Kamenev led the opposition to Lenin's call for the overthrow of the Provisional Government. In *Pravda* he disputed Lenin's "assumption that the bourgeois democratic revolution has ended," and warned against utopianism that would transform the "party of the revolutionary masses of the proletariat" into "a group of communist propagandists." A meeting of the Petrograd Bolshevik Committee the day after the April Theses appeared in *Pravda* voted 13 to 2 to reject Lenin's position. But now Lenin went to work, by sheer force of personality and argument, to win the party leadership over to his own way of thinking. He was, after all, "the celebrated master of the order," as Sukhanov described him, "toward whom they displayed a really extraordinary piety." He was distinctly a father-figure: at forty-eight, he was ten years or more the senior of the other Bolshevik leaders. And he had a few key helpers—Zinoviev, Alexandra Kollontai, Stalin (who was quick to sense the new direction of power in the party), and, most effective of all, Yakov Sverdlov.

Sverdlov was a thirty-two-year-old veteran of the revolutionary profession. Though his father was only a print shop operator he received the secondary education of an intellectual in a *gymnasium,* and then like so many contemporaries finished his education in the revolutionary underground and in prison. A short and frail man, he nonetheless struck his colleagues with what Trotsky described as his "manner that gave the impression of significance and quiet strength." With his sharp face, black beard, and glasses, Sverdlov looked like Trotsky, and he has even been mistaken for Trotsky in the paintings that Stalin later commissioned to illustrate the rewritten history of the party. Sverdlov —along with Stalin—became one of Lenin's key agents in Russia, until both were arrested in 1913. They were exiled to Siberia and lived together for a time, rather to Sverdlov's discomfort. After the February Revolution Sverdlov started to work with the Bolshevik organization in the Ural region, when Lenin called him to Petrograd to become the secretary of the whole party. He had just the qualities Lenin needed— selfless devotion, imperturbable nerves, and a fabulous memory that contained, according to Lunacharsky, "practically a biographical dictionary of the communists." Sverdlov was the indispensable man in the Bolshevik organization from April right on through the revolution. He chaired the meetings, ran the office, disbursed the funds, kept in touch with the provinces, and supervised much of the party's agitation among the Petrograd workers and soldiers. If the Bolshevik Party was less disorganized than its rivals it was largely Sverdlov's accomplishment.

Another source of support for Lenin's radical line, and a decisive arm of Bolshevik action later on, was the "Military Organization under the Central Committee." This body was set up shortly after the February Revolution with the dual function of training the workers' Red Guard units and propagandizing among the troops of the Petrograd garrison. Its initiator and chief, with headquarters in the Ksheshinskaya mansion, was Nikolai Podvoisky, a stern-looking but enthusiastic Bolshevik undergrounder, thirty-six years old. Podvoisky could hardly wait for the barricades to go up again; in March, an associate recalled, he was "the first to pronounce the phrase, bold for that time, 'The revolution has not ended, it has just begun.'" With his aides, many of them active officers or noncoms, Podvoisky started a newspaper in mid-April (the *Soldiers' Pravda*), and did his best to keep up with the rapidly widening opportunity for agitation in the army.

Supported by the most fervent of the Bolsheviks, and demonstrating the same powers of command that were so striking again in the fall, Lenin began a whirlwind campaign to win the party firmly to his revolutionary point of view. He started with a furious stream of articles in *Pravda* reiterating his attack on the Provisional Government. At the same time his closest sympathizers arranged small meetings in their apartments so that Lenin, with the withering blast of his invective, could shame the Bolshevik activists a few at a time away from the line of peaceful opposition. Then, circumventing the Bolshevik City Committee, Lenin went directly to the district organizations of the party to get their endorsement. He had his way at this level in a matter of days. When a city-wide conference of district delegates met on April 14 and 15, he had enough strength to win a slight majority for his April Theses against the opposition of Kamenev. Five days later Lenin's hand was immeasurably strengthened by the first of the many revolutionary crises that shook the Provisional Government.

❋   ❋   ❋

April 18—May 1 by the Western calendar—was celebrated as Free Russia's first May Day by millions of ecstatic revolutionaries all over the country. Bolshevik slogans were prominent among the demonstrations in Petrograd—"Down with the war!" "Peace without annexations and indemnities!" "Land to the peasants!" "All power to the soviets!" This happened to be the day that Foreign Minister Milyukov sent a note to the governments of the Allied powers assuring them that Russia would live up to her treaty commitments to fight the war to a victorious conclusion.

On the 20th, Milyukov's note was made public, to the accompaniment of intense popular indignation. One of the Petrograd regiments, stirred up by the speeches of a mathematician who happened to be serving in the ranks, marched to the Marinsky Palace (the seat of the government at the time) to demand Milyukov's resignation. The movement quickly spread that evening and the following day, with the encouragement of the Bolshevik City Committee and Military Organization under the frank slogan, "Down with the Provisional Government." General Lavr Kornilov, commanding the garrison, wanted to use force to keep order. The soviet advised restraint, but nevertheless there were clashes and deaths, the first blood since the fall of the Tsar.

This disturbance of the April Days alarmed everyone from the government to the Bolsheviks. Lenin recoiled from the risky spontaneity of the riots and scolded the Bolshevik Petrograd Committee, scarcely won over to revolution, for "adventurism." The Mensheviks and SRs who led the Petrograd Soviet began to look less happily at the crowds who demonstrated in their name, and offered their help to the government to keep order. The Provisional Government realized that it could not carry on without concessions to the populace and the gesture of popular support that only the Petrograd Soviet could supply. A coalition government was the natural outcome, and it became a reality on May 5 after Milyukov and Guchkov were pressured into resigning from the cabinet. Tereshchenko replaced Milyukov as Foreign Minister, and Kerensky moved up from Justice to the War Ministry, while five Mensheviks and SRs from the soviet stepped into the cabinet to share the shaky powers and staggering problems of the administration.

While the conservatives and moderate socialists were closing ranks to try to maintain order, Lenin was consolidating his leadership of the Bolshevik Party and his line of controlled revolution. From the 24th to the 29th of April, in the Women's Medical Institute, the party held a formal nationwide leadership conference, the first it had ever been able to call in Russia. About 150 delegates attended, representing eighty thousand members—nearly a threefold growth since February. Sverdlov, in his new eminence, presided, when he was not arranging meals and rooms for the delegates and lobbying for Lenin. The issue of further revolutionary action continued to bother many party leaders, and Kamenev and Rykov continued to protest that Russia was unready, according to Marxism, to venture into the proletarian revolution. But Lenin easily carried the day on his fundamental points—opposition to the war, rejection of unity with the Mensheviks, adoption of the goal, through means as yet unspecified, of "all power to the soviets." A new Central Committee of nine men was elected, headed by Lenin, Zinoviev, Sverdlov, and Stalin (who became chief editor of *Pravda*). Kamenev and three of his supporters (including Nogin) had to be included to appease the opposition and prevent a split. Finally there was a new man, Ivan Smilga, the ardent young (twenty-five) scion of a family of Baltic barons, who took charge of the key Bolshevik organization among the Russian soldiers and sailors stationed in Finland.

*   *   *

Offering their party as a vehicle for the most uncompromising popular demands, the Bolsheviks were rewarded with a great spurt of growth. Up to the February Revolution the party had been scarcely more than a sect, with no more than twenty or thirty thousand members in the whole country. When a count was taken by the party congress held in August the claimed membership came to nearly 250,-000. Twenty per cent of the members were strategically concentrated in Petrograd, and another 20 per cent in Moscow. The party's appeal in all the new forms of electoral democracy—the soviets, the factory committees, the soldiers' councils—rose even faster. By summer the Bolsheviks had easily eclipsed the Mensheviks and become the number-one party in the leading cities; in the country as a whole they were outpaced only by the Socialist-Revolutionaries, who had the spontaneous loyalty of Russia's vast but inchoate peasant masses.

Growth created certain problems for the conspiracy-oriented party

of Lenin. As a mass movement the Bolshevik Party no longer con-
formed to Lenin's original model of a core of professional revolutionaries, nor was the narrow disciplined movement really justified under
the sudden new conditions of freedom in Russia. It was hard to keep in
touch with the party's burgeoning organizations around the country, let
alone control them. Sverdlov was invaluable, with his memory for
people and his ability to recommend individuals to the local party
organizations as officers and delegates (a practice that became the key
to the Communist dictatorship later on). Somehow, with only half-a-
dozen women working for him, Sverdlov managed to run the party
secretariat in the Ksheshinskaya mansion, maintain the records and
correspondence, collect dues from the local organizations, and handle
the organizational chores he was tossed in Petrograd itself. The party
press, apparently benefiting more directly from outside funds chan-
nelled through Molotov, did better: *Pravda* circulated in the hundreds
of thousands, and special regional and military newspapers carried the
Bolshevik word all over the country.

A particularly valuable element in the Bolshevik Party's growth was
the absorption of the left-wing anti-war Mensheviks of the Interdistrict group. From Trotsky on down these people gave Lenin valuable
oratorical talent and a further boost for his policy of revolutionary
hostility to the war and the Provisional Government. Trotsky, still the
popular hero of 1905, reached Russia by ship from New York on May
4, after a couple of weeks of unexpected detainment by the British
authorities when his ship put in at Halifax, Nova Scotia. On arrival in
Petrograd he immediately got himself elected to the soviet, put aside
his past differences with Lenin, and plunged into the whirl of revolutionary agitation. "I told Lenin," Trotsky wrote, "that nothing sepa-
rated me from his April Theses and from the whole course that the
party had taken since his arrival." The two agreed, however, that
Trotsky would not join the Bolshevik Party at once, but would wait
until he could bring as many as possible of the Interdistrict group
and the left-wing Menshevik followers of Martov into the Bolshevik
ranks. The Interdistrict organization had particularly good ties with
the garrison, and its leading figures—Trotsky, Lunacharsky, Uritsky,
Antonov-Ovseyenko, Riazanov, Yurenev—gave effective aid to the
Bolsheviks in winning a hold on the troops. The actual merger of the

Interdistrict people with the Bolshevik Party, voted at the party congress in August, only formalized three months of close collaboration.

As early as May the combination of Bolshevik agitation and popular dissatisfaction began to produce important results. The soviet of the island naval base of Kronstadt, outside Petrograd, repudiated the authority of the government. The Bolsheviks gained ground steadily in the Petrograd Soviet, thanks to the practice of unrestricted recall and reelection of deputies by the factories and regiments, and on May 31 a Bolshevik resolution on transferring power to the soviets won a majority in the Workers' Section of the soviet. Simultaneously a city-wide conference of factory committees heard Lenin extoll workers' control in industry, and gave the Bolsheviks an overwhelming endorsement. The trend in the capital was clear when the First All-Russian Congress of Soviets convened on June 3 to formulate the long-run aims of the revolution. Lenin had reason for his confident words to the assembled delegates.

To impress the Congress with the growing strength of the Bolsheviks, and exploit the limitations of Kerensky's new "Declaration of Soldiers' Rights," the Bolshevik Military Organization proposed an armed demonstration by the pro-Bolshevik regiments of the garrison. In fact the men of the Pavlov Regiment, constantly in the revolutionary vanguard from February to October, took the initiative to plan such a show of strength. The cautious Bolsheviks—Kamenev and Nogin, joined by Zinoviev on this issue—were skeptical of the plan, while Smilga wanted to turn it into a *coup d' état*. Lenin agreed to the idea as a political probing action, and on June 8 a large conference of the Central Committee with the Petrograd district leaders voted (against the continuing opposition of the Kamenev group) for a peaceful—though armed—mass demonstration against "the counterrevolution" on the 10th. On the 9th, bolstered by the election returns that gave Bolsheviks majority control of the Vyborg district government, the party passed out leaflets with its slogans for the demonstration—"Down with the Tsarist Duma!" meaning the conservative ministers; "All Power to the Soviets!" "Time to End the War!" "Bread! Peace! Freedom!"

At this juncture the moderate leaders of the soviets, repeatedly stung by Lenin's attacks on them at the Congress, finally took alarm. The Executive Committee of the Petrograd Soviet, seconded by the Congress of Soviets itself, banned the proposed demonstration. Lenin backed down, and with some effort the Bolshevik agitators managed to persuade the troops not to move. They made up for lost ground a week later when the Congress of Soviets called a demonstration of support, only to see half a million pro-Bolshevik workers and soldiers take over the streets of the city.

The same day, June 18, Kerensky broke the calm on the Eastern Front by ordering the Russian army into an offensive. General Kornilov, now commanding the forces facing the Austrians, scored some early successes, but as the going got harder, many Russian units refused to go into battle, and a wave of desertions began. Tension immediately mounted in Petrograd, so much so that the Bolshevik Military Organization, fearing a premature clash, had to appeal to the troops not to demonstrate without orders. The First Machine-Gun Regiment refused to allow the transfer of some of its men to the front. At the same time, a wave of strikes broke out in the Petrograd factories, as inflation raced ahead of wages and social reform lagged. In this atmosphere, on June 24, the Congress of Soviets adjourned, having failed to resolve any of the problems that beset the country. Two days later representatives of the mutinous front regiments arrived in Petrograd, and the most volatile units of the garrison reached the point of open revolt.

✻   ✻   ✻

The spark that touched off the explosion of July was a cabinet crisis. The conservative members of the government, highly nationalistic, opposed the growing passion of the country's non-Russian minorities for autonomy, and on July 2, after a majority of the cabinet voted to yield to the Ukrainians' demand for home rule, four Kadet ministers resigned in protest. This crack in the government's ranks was a signal for action to the people who wished an end to the regime altogether. Trotsky and Lunacharsky happened to be speaking at a Sunday afternoon "meeting-concert" of the First Machine-Gun Regiment, on their usual theme of power to the soviets. The machine gunners were more excited by their own speakers, particularly the Bolshevik noncom Mikhail Lashevich, and decided that the time had come to take the slogan seriously. The next morning, despite all the efforts to dissuade them by speakers from the Bolshevik Military Organization, they sent delegations to call the other regiments, the Kronstadt sailors, and the Putilov workers to join an armed demonstration for the soviet power. By evening on July 3 a seething mob had gathered in front of the Bolshevik headquarters. Speakers from the Bolshevik Military Organization appeared on the balcony of the Ksheshinskaya mansion and tried to quiet the crowd, only to be booed. The Bolshevik Central Committee, which had resolved against a demonstration, quickly decided to put itself in the lead of the movement rather than lose control altogether, and the troops were led off to the Tauride Palace to demonstrate before the soviet.

For the next thirty-six hours Petrograd was in a state of mob anarchy such as the city had not seen since the February Revolution. Matters became especially tense on the 4th when several thousand armed Kronstadt sailors came to town. There were attempts to arrest government ministers, and numerous confused armed clashes between rebel and loyalist forces, with several hundred casualties resulting. What did it all mean? The government was convinced that the Bolsheviks were trying to seize power, and some historians still hold to this view. The Bolsheviks themselves emphatically denied any such intention, and the detailed record for most of the period supports their contention that as in April they were trying to restrain their followers rather than incite them. When the riots started Lenin was not even in Petrograd—he returned from a rest at Bonch-Bruevich's *dacha* (country house) in Finland on the morning of the 4th. Did the Bolsheviks decide at the last minute to see what they could do? The Bolshevik Military Organization was both independent and impatient; Podvoisky complained in retrospect, "Up to the July Days the majority of the party . . . still hoped for bloodless 'concessions' by the bourgeoisie to the supporters of power to the proletariat. Nevertheless, the Military Organization continued quietly to direct the fighting organizations." Did the Central Committee have insurrection in mind when they called the Kronstadt sailors in? Or had they no alternative except to approve the march? "Perhaps we should try it now," Lenin is supposed to have said when he found the city in chaos, but he must have answered his own question in the negative, fearing the resistance of the rest of the country. If he had planned to overthrow the government at this point, nothing could have stopped him—but he was waiting for a better time, he told a friend, "no later than the fall." The Bolsheviks made no move to take over when they had both the soviet and the Provisional Government at their mercy, and the arrival of loyal troops late at night on the 4th put an end to the possibilities of insurrection. The Central Committee cancelled all further demonstrations.

To neutralize the Bolsheviks' potential challenge, the government had been preparing a political bombshell. Since May military intelligence had been intercepting evidence of Lenin's financial connections with the Stockholm agents of the German Foreign Ministry. The material was given to two journalists—the ex-Bolshevik Alexinsky and the SR Pankratov—to work up a statement that could be used when the time was ripe, while the authorities prepared to trap the whole Bolshevik network. In the panic of July 4, to the consternation of his cabinet colleagues, the SR Minister of Justice Pereverzev (Kerensky's replacement) made the letter public. Basically there were two allegations—one from a former Russian prisoner of the Germans, one Yermolenko, who claimed he was a German agent and knew Lenin to be one too. This story was probably a fiction, and this made it possible to cast doubt on the other, more serious charge of German subsidy of the Bolsheviks through Hanecki in Stockholm.

The cabinet tried to hold up what it regarded as premature publication of the charges against the Bolsheviks, but unsuccessfully. One conservative paper published the Alexinsky-Pankratov statement on July 5, and the others followed suit on the 6th. The opportunity for some important arrests was lost, but politically the publication of the letter was a near-disaster for the Bolsheviks. There was a revulsion of feeling against them, in popular as well as political circles; Lenin was widely believed to be a "German spy."

Ever since then, both before and after the October Revolution and even down to the present day, the German connection has been a cornerstone of the most violent arguments against Lenin's movement. It has always been absolutely denied by the partisans of the Bolsheviks, but not very convincingly. The German archives that became available after World War II made it clear that the Kaiser's government had discreetly been doing everything it could to support the Bolsheviks in order to undermine the Russian war effort. In a note he wrote to the General Staff after the Bolshevik Revolution, Germany's

Foreign Minister Kuhlman did not hesitate to claim a share of the credit: "It was not until the Bolsheviks had received from us a steady flow of funds through various channels and under varying labels that they were in a position to be able to build up their main organ, *Pravda*, to conduct energetic propaganda and appreciably to extend the originally narrow basis of their party."

Did the receipt of German money make Lenin an "agent"? This is one of the most controversial questions in the entire history of the revolution, and the answers range from the official Soviet denial of any such help, to the contention that Lenin's every move was guided by his German paymaster. (The famous "Sisson Documents," published in America after the revolution to support this latter contention, were ultimately proved by George Kennan to be forgeries.) The practice of subsidizing foreign political movements is certainly not uncommon among modern governments. The most reasonable judgment is that the Bolsheviks—and also the left-wing Mensheviks and Left SRs—received considerable German funds, but indirectly, without specific conditions or instructions, and perhaps without definite knowledge about the source. It was Justice Minister Pereverzev himself who gave one of the fairest estimates of Lenin's state of mind: "Lenin is an almost mad fanatic who has never been and is not now interested in knowing from what sources he receives offers of funds for the struggle on behalf of his ideals." Lenin's devotion to the cause of revolution was far more profound than any link to a temporary source of support. Between him and the German government there was only a momentary parallel interest, cynically exploited by both sides. After the July Days, as far as the German archives show, when the public accusations against Lenin made it risky to support him, the supply of funds ceased, and the Bolsheviks were on their own.

The sensational impact of the German-agent charges made it easy for the Provisional Government to proceed with forceful action against the Bolshevik organization. Loyal troops raided both the editorial and printing offices of *Pravda* on the 5th and put the Bolshevik press out of business for the next three weeks. The following day, the 6th, government forces drove the Bolsheviks out of their headquarters, the Ksheshinskaya mansion, and disarmed the last rebels holding out in the Peter-Paul fortress. The Bolshevik City Committee wanted to call a general strike of protest, but Lenin vetoed this desperate suggestion. He and Zinoviev went into hiding, and moved each night to a different sympathizer's apartment. (One was Sergei Aliluev, Stalin's future father-in-law.)

Although the 6th was a successful day for the government in the capital city, there was ominous news from the battle front in Galicia. A German counterattack turned the sagging Russian offensive into a bloody rout. The discipline and morale of the Russian army thenceforth evaporated all the faster, and the army soon ceased to be an effective fighting force. But the disaster did not diminish Kerensky's stature among his government colleagues, who voted him in as Prime Minister to succeed Prince Lvov on July 8.

It was the night following the German attack when the government issued orders for the arrest of Lenin and his principal lieutenants and raided their apartments. To avoid apprehension, Lenin and Zinoviev took a train to the suburban village of Razliv, where they hid for the next month, first in a barn and then in a forest lean-to. (This episode figures heavily in the Soviet mythology, with never a hint that Zinoviev went along with Lenin.) Kamenev, Kollontai, and several members of the Bolshevik Military Organization were caught and jailed in the Kresty Prison near the Finland Station, along with the oratorical stars of the Interdistrict Committee—Trotsky, Lunacharsky, and Antonov. Trotsky, sitting in jail, "sometimes got fired up with revolutionary impatience," according to his cell-mate, Ensign Raskolnikov of Kronstadt. "Maybe we should have made an attempt to seize power after all," Trotsky mused. "Would the front have supported us right away? Then all the events would have taken a different turn."

Lenin came to the same conclusion: "All hopes for a peaceful development of the Russian Revolution have definitely vanished," he wrote. "The objective situation is this: either a victory of the military dictatorship with all it implies, or a victory of the decisive struggle of the workers. . . . The slogan of all power passing to the soviets was a slogan of a peaceful development of the revolution, possible in April, May, June, and up to July 5–9, i.e., up to the time when actual power passed into the hands of the military dictatorship. Now this slogan is no longer correct." The moral he drew from the events was a confirmation of his own basic proclivities: "No constitutional or republican illusions of any kind; no more illusions of a peaceful way." His aim was simple: "Only the passing of power into the hands of the proletariat, supported by the poorest peasantry, in order to carry out in practice the program of our party."

*   *   *

While the outcome of the July Days had given the Provisional Government a new lease on life from the standpoint of keeping order, politically it was coming apart at the seams. On July 7 Prince Lvov resigned as Prime Minister, declaring that he could no longer accept the radical desires of his cabinet—to legalize the peasants' land seizures and to promulgate a Republic without waiting for the Constituent Assembly. The man Lvov endorsed to give the country a new and stronger authority was War Minister Kerensky: "In the army he is a recognized leader, he is a symbol of the revolution for the whole country. He possesses real power already, and among the socialists he is perhaps the only man of action."

Kerensky, assuming the uniform and stance of a military leader, was a much more exciting figure, though inclined to snap judgments and (according to some sources) occasional hysterical collapses. He immediately accepted his mandate from the cabinet, and under his energetic, if erratic, leadership the Provisional Government showed new vigor for a time. His first move as Prime Minister was to tour the battlefront and restore the death penalty for disobedience in action. On July 18 he appointed a new Commander in Chief of the army, General Kornilov, the more-or-less hero of the June offensive. On the domestic front, Kerensky ordered an end to illegal land seizures. To enhance the majesty of the government he moved its seat from the Marinsky Palace to the former official residence of the Tsars—the mammoth eighteenth-century Winter Palace, fronting on the Neva in the center of Petrograd. The All-Russian Central Executive Committee of the soviets gave its unqualified endorsement to Kerensky's "dictatorship" and voted to endorse "unlimited powers" for the government to fight the twin threats of "counterrevolution" and "anarchy." Nevertheless the prestige of the socialists was clipped somewhat when the meeting place of the Petrograd Soviet and the All-Russian Central Executive Committee was moved from the Tauride Palace to a former girls' boarding school, the Smolny Institute, on the eastern edge of the city.

Kerensky's relations with the politicians were more difficult. When his efforts to form a new cabinet were held up by bickering between the Kadets and the soviet leaders, he threatened to quit, and finally won a free hand; on July 23 he was able to announce Russia's second coalition cabinet, evenly balanced between conservatives and moderate socialists. The latter were relieved and hopeful, though their top leaders avoided serving in the cabinet. There was less enthusiasm for Kerensky's efforts on the part of the Right: "The list of ministers invited by A. F. Kerensky to save the revolution has been made public," announced the conservative paper *Novoe Vremia* (*New Time*). "There are no indications that they will be equal to such heroic action."

For the time being Kerensky had disposed of the threat from the Left. The Bolshevik Party was badly shaken by the events of the July Days and the government's measures of repression. The party had lost its headquarters and its press; its leaders were in hiding or in jail; the Central Committee had ceased to function. Sverdlov had to transfer the party office to a dingy tenement on Finland Prospekt in the Vyborg district. Outside of this Bolshevik stronghold many of the party's followers were wavering in their allegiance because of the German-agent accusations. Only one party unit showed much life before the end of July—the Military Organization, which resumed its work among the troops and started a new newspaper, *Rabochi i Soldat* (*Worker and Soldier*). This was the party's only organ in Petrograd until the middle of August.

On the 26th of July the Bolsheviks managed to convene the party congress which they had called more than a month before. Under the protection of the Vyborg district workers, 157 voting delegates from all over the country assembled in a workers' club for the first such gathering since the revolution began—in fact, though it was called the Sixth Congress of the Social Democratic Party, it was the first Bolshevik Congress since their final break with the Mensheviks in 1912. With the help of notes sent by Lenin, Sverdlov and Stalin led the proceedings, which lasted for a week. But under the circumstances—a conspiratorial meeting with the top leadership missing—the congress could not accomplish very much. Its most important step was to formalize the merger of the Interdistrict Committee with the Bolshevik Party, finally making Trotsky and all his associates (in and out of jail) Bolshevik Party members. There was renewed debate about program when the cautious wing of the party protested Lenin's abandonment of the slogan of the soviets, but revolutionary enthusiasm in the spirit of "permanent revolution" carried the day. Despite the setback of the July Days, the bolder wing of the party had become more zealous than ever. "We are going to have a great new upsurge of the revolutionary wave," announced Nikolai Bukharin, a rising theoretician and leader of the radical wing in Moscow. He was ready for "revolutionary war" to "light the fire of world socialist revolution." Nothing yet was said about the manner of a Bolshevik take-over, though it was both desired and expected.

Midway in the congress, alarmed over possible arrest, the delegates hastened to reorganize the Bolshevik Central Committee. They re-elected all but one of the April members—Lenin, Zinoviev, Kamenev, Sverdlov, Stalin, Nogin, Smilga, and V. P. Milyutin, an old under-grounder who consistently backed Kamenev. Several other old Bolshevik provincial leaders were added, including Rykov and Bukharin in Moscow. Two were wartime recruits to Bolshevism, Alexandra Kollontai and the Pole Felix Dzerzhinsky, a high-strung fanatic who took charge of liaison with the Bolshevik Military Organization. There were two representatives of the Interdistrict group, Trotsky and Uritsky. (Another Interdistrict man, Adolf Ioffe, an old journalistic collaborator of Trotsky's, was made a candidate member.) Also included was Stalin's new co-editor of *Pravda*, Grigori Sokolnikov, a twenty-nine-year-old Bolshevik friend of Trotsky. Andrei Bubnov, long a Bolshevik activist, was promoted from candidate to full member. This was the leadership that took the party into the revolution, though at this point the day of victory still seemed remote.

CHAPTER FOUR

The Leader Decides

Wʜᴇɴ the Petrograd-Helsingfors express train reached the border between Russia proper and Finland on the evening of August 9, 1917, it stopped for the customary check of the passengers' travel documents. As usual, the locomotive—it was number 293, with a Finnish engineer named Yalava and his fireman in the cab—uncoupled and moved off to replenish its supply of water and firewood, while the passsenger cars were left standing for the inspection. The fireman this time was not the usual man—though, sturdy and clean-shaven, he could have passed for a typical Petrograd worker. He was a fugitive from justice, travelling with false papers identifying him as Konstantin Ivanov, worker at the Sestroretsk munitions plant. In fact, the man was Lenin, in worker's clothes, with a wig on his well-known pate, fleeing to the separate jurisdiction of Finland to be safer from arrest by Kerensky's police.

The ruse was successful and Lenin reached Finnish territory undetected. He stayed two or three days in a sympathizer's forest cabin near the border. Then, disguised as a Lutheran minister, he was conducted to Helsingfors and hidden safely in the apartment of the socialist police chief. Undaunted by the temporary setback to his hopes, Lenin immersed himself in the revolutionary political theory that had occupied him in earlier periods of exile. In a couple of weeks he had finished his major theoretical opus, published after its author was already ruler of Russia, under the title *State and Revolution*.

This book was a curiously utopian restatement of Marx and Engels on the need to destroy the "bourgeois state machinery" and replace it with the power of "the armed people." Lenin took a phrase Marx used once or twice, "the dictatorship of the proletariat," and made it the cornerstone of his doctrine—expropriation of the landlords and capitalists, suppression of the political rights of "exploiters," replacement of the old bureaucracy with elected officials paid no more than "workmen's wages." Finally, when class differences had been completely abolished, the state could at last be fully democratic—but there would be no more need for it: in the rosy future society of proletarian good-fellowship, the state would "wither away."

All this was purely theoretical speculation at the time. Kerensky appeared to have the revolutionaries firmly circumscribed, while he leaned himself in the opposite direction to win the confidence of the conservatives. But the latter were not easily appeased, and sought some way to put an end to the soviets and the "anarchy" they represented. The result was a new crisis for the government, of a sort that changed the whole course of the revolution.

Early in August, Kerensky's commander in chief General Kornilov was persuaded by some of the conservatives, particularly among the Kadets, that he had to assume a responsible political role himself, to preserve social order and the national honor. He prepared a program that he hoped to force on Kerensky, to overhaul the Provisional Government, destroy the soviets and the anarchy they represented, restore discipline in the army and retrieve the military prestige of Russia. He said to an associate, "It is time to hang the German agents and spies with Lenin at their head, to disperse the Soviet of Workers' and Soldiers' Deputies and scatter them far and wide." For himself, Kornilov asserted, like so many self-appointed saviors, "I have no personal ambition, I only wish to save Russia, and will gladly submit to a strong Provisional Government, purified of all undesirable elements."

On or about August 20, just as the city of Riga was falling to a new German attack, Kornilov ordered a corps of cavalry to concentrate where it could move on Petrograd. Kerensky, it seems, thought this was useful as a counterweight to the Bolsheviks, and he was only made aware belatedly that he himself was the immediate intended victim. On the 27th, in the face of a new cabinet crisis (the Kadet ministers, sympathizing with Kornilov, resigned), Kerensky wired Kornilov to relieve him of his command. Kornilov answered by ordering his troops to move.

The next few days saw an extraordinary shift in political alignments in the capital. For the moment the Bolsheviks were no threat to the moderates; the danger came from the Right, and there were plenty of historical precedents, particularly from nineteenth-century France, for considering the danger of counterrevolution a grave one. The moderate-dominated Central Executive Committee of the Soviets announced on the 27th the formation of a "Committee for the Struggle with the Counterrevolution," with Bolshevik participation. For once, the Bolsheviks of the Petrograd Soviet, led by Sokolnikov and Riazanov, cooperated wholeheartedly with their rivals to mobilize the populace and garrison for the defense of Petrograd. The jailed Bolsheviks were one after another released on bail. Kerensky had wavered in the face of Kornilov's move, but under pressure of the Central Executive Committee he stiffened his stand, and sanctioned the issue of arms to the workers. The Red Guards sprang to life again, and the Bolshevik Military Organization had a field day extending its links among the troops and workers. Some factories and regiments established continuing ties —notably the Putilov workers and the Pavlov Regiment. Sverdlov moved the party secretariat to better quarters that his wife rented from a religious order (shades of the Jacobins!) next door to their own apartment on Furshtadtskaya Street not far from the soviet headquarters in the Smolny Institute. For weeks the Bolsheviks joked that their revolution was being hatched "under the cross of the Lord."

The defense of Petrograd against Kornilov was more psychological than military. While the railroad workers sabotaged the movement of Kornilov's troop trains, agitators from the soviet met the Caucasian and Cossack cavalrymen at the railroad stations along the way to warn them of Kornilov's counterrevolutionary aims. By August 30 Kornilov's force, small to begin with, was stalled and disorganized, and the advancing columns dissolved into a congeries of debating circles. The coup from the Right had collapsed, though it left a legacy of confirmed fear among all the socialist parties that another rightist attempt could be expected at any time. Lenin's statement of the two dictatorial alternatives seemed increasingly real.

❖   ❖   ❖

At the news of the Kornilov affair Lenin quickly awoke from his reverie of anarchistic theorizing. On August 30 he wrote to the Bolshevik Central Committee in Petrograd, "Events are developing with a speed that is sometimes dizzying. . . . Kornilov's revolt is an altogether unexpected . . . and almost unbelievably sharp turn in the course of events." Lenin was already calculating how to turn the alliance of the Left and the government to his own advantage, though what worried him most was the possibility that his followers would think no further revolution necessary: "One must be extremely cautious lest on lose sight of principles." Some Bolsheviks, he thought, were being carried away by the idea of conciliation. "We are fighting against Kornilov, even *as Kerensky's troops do,* but we do not support Kerensky. *On the contrary,* we expose his weakness. . . . An active and most energetic, really revolutionary war against Kornilov . . . by itself may lead *us* to power, though we must *speak* of this as little as possible in our propaganda (remembering very well that even tomorrow events may put power in our hands, and then we shall not relinquish it)."

Events continued to move, as Lenin said, at dizzying speed. Kerensky made himself Commander in Chief on August 30, and on September 1 his representatives arrested General Kornilov. The same day, still unable to put a new coalition cabinet together, Kerensky announced a temporary "Directory" of five men—himself, Foreign Minister Tereshchenko, the new War Minister General Verkhovsky (promoted for standing with the government against Kornilov), Navy Minister Admiral Verderevsky, and the Menshevik Interior Minister Nikitin. Kerensky also proclaimed what had long been taken for granted—that Russia was officially a Republic.

In the meantime, on August 31, the Bolsheviks for the first time won an absolute majority in the Petrograd Soviet, workers' and soldiers' sections voting together. At issue was a resolution from the Bolshevik Central Committee, drafted by Kamenev (just out of jail), which blamed the Provisional Government for the Kornilov trouble and called for a government "of representatives of the revolutionary proletariat and peasantry." The soviet agreed, by a vote of 279 to 115, 51 abstaining. With this the Bolsheviks had won their strategic base for revolution, no less important than the Commune of Paris in the overthrow of the French monarchy in 1792.

With his characteristic flexibility, Lenin quickly proposed a new tactic to exploit this success. The Bolsheviks' cooperation with the other socialist parties during the Kornilov affair, he suggested in an article he called "On Compromises," could become the model for "a peaceful development of the revolution—a possibility that is extremely rare in history and extremely valuable." For the sake of such an achievement the Bolsheviks would "return to the pre-July demand of all power to the soviets, a government of SRs and Mensheviks responsible to the soviets." For their part, "the Bolsheviks . . . would refrain from immediately advancing the demand for the passing of power to the proletariat and the poorest peasants, from revolutionary methods of struggle for the realization of this demand." With rapid new Bolshevik gains in the soviets, it was natural enough that Lenin should return to his old strategy. Two days later, on September 3, Lenin wrote a postscript to say that because the Mensheviks and SRs had not moved against Kerensky, the peaceful revolution might not be possible after all. Kerensky lost no time in showing his own view of the Bolsheviks: he ordered their press suppressed again on September 2,* and followed this with an order on the 4th—quite unenforceable—that all unofficial organizations formed to fight Kornilov give up their arms and dissolve.

What the Mensheviks and SRs did undertake to do in the wake of the Kornilov fiasco was to start some serious planning of a permanent democratic government. Rather than wait for the Constituent Assembly (the elections and convocation had been postponed by the cabinet from September to November, at the behest of the Kadets), the All-Russian Central Executive Committee issued a call on September 3 for a "Democratic Conference" to convene in Petrograd the following week. It would include participants from every sort of organization around the country—the soviets themselves, local governments, the trade unions, the peasants' cooperatives. In the minds of its sponsors the conference would prepare the ground for a "homogeneously socialist" cabinet (i.e., including all the socialists but no one else) and thus terminate the issue of coalition with the "bourgeois" Kadets that was splintering the moderate socialists.

* The Bolshevik daily had been revived on August 13 as *Proletarii* (*The Proletarian*); suppressed August 24; and reopened August 25 as *Rabochi* (*The Worker*). On September 3 it reappeared as *Rabochi Put* (*The Worker's Path*), the name it bore until the revolution permitted *Pravda* to reappear on the masthead.

The Bolshevik Central Committee had to take a stand on the Democratic Conference without any guidance from Lenin. It immediately resolved to get as many Bolsheviks as possible into the conference to make the voice of the workers and poor peasants a strong one. In this direction the party had a stroke of good fortune when Trotsky was released from prison on bail of 3,000 rubles the next day, the 4th. (He took an apartment with his wife and two sons in a bourgeois district where the neighbors were openly hostile—until one day a Bolshevik sailor came to visit and put the fear of the proletariat into them.) Trotsky and Kamenev were quickly appointed to join Stalin and Sokolnikov as editors of the party press, and along with Lunacharsky, Trotsky undertook to harangue an unending series of mass meetings in the wooden theater on the Petrograd Side known as the Circus Modern. He returned to the Petrograd Soviet and at once became the leader of the Bolshevik group.

On September 5 the Moscow Soviet followed the lead of the Petrograd Soviet and passed a Bolshevik resolution for the first time. On the 9th the Petrograd Soviet, on Trotsky's motion, reaffirmed its Bolshevik vote, 519 to 414 with 67 abstaining. Chairman Chkheidze and the moderates who had dominated the soviet's Executive Committee ever since February took this as a vote of no confidence, and resigned. The same day, a regional congress of soviets in Finland—representing mainly the Russian forces there—gave the Bolsheviks a majority and made Antonov their chairman. With this trend clear, Lenin placed his bets squarely on the soviets to create a new revolutionary power and also, as he was explaining at length in *State and Revolution,* to become the basis of the permanent future government.

"The main question of every revolution is, undoubtedly, the question of state power. In the hands of which class power lies—this decides everything," Lenin wrote for *Rabochi Put.* "Either disruption of the soviets and their ignominious death, or all power to the soviets, I said before the All-Russian Congress of Soviets early in June, 1917, and the history of July and August has thoroughly and convincingly confirmed the correctness of these words. . . . The soviets of workers', soldiers', and peasants' deputies are particularly valuable because they represent a new *type* of state apparatus, which is immeasurably higher, incomparably more democratic." In his typically black-and-white fashion he asserted, "Experience has shown that there is no middle road.

Either all power to the soviets, and a full democratization of the army, or a new Kornilov affair." In additional articles Lenin disposed of the Constituent Assembly—power should be taken by the soviets beforehand, to guarantee "democratic" elections. And there need be no civil war, contrary to the charges of the party's enemies: "A peaceful development of the revolution is *possible* and *probable* if all power passes to the soviets."

The Bolsheviks in Petrograd took Lenin's return to the slogan of soviets and peaceful revolution as a counsel of moderation. The Petrograd City Committee met on September 10 to allay some objections to Bolshevik participation in the Democratic Conference. Over the protest of Bubnov, the Central Committee member who edited the paper of the Military Organization and was also detailed for liaison with the local Petrograd leadership, the city committee agreed that the party should take part in the conference and make the most of it as a propaganda forum. "It is too early to speak of the struggle for power," said Vladimir Nevsky, a member of the Military Organization where awareness of the odds against an uprising was much keener since July. "We must speak about a long process. . . . Now we need to think about education of the proletariat," added a representative of the workers. On September 12 the Bolshevik papers printed announcements to the workers and soldiers cautioning them not to yield to "provocations" and to refrain from random demonstrations. The Democratic Conference itself got under way the 14th at the Alexandrinsky Theater (now the Pushkin Theater) in Petrograd, and remained in session for more than a week.

For all its high hopes, the Democratic Conference could not arrest the splintering that was taking place among all the moderate political groups. While Kerensky offered—or threatened—to let the socialists form a government, the right wing of the Mensheviks and SRs refused to break with the Kadets. Kamenev promised that the Bolsheviks would support a socialist government—but only until the next Congress of Soviets. Nothing showed how fast the government was sinking more clearly than the reaction of the sailors Kerensky sent to the conference to guard it against the Bolsheviks—they wanted to protect Trotsky instead after they heard him speak. Out of it all, wrote the Menshevik leader Dan, "We got no coalition government, but only a coalition abortion."

The Kornilov affair and the Democratic Conference precipitated a development in the party of the SRs that was highly favorable to the Bolsheviks—the open split between the SR left wing and the rest of the party. Led by the intransigent Boris Kamkov and a frail but dynamic young woman, Maria Spiridonova, and fired by a tradition of peasant anarchism, the Left SRs repudiated the Provisional Government and took a stand on land and peace scarcely different from the Bolsheviks. They attracted the lion's share of the SR following in the army; by August they had the upper hand in the Soldier's Section of the Petrograd Soviet. In September they captured the Petrograd city organization of the SR party. After the Democratic Conference the Left SRs were to all intents and purposes an independent party, cooperating closely—they thought—with the Bolsheviks.

The trend toward a new revolutionary crisis was clear to many observers. The American Ambassador David Francis wrote to a friend on September 11, "The greatest menace to the present situation is the strength of the Bolshevik sentiment which, intoxicated with its success (attributable in no small degree to the failure of the Kornilov movement), may attempt to overthrow the present Provisional Government and administer affairs through its own representatives. If such a condition should eventuate, failure will undoubtedly ensue in a short time, but meanwhile there may be bloodshed."

Up to now, for all his revolutionary exhortation, Lenin had said little about the way power was to be transferred to the soviets, the proletariat, and—the Bolsheviks. Emboldened by the manifest upsurge in Bolshevik support around the country, but perhaps fearful that the moderates in the Democratic Conference might produce an attractive alternative, Lenin decided to cast the die. "Having obtained a majority in the Soviets of Workers' and Soldiers' Deputies of both capitals [Petrograd and Moscow], the Bolsheviks can and must take power into their hands," he announced to the Bolshevik Central Committee in the first of two ringing letters written in Helsingfors between September 12 and 14. The masses were with the Bolsheviks, or would be soon enough. If the party waited for the Constituent Assembly, Kerensky would surrender Petrograd to the Germans (a theme from which the Bolsheviks later made great capital). The Bolshevik delegates assembling for the Democratic Conference could function as a party congress; "this congress must (whether it wishes to do so or not) decide the *fate of the revolution*. The main thing," concluded Lenin, was "to place on the order of the day the *armed uprising* in *Petrograd and Moscow. . . .* We will win *absolutely* and *unquestionably*."

In the companion letter Lenin attacked the theoretical objection that insurrection was not Marxism but "Blanquism"—the conspiratorial heresy of the French socialist Auguste Blanqui. The "vanguard of the revolution" and "all the objective prerequisites for a successful uprising" were ready. He alleged—with no foundation—that the Allies were contemplating a separate peace with Germany so that the Kaiser's forces could stifle the Russian Revolution; but somehow the victorious Bolsheviks could themselves get a truce from Germany—"and to secure a truce at present means to conquer *the whole world*." "We must prove," Lenin went on, "that we accept, and not only in words, the idea of Marx about the necessity of treating uprising as an art." It was the time for "*action*, not writing resolutions"; go to the factories and barracks—"the pulse of life is there"; then, "we shall correctly estimate the best moment to begin the uprising." His conclusion was to the point:

> Without losing a single moment, organize the staff of the insurrectionary detachments; designate the forces; move the loyal regiments to the most important points; surround the Alexandrinsky Theater [i.e., the Democratic Conference]; occupy the Peter-Paul fortress; arrest the general staff and the government; move against the military cadets, the Savage Division, etc., such detachments as will die rather than allow the enemy to move to the center of the city; we must mobilize the armed workers, call them to a last desperate battle, occupy at once the telegraph and telephone stations, place *our* staff of the uprising at the central telephone station, connect it by wire with all the factories, the regiments, the points of armed fighting, etc.
>
> Of course, this is all by way of an example, to *illustrate* the idea that at the present moment it is impossible to remain loyal to the revolution *without treating insurrection as an art*.

Smilga, the Bolshevik chief in Helsingfors, took Lenin's letters to Petrograd on the 15th and turned them over to Krupskaya, who had remained in the city. She gave them to Stalin, who read them to the members of the Central Committee assembled in Sverdlov's apartment. The letters were heard with "bewilderment." As Bukharin recalled it:

> We gathered and—I remember as though it were just now—began the session. Our tactics at the time were comparatively clear: the development of mass agitation and propaganda, the course toward armed insurrection, which could be expected from one day to the next. When I entered, Milyutin came suddenly to meet me and said, "You know, comrade Bukharin, we've received a little letter here."
>
> The letter read as follows: "You will be traitors and good-for-nothings if you don't send the whole [Democratic Conference Bolshevik] group to the factories and mills, surround the Democratic Conference and arrest all those disgusting people!" The letter was written very forcefully and threatened us with every punishment. We all gasped. No one had yet put the question so sharply. No one knew what to do. Everyone was at a loss for a while. Then we deliberated and came to a decision. Perhaps this was the only time in the history of our party when the Central Committee unanimously decided to burn a letter of Comrade Lenin's. This instance was not publicized at the time.

Kamenev proposed replying to Lenin with an outright refusal to consider insurrection, but this step was turned down. Finally it was decided to postpone any decision, and only by the close tally of 6 to 4 with 6 abstentions did the Central Committee resolve to keep one copy of each letter for the record. Word of Lenin's demands quickly spread through the Bolsheviks in the Democratic Conference, but the Central Committee acted for the time being as though nothing had happened.

While Lenin was moving from Helsingfors to Vyborg (still in Finland—not to be confused with the "Vyborg" district of Petrograd where he hid later) to be in somewhat closer touch with his followers, the Bolshevik leaders in Petrograd continued to call for the peaceful assumption of power by the soviets. They were encouraged further by their capture of the Executive Committee of the Moscow Workers' Soviet on September 19, though the man the Moscow Bolsheviks installed as chairman of the soviet was Kamenev's cautious supporter

Nogin. Trotsky addressed the Petrograd Soviet on September 20 with the demand that a new nationwide Congress of Soviets be convoked to decide on the transfer of power to the soviets. The next day the soviet passed a resolution to this effect, together with an attack on the Democratic Conference as unrepresentative, and it summoned all the other soviets to mobilize their defenses against the "counterrevolution."

On the 21st, for the first time since the Kornilov affair, the old lines of cleavage reappeared in the Bolshevik Central Committee when some of the members proposed that the party stage a walkout from the Democratic Conference. The cautious wing won a majority and rejected the proposal. Action also had to be taken on the decision by the conference to convoke a provisional legislative body, to be known as the "Council of the Republic." (More familiarly termed the "Pre-Parliament," the Council of the Republic convened October 7, and it was still in session when the Provisional Government was overthrown on October 25.) On the question whether to participate in the Pre-Parliament the Central Committee split almost evenly. Rykov reported for the Bolshevik moderates, and Trotsky for the bolder group. Trotsky prevailed by a vote of 9 to 8 to boycott the Pre-Parliament altogether, but because of the evenness of the division the Committee then decided to refer the whole question to the gathering of Bolshevik members of the Democratic Conference which was scheduled to meet later the same day.

Trotsky and Rykov again presented their respective cases to this larger assemblage. Trotsky was supported, interestingly enough, by Stalin, while Rykov was backed by Kamenev. This time, with the preponderance of less venturesome provincial delegates, the vote went to the opponents of boycotting the Pre-Parliament, by a count of 77 to 50. Nogin expressed the relief of the cautious Bolsheviks: boycotting the Pre-Parliament would be an "invitation to insurrection" that he was not ready to contemplate. A lesser Bolshevik named Zhukov confided to the Mensheviks, "We haven't forgotten the July Days and won't commit any new stupidity." Lenin, now in Vyborg, Finland, was increasingly disturbed at the temporizing of the Petrograd leadership, with one exception that came to his attention: "Trotsky was for the boycott: Bravo, Comrade Trotsky!" Otherwise, "At the top of our party we note vacillations that may become ruinous."

The counsel of caution was strengthened from an unexpected quarter on the 23rd when Zinoviev began attending the Central Committee meetings for the first time since the July Days. The experience of the summer had brought him to the conclusion that any attempt at an uprising would end as disastrously as the Paris Commune of 1871; revolution was inevitable, he wrote at the time of the Kornilov crisis, but the party's task for the time being was to restrain the masses from rising to the provocations of the bourgeoisie. This drastic change of mood on the part of the man recently so close to Lenin was perhaps intensified by chagrin that he had been displaced by Trotsky as the Bolsheviks' number-two leader. Though he was still wanted by the police, Zinoviev joined Kamenev to lead an unyielding campaign against Lenin's call for armed insurrection.

While the Bolsheviks debated the Pre-Parliament, the All-Russian Central Executive Committee of the soviets was wrangling over the Bolshevik demand for a new Congress of Soviets. The Bolsheviks wanted a congress in two weeks, and threatened to call their own if the CEC did not act. The CEC yielded on September 23 and issued a call for the Second All-Russian Congress of Soviets to convene in Petrograd on October 20.

Lenin was irked that this date was so far off and wrote, "The Congress of Soviets has been postponed [*sic*] till October 20. At the tempo of Russian life at present, this almost means postponing it to the Greek Calends," i.e., indefinitely. But the Bolsheviks in Petrograd began immediately to exploit the opportunity which the calling of the Soviet Congress gave them. On September 24 a conference of the Central Committee, the Petrograd City Committee, and the Bolshevik members of the Democratic Conference heard a report by Bukharin on the impending "open clash of classes" and the aim of "all power to the soviets." The conference resolved that it was now the task of the "party of the proletariat" to fight off the bourgeoisie and secure the transfer of power to the soviets. Work in the Pre-Parliament would only be "auxiliary" to this. But still nothing was being said in these secret gatherings about armed insurrection.

Monday September 25 saw a crystallization of leadership on both sides, government and revolutionary. Kerensky was finally able to announce the formation of a new provisional cabinet, more than half new men, largely from the Kadets and other moderate groups, plus three Mensheviks and two SRs. The same day the Petrograd Soviet resumed business, now that its leaders were no longer involved in the Democratic Conference, and finally elected a new Executive Committee to replace the body that had resigned September 9. The results, reflecting six months of revolutionary upsurge, were as follows: Workers' Section —Bolsheviks, 13; SRs, 6; Mensheviks, 3; Soldiers' Section—Bolsheviks, 9; SRs, 10; Mensheviks, 3. Bolsheviks held exactly half the total, and with the support of the left-wingers among the SRs, had a good working majority. The first step of the new majority was to install Trotsky as chairman of the soviet. (A week or two later the Soldiers' Section elected as its leader Andrei Sadovsky, an activist of the Bolshevik Military Organization.) Predictably the soviet passed a resolution offered by Trotsky condemning the counterrevolutionary nature of Kerensky's new coalition cabinet, and calling on the masses to struggle through the soviets for revolutionary power.

This was still not enough for Lenin. From Vyborg he wrote to Smilga in Helsingfors that the Petrograd Bolsheviks "have declared war on the government" but did nothing except "pass resolutions." He reiterated his demand that the party prepare for an armed uprising, with emphasis on the role of the soldiers and sailors in Finland, whom Lenin now thought most reliable to the Bolshevik cause. "History has made the *military* question now the fundamental *political* question. I am afraid that the Bolsheviks forget this . . . , hoping that 'the wave will sweep Kerensky away.' Such hope is naive: it is the same as relying on chance. On the part of the party of the proletariat this may prove a crime." He would not consider waiting for the newly summoned Congress of Soviets to take decisive action. Instead he demanded "all power to the Petrograd Soviet *now,* later to be transferred to the Congress of Soviets. Why should we tolerate three more weeks of war and Kerensky's 'Kornilovist preparations'?"

Along with this Lenin composed a long article, "Will the Bolsheviks Retain State Power?", to apply his propositions of *State and Revolution* —destruction of the "bourgeois" state, and management of capitalist enterprise by the workers—to the immediate situation in Russia. The masses, Lenin argued, "will support a purely Bolshevik government"; the police machinery of the old government could be replaced by the soviets, and the banking system could be taken over and used as the lever to control industry. Power had to go to one class or another; civil war was inevitable; and victory was within the Bolshevik grasp: "There is no force on earth which can prevent the Bolsheviks, *if only they do not allow themselves to be cowed* and are able to seize power, from retaining it until the final victory of the world socialist revolution."

CHAPTER FIVE

The Party Persuaded

For all his fulminations against the counterrevolution and the petty-bourgeoisie, Lenin had not succeeded by the end of September in moving his own party toward the goal of a violent seizure of power. On September 29 the Central Committee did no more than pick candidates for the anticipated election to the Constituent Assembly and approve a statement by Zinoviev on the Congress of Soviets. Published the next day as an "Appeal of the Central Committee of the RSDWP (B) to the Workers, Soldiers, Sailors and Peasants with a Summons to Struggle for the Transfer of Power into the Hands of the Soviets," Zinoviev's document put the Bolsheviks squarely behind the Congress of Soviets and the Constituent Assembly, and depicted Kerensky and the proposed Pre-Parliament as a counterrevolutionary threat to both. Welcoming new allies—the left wings of both the Mensheviks and SRs "whom we call on to struggle hand in hand with us for the interests of the workers and peasants, for a democratic peace, for the power of the Soviets"—Zinoviev cautioned against premature "isolated actions."

This was exactly the attitude Lenin meant to condemn. The same day, the 29th, he decided to spell out as much of his insurrectionary reasoning as he dared in published form. The article, entitled "The Crisis Has Matured," was printed in *Rabochi Put*, minus one section that the editors cut out and lost and a particularly frank conclusion which Lenin marked only for "distribution" to the party leadership.

"There is no room for doubts," Lenin wrote for the public. "We are on the threshold of a world proletarian revolution." And it was, he made clear, the mission of the Russian Bolsheviks to take the lead in this revolution. He enumerated again all the circumstances that made Russia ripe for a new revolution—"a peasant uprising is growing"; "the counterrevolutionary forces are approaching the last ditch"; "we witness finally the vote in Moscow where fourteen thousand out of seventeen thousand soldiers voted for the Bolsheviks." Everything pointed to revolution, save the irresolution of the Bolshevik leaders themselves. Lenin's great fear was that his lieutenants would content themselves with a legal approach to power:

> There is not the slightest doubt that the Bolsheviks, were they to allow themselves to be caught in the trap of constitutional illusions, of "faith" in the Congress of Soviets and in the convocation of the Constituent Assembly, of "waiting" for the Congress of Soviets, etc.—that such Bolsheviks would prove *miserable traitors* to the proletarian cause.

In Germany two sailors had been shot for leading a food protest at Kiel. Lenin took this as a revolutionary signal for the Bolsheviks to do their international duty. "To 'wait' for the Congress of Soviets, etc., under such conditions means *betraying internationalism*, betraying the cause of the international socialist revolution."

All this obvious revolutionary agitation appeared in print on October 7, more than a week after it was written. In the addendum reserved for party eyes only, Lenin bore down on the resistance to his views:

> What, then, is to be done? We must *aussprechen, was ist* [Lenin liked to use German for emphasis], "say what is," admit the truth, that in our Central Committee and at the top of our party there is a tendency in favor of *awaiting* the Congress of Soviets, *against* an immediate uprising. We must *overcome* this tendency or opinion.
>
> Otherwise the Bolsheviks would *cover themselves with shame forever;* they would be *reduced to nothing* as a party.
>
> For to miss such a moment and to "await" the Congress of Soviets is either absolute idiocy or complete betrayal.

This suggests how slender was Lenin's regard for the revolutionary institution of the soviets, when he felt the pressure of time to strike against Kerensky's government before it could put down the rampaging peasants. "Weeks and even days now decide everything." October 20, the date set for the Congress of Soviets, was too late. In a footnote Lenin wrote, "To 'call' the Congress of Soviets for October 20, in order to decide upon the seizure of power—is there any difference between this and a foolishly 'announced' uprising? Now we can seize power, whereas October 20–29 you will not be allowed to seize it."

Lenin thought the details of an uprising would be simple. "We can launch a *sudden* attack from three points, from Petrograd, from Moscow, from the Baltic Fleet." He sketched again the course the insurrection would actually take: "We have thousands of armed workers and soldiers in Petrograd who can seize *at once* the Winter Palace, the General Staff building, the telephone exchange and all the largest printing establishments. . . . *The troops will not advance* against the government of peace. . . . Kerensky will be compelled to *surrender.*" Aware that his followers were not responding to his argument, Lenin ended the letter on a high pitch of indignation:

> Seeing that the Central Committee has *not even bothered to answer* my writings insisting on such a policy since the beginning of the Democratic Conference [two weeks before], that the Central Organ is *deleting* from my articles references to such glaring errors of the Bolsheviks as the shameful decision to participate in the Pre-Parliament, the offer of seats to the Mensheviks in the Presidium of the Soviets, etc., etc.*—seeing all that, I am compelled to recognize here a "gentle" hint as to the unwillingness of the Central Committee even to consider this question, a gentle hint at gagging me and at suggesting that I retire.

To reply to this "hint" Lenin issued a political ultimatum (and, incidentally, claimed a right of opposition that he accorded no one else):

> I am compelled to *tender my resignation from the Central Committee,* which I hereby do, leaving myself the freedom of propaganda *in the lower ranks* of the party and at the party congress.

* A reference to the Petrograd Soviet and the installation of a Bolshevik-dominated presidium on September 25. For Lenin the bottle was always half empty rather than half full.

> For it is my deepest conviction that if we "await" the Congress of Soviets and let the present moment pass, we *ruin* the revolution.

Lenin followed his threat to resign from the Central Committee with a stream of almost daily communications to the party in Petrograd. He completed "Will the Bolsheviks Retain State Power?" and sent it for publication in the party's revived theoretical journal, with a blistering postscript denouncing everyone who thought the revolution might better succeed by holding to the defensive rather than taking the offensive. He wrote a letter on October 1 addressed to all the top party committees, to warn that the moderates of the All-Russian Central Executive Committee would postpone the Congress of Soviets: "The Bolsheviks are wrong to await the Congress of Soviets, they must take power *right away*." The Bolsheviks should strike forthwith to start the world revolution and prevent the imperialists from ganging up on Russia. "Delay is a crime. To wait for the Congress of Soviets is a child's game of formality, a shameful game of formality, treason to the revolution." A quick stroke might even be bloodless: "If it is impossible to take power without insurrection, we must proceed to insurrection immediately. It may very well be that right now it is possible to take power without insurrection." The Moscow Soviet, Lenin thought, could easily take over the city and declare itself jointly with the Petrograd Soviet to be a revolutionary government. "Victory is assured, and the chances are nine out of ten that it will be bloodless. To wait is a crime against the revolution."

*   *   *

Despite the pressure of Lenin's exhortations the Bolshevik Central Committee was still equivocating. On October 3 they heard a report from the Moscow representative G. I. Lomov, who had been one of the revolutionary enthusiasts all along. Lomov was optimistic: "Everywhere we occupy an opportune position"—he did not say exactly for what, but the Committee was so disturbed that the members decided not to have any debate on his report. At the same time, for the sake of "continuous and close liaison," they invited Lenin to move from Finland back to Petrograd. As far as the record up to this point suggests, the Central Committee probably hoped to persuade Lenin how uncertain the political situation was and thus get him to stop his demands for insurrection. Lenin lost no time in returning as soon as arrangements could be made to smuggle him back across the provincial border.

In anticipation of Lenin's arrival the Central Committee decided on October 5 to reschedule the planned "Congress of Soviets of the Northern Region" (mainly the Petrograd province plus Estonia and Finland), shifting it from Helsingfors to Petrograd and delaying its opening two days, to October 10. The congress, dominated by Bolshevik delegates, would give the party a public forum to announce any decisions taken by the Central Committee when it met with Lenin. Other regional congresses of soviets in the series then underway gave a somewhat spotty picture of Bolshevik strength—domination in the soviets of the Urals, the Volga region, and Siberia; a narrow victory in the Moscow region; a minority in the central provincial capitals, most of the non-Russian regions, and the army outside of the Northern Region.

While the Bolshevik Central Committee waited to hear from Lenin, it postponed the party congress that it had called two weeks before for October 17—and in fact there never was a party congress, until four months after the revolution. At the same time the Central Committee returned to an issue that revealed the advance pressure of Lenin's impending arrival—whether to take part in the Pre-Parliament. The Bolshevik conference of September 21 had voted to participate, as an opposition, in the Pre-Parliament; now the Central Committee reversed this position. The Bolshevik delegates would go, read a revolutionary resolution, and stage a walkout the very first day. The editors of the party press (Stalin, Trotsky, and Sokolnikov) were instructed to draft the declaration; actually it was Trotsky who wrote it out. One man only voted against this plan—Kamenev. (Zinoviev would no doubt have joined him, but was not present at the meeting.) A significant political pattern appeared here, and persisted in the Central Committee until the actual seizure of power: vocal opposition crystallized in a small minority, a few activists backed Lenin, and other reluctant individuals merely dragged their feet but did not stand up to incur Lenin's open wrath. Kamenev, representing the opposition, was provoked into a stand so strongly against Lenin that he cut himself off from possible support among the foot-draggers. He wrote out a note of protest against the implied insurrection:

Dear Comrades:

I maintain that your decision on walking out from the very first session of the "Council of the Russian Republic" predetermines the tactics of the party for the immediate future in a direction which I personally consider extremely dangerous for the party. Though I submit to the decision of the party, at the same time I ask the comrades to release me from my duties in the representative organs (the CEC, etc.) and give me some other kind of work.

While the Bolsheviks wrestled with Lenin's demands for action, volatile new fuel was spilled on the revolutionary fires of Petrograd by the leaders of the Provisional Government. At a closed meeting during the night of October 4–5, Kerensky's cabinet discussed the danger of a German offensive against Petrograd, following the enemy's successful amphibious operation to occupy the Baltic islands off Estonia. Nikolai Kishkin, the Kadet Minister of Welfare, brought in a plan to transfer the seat of government to Moscow and declare Petrograd part of the zone of military operations. The Petrograd Soviet and the Central Executive Committee, being private organizations, would be left to fend for themselves.

The idea of moving the capital was taken by the socialist members of the cabinet as a transparent plot to cut off revolutionary influence on the government and the forthcoming Constituent Assembly. They protested vigorously, and in consequence the cabinet made no decision at all, but put the transfer plan off until the Pre-Parliament could consider it. However, the discussion quickly leaked out to the public, in a version that had the Provisional Government plotting to surrender Petrograd to the Germans so that the enemy forces could extinguish the fire on the hearth of the revolution. As in the summer of 1792 in France, the menace of invasion and the fear of treason combined to panic the capital into a new revolutionary mood, and the Bolsheviks quickly made the most of it. *Rabochi Put* carried the evacuation story on October 6, and Trotsky went into a session of the Soldiers' Section of the Petrograd Soviet the very same day with a resolution, adopted unanimously:

The Soldiers' Section of the Petrograd Soviet of Workers' and Soldiers' Deputies categorically protests against the plan to transfer the Provisional Government from Petrograd to Moscow, since such a transfer would mean abandoning the revolutionary capital to the whim of fate.

If the Provisional Government is not able to defend Petrograd, then it should either conclude peace or yield its place to another government.

The move to Moscow would mean desertion from a responsible post of battle.

All the past week Lenin had been writing more notes and letters to rouse support for his uprising among the top Bolshevik Party committees. He got more response in Moscow, where the romantic Bukharin and his old school friend Osinsky spoke vigorously for radical action. Sensing this mood, Lenin suggested again that Moscow might show the way to insurrection while Petrograd faltered. He jotted down some theses for the planned party congress (before he learned it was postponed) to reiterate his opposition to participating in the Pre-Parliament and his concern about "vacillations . . . at the top of our party, a 'fear,' as it were, of the struggle for power, an inclination to substitute resolutions, protests, and congresses in place of this struggle." This was written before the opposition by Zinoviev and Kamenev became a matter of record, and it shows Lenin's feeling that practically the whole party leadership wanted to avoid an armed test of strength. Lenin repeated his stress on a revolution through the soviet—"a refusal now on the part of the Bolsheviks to transform the soviets into organs of uprising would be a betrayal both of the peasantry and of the cause of the international socialist revolution." But he refused adamantly to let the uprising depend on the Congress of Soviets. He feared exposing the party's plans by tying them to the date of the congress, but more fundamentally he asserted,

It is necessary to fight against the constitutional illusions and against hopes placed in the Congress of Soviets, to reject the preconceived idea of "waiting" for it at all cost. . . . The Bolsheviks have in their hands the soviets of both capital cities; if they refused to carry out this task and became reconciled to the convocation of the Constituent Assembly (which means a concocted Constituent

Assembly) by the Kerensky government, they would reduce all their propaganda for the "power to the soviets" slogan to empty phrases and, politically, would cover themselves with shame as a party of the revolutionary proletariat.

In other words, soviets were good organs of power as long as they were certain to respond quickly under Bolshevik control; but as a practical matter, if delay or weakness were entailed, they should be disregarded.

Lenin's latest letters were taken to a meeting of the Petrograd City Committee on the evening of October 5. With good reason Lenin sensed that this body would support him more readily and give him leverage against the Central Committee. But his directive for insurrection was eloquently opposed by Moisei Volodarsky, a former Interdistrict man and a popular leader in the soviet. "There are two sides to this question," Volodarsky warned. "I think that we, a party of genuine revolutionaries, could in no case take power and hold out more than one or two months." Petrograd and Finland were not the whole country. "We must not force events. . . . This policy is doomed to certain collapse. . . . We can take power only in a state of desperation." The masses would have to learn that it was the government who opposed the Congress of Soviets and the Constituent Assembly. Then the Bolsheviks could act, but for the time being, "Ilyich's course seems to me extremely weak."

Volodarsky was backed up by Lashevich of the Military Organization, another man who had sobered up since July: "The strategic plan proposed by Comrade Lenin is limping on all four legs. . . . Let's not fool ourselves, comrades. Comrade Lenin has not given us any explanation why we need to do this right now, before the Congress of Soviets. I don't understand it. By the time of the Congress of Soviets the sharpness of the situation will be all the clearer. The Congress of Soviets will provide us with an apparatus; if all the delegates who have come together from all over Russia express themselves for the seizure of power, then it is a different matter. But right now it will only be an armed uprising, which the government will try to suppress." In any case the party would not have to wait long. "We are sitting on a volcano. Every morning when I get up I wonder, 'Hasn't it begun yet?' "

Smilga was present to defend Lenin's view—"Actually we have long been in power already." But even this young firebrand toned down the insurrectionary line a little: it did not mean "the seizure of power tomorrow," but only the basic strategy. Both he and Sokolnikov, who spoke for the Central Committee, emphasized the role that the Congress of Soviets would play, quite contrary to Lenin's warning about "constitutional illusions." Said Sokolnikov, "The Congress of Soviets in itself constitutes the apparatus which we can use," while the tranfer of the government from Petrograd to Moscow would provide "the excuse for battle." "If only Lenin were here," someone lamented.

*　　*　　*

On Saturday, October 7—already the 20th by the Western calendar— a cold Baltic rain was soaking into the slush of an early Petrograd snowfall. This was the day set for the Pre-Parliament to convene and start planning a democratic Russia—with the Bolsheviks determined to blow up the first session with their walkout. It was the day *Rabochi Put* came out with Lenin's long article, "Will the Bolsheviks Retain State Power?"—the first published hint that he would not wait for the Congress of Soviets. And it was the day Lenin took the afternoon train in Vyborg that would bring him back to Petrograd to impose his will on his hesitant followers.*

A conference of the Bolshevik rank and file of Petrograd, also opening on the 7th, received Lenin's theses on the "vacillation" among the party leadership, but there is no record of any response. Reports from the district indicated that the masses were still not enthusiastic for armed uprising. A letter Lenin wrote specifically for the conference, taking up the issue of the evacuation of Petrograd, was not read to those assembled until their last session on October 11. In this message Lenin alleged that "a *conspiracy* has been formed between the Russian and the English imperialists, between Kerensky and the Anglo-French capitalists, to surrender Petrograd to the Germans and *thus* to stifle the Russian Revolution." He called again for Moscow to start the uprising and submitted to the conference a draft resolution on revolutionary

---

* There has been considerable controversy among Soviet historians about the accuracy of this date for Lenin's return from Finland. Both Eino Rakhia, who accompanied him, and Mme. Fofanova, who put him up in her apartment, give earlier dates in their recollections, but these appear to be errors of memory. A great deal of circumstantial evidence plus Krupskaya's account and the engineer's logbook make it hard to dispute the October 7 date.

action. Lenin's draft accused Kerensky of plotting with the Kornilovites and the English and French to sell Petrograd out to the Germans and "urgently requested" the Bolshevik Central Committee to take the lead in an uprising. Again Lenin trampled on his own principle of party discipline, by trying to use a local party meeting to put pressure on the Central Committee and force it to change its line. But there is no evidence that the Petrograd conference took any positive action on Lenin's draft.

The sixty-six Bolshevik delegates chosen to participate in the Pre-Parliament caucused in the afternoon of the 7th at the Smolny Institute. Apparently they assumed that the Pre-Parliament, like every other Russian institution, would start late. But promptly at 5 P.M. Kerensky opened its proceedings at the Marinsky Palace, the somber neoclassical structure earlier occupied by the government ministers. The SR leader of the peasant soviets, Avksentiev, was elected permanent chairman of the body, and Yekaterina Breshko-Breshkovskaya, the seventy-three-year-old "little grandmother of the Russian Revolution," gave the opening address. Moderate socialists heavily predominated over the conservative elements. The Bolsheviks were missing—they were still wrangling in their caucus over whether to go through with the strategy of a walkout during the first session, or, as Kamenev and Riazanov urged, to stay on after all, until the other parties offered a provocative issue for the walkout. Trotsky had to argue again for the walkout, and won by only a few votes.

When the Bolsheviks finally joined the assembled Pre-Parliament of over five hundred members, they found the gathering in a state of extreme nervousness over what the Bolshevik Party would do. Trotsky was nervous too, uncertain whether he could keep his own ranks together. He bided his time; then, when the first session was about to adjourn, he rose to read his prepared statement indicting the Kerensky government for plotting against peace and democracy:

> The officially proclaimed aims of the Democratic Conference summoned by the Central Executive Committee of the Soviets of Workers' and Soldiers' Deputies consisted of the abolition of the irresponsible personal regime that nourished the Kornilov movement, and the creation of a responsible power able to liquidate the war and guarantee the convening of the Constituent Assembly after

the designated interval. Meanwhile, behind the back of the Democratic Conference and by means of backstage deals between Kerensky, the Kadets and the leaders of the SRs and Mensheviks, results were arrived at which were directly opposed to the officially proclaimed aims.

In apparent reference to the more conservative coalition cabinet formed on September 25, Trotsky went on to allege, "A power was created in which and around which avowed and secret Kornilovists play a leading role." The peasant movement was about to be put down, and the war was to be cruelly continued. In particular Trotsky pressed the charge that Petrograd was to be evacuated in order to "smother" the revolution:

> The idea of surrendering the revolutionary capital to the German troops does not evoke the least indignation among the bourgeois classes; on the contrary, it is accepted by them as a natural link in the general policy, which is to facilitate their counterrevolutionary plot.

Defiantly Trotsky ended his speech amidst an uproar of shouts and profanity from the conservative representatives:

> We, the faction of Bolshevik Social Democrats, declare: with this government of national betrayal and with this council [the Pre-Parliament] that tolerates counterrevolution we have nothing in common. . . .
>
> Quitting the Provisional Council, we appeal to the vigilance and courage of the workers, soldiers and peasants of all Russia.
>
> Petrograd is in danger! The revolution is in danger! The nation is in danger!
>
> The government aggravates this danger. The ruling parties help it.
>
> Only the people themselves can save themselves and the country. We turn to the people.
>
> All power to the Soviets!
>
> All the land to the people!
>
> Long live an immediate, honorable, democratic peace!
>
> Long live the Constituent Assembly!

On this retrospectively ironic note of democratic nationalism the Bolsheviks walked out of the Council of the Republic and prepared to hear the revolutionary plans of their leader, who was returning to Petrograd at that very hour. The Pre-Parliament was left to argue bitterly and inconclusively the emotional matter of peace or war; so much feeling arose over the rumors of moving the capital that the question had to be removed from the assembly's agenda altogether.

❋   ❋   ❋

While democratic Russia was debating itself to death, out at the border checkpoint of Beloostrov the same Konstantin Ivanov who fled to Finland in August was returning in the same disguise, once again with engineer Yalava in locomotive 293. With his bodyguard Rakhia, Ivanov-Lenin got off the train when it reached the Udelnaya suburban station in the northern outskirts of Petrograd. They were met at the station by another Finnish Bolshevik named Kalske, the man Zinoviev was staying with not far away. Lenin's first move was to go with Kalske to see Zinoviev. "Entering the apartment and meeting Comrade Zinoviev," Kalske recalled, "he began an animated conversation, and at least as far as I recall Vladimir Ilyich was not entirely happy with the tactics of the comrades who had been leading our party."

From Kalske's building Lenin did not have far to walk to the apartment house where he was to hide. It was number 1 Serdobolskaya Street, on the corner of Sampsonievsky Boulevard (now Karl Marx Boulevard), to the north of the ardently Bolshevik working-class slums of the Vyborg district. The apartment of four small rooms on the fourth floor belonged to a young widow, Margarita Fofanova, of a well-to-do family of the intelligentsia. She was a student of the agarian problem, and had become a Bolshevik deputy to the Petrograd Soviet. Mme. Fofanova had known Lenin's wife in an adult education project since April, and often put Krupskaya up for the night in her apartment. Early in August Krupskaya had sent Fofanova a request to make the apartment ready as a hiding place for Lenin. Mme. Fofanova thereupon arranged for her children to be sent to stay with her parents at Ufa in the Urals, and dispensed with her customary domestic help. Lenin had been given a key, and slipped quickly into the apartment. When Mme. Fofanova met him, the first thing he spoke of was possible escape routes (he settled on the balcony and the rain pipe). She installed Lenin in one of her bedrooms, of old-fashioned bourgeois decor with flowered curtains and wallpaper, a brass bed, a washstand with its china pitcher and basin, a small shelf of books, and an old picture map of pre-war St. Petersburg.

For two and a half weeks, in the eye of the revolutionary hurricane, Lenin spent his days in the quiet of the Fofanova apartment, with frequent evenings out to confer with the other Bolshevik leaders. Forty years afterward Mme. Fofanova published a chatty account of Lenin's days with her and told of his fascination with her library on agriculture and forestry. Some biographers are tempted to suggest that the relationship of Lenin and his hostess went beyond the intellectual, but this conjecture is dimmed by the fact that Lenin's wife was staying just a mile away down at the Bolsheviks' Vyborg district headquarters. She came frequently to the apartment to transmit messages (there was no telephone in the apartment), and at least once remained overnight.

The day after Lenin moved in on Serdobolskaya Street, he went back to work drafting notes and statements to bring the Bolshevik Central Committee over to his line on insurrection. He wrote an impassioned letter, labelled "Advice from an Onlooker," urging the Central Committee once again to apply the "art" of insurrection: they should try to seize power, in the next two days, before the scheduled meeting of the Congress of the Northern Soviets on October 10. He quoted Danton—"Audacity, more audacity, and still more audacity"—and he reiterated the simple strategy he had outlined a week before, of seizing the key points in the capital city. "The success of both the Russian and the world revolution," asserted this Slavic prophet of Marxian necessity, "depends upon two or three days of struggle."

To the Bolshevik contingent assembling to dominate the Congress of Northern Soviets, Lenin sent a special appeal:

> Comrades! Our revolution is passing through a highly critical time. This crisis coincides with the great crisis of a growing worldwide socialist revolution and of a struggle against it by world imperialism. The responsible leaders of our party are confronted with a gigantic task; if they do not carry it out, it will mean a total collapse of the internationalist proletarian movement. The situation is such that delay truly means death.

Here was a true doctrine of the historical decisiveness of the *coup d'é-tat,* belying all the economic proof of inevitable proletarian victory. For moral support, Lenin referred with some exaggeration to the troubles of the German navy at Kiel: "It cannot be doubted that the mutiny in the German navy is a sign of the great crisis of the rising world revolution." But the real mission was for the Russians: "Yes, we shall be real betrayers of the International if, at such a moment, under such favorable conditions, we reply to such a call of the German revolutionists by mere resolutions."

He repeated his charge that Kerensky was plotting to deliver Petrograd to the Germans, now with more plausibility, for one of the Sunday morning papers had reported a speech by the conservative ex-president of the Duma, Rodzianko, calling for just this. Lenin wrote, "We must not wait for the All-Russian Congress of Soviets, which the Central Executive Committee may postpone till November; we must not tarry, meanwhile allowing Kerensky to bring up still more Kornilovist troops. Finland, the fleet, and Reval [now Tallinn, the Estonian capital and naval base] are represented at the Congress of Soviets [i.e., the Northern Soviets]. Those, together, can bring about an immediate movement towards Petrograd. . . ." He was improvising a new strategy—attack on the capital by pro-Bolshevik soldiers and sailors from the Baltic bases, instead of primary reliance on a coup inside Petrograd. "Such a movement has ninety-nine chances in a hundred of bringing about within a few days the surrender of one section of the Cossack troops, the destruction of another section, and the overthrow of Kerensky, since the workers and the soldiers of both capitals [Petrograd and Moscow] will support such a movement. Delay means death."

On Monday October 9th, as Petrograd rumbled with rumors of the government's evacuation, Army Headquarters in the city threw the fat in the fire by issuing a general order for about a third of the garrison regiments to prepare to move out to the front. Kornilov had issued a similar order as part of his attempted coup, and the soviet people instantly assumed that another rightist plot was being set in motion. The soviet's liaison men at headquarters rushed to Smolny with the news, and the Executive Committee of the Petrograd Soviet met at once to plan some sort of counteraction. Immediately the Bolsheviks and non-Bolsheviks fell to arguing. The Bolshevik members proposed that a "revolutionary headquarters" be set up to organize the defense of Petrograd and prevent the removal of the garrison. The Mensheviks and SRs protested that such a headquarters would create a dual command and actually weaken the defense of the city. To head off such a danger, the Mensheviks offered an alternative proposal, calling for a committee of the soviet to cooperate with the Headquarters of the Military District. This would be supplemented by a "committee of revolutionary defense" intended to "make a study of the question of the defense of Petrograd and its approaches, and work out a plan for the protection of the city with the active support of the working class." Surprisingly, the Mensheviks carried the Bolshevik-dominated Executive Committee, by a vote of 13 to 12, and it was their proposal that therefore went before the full body of the Petrograd Soviet that evening.

Trotsky, as chairman, started off this session of the soviet with a rousing defense of the Bolsheviks' walkout from the Pre-Parliament two days before. "Long live the direct and open struggle for a revolutionary government in Russia. Long live peace for all nations," was his concluding appeal. The soviet thereupon voted to condemn the Pre-Parliament as "counterrevolutionary" and to approve the Bolshevik walkout: "The salvation of Petrograd and the country lies in the transfer of power into the hands of the soviets."

Bitter debate ensued over the withdrawal of the troops from Petrograd. Heeding Trotsky's warning of the "Kornilovite" menace, the soviet rejected the Menshevik resolution sent in by its executive committee and instead adopted a Bolshevik statement:

> The Petrograd Soviet authorizes the Executive Committee to organize a revolutionary committee of defense, which would concentrate in its hands all information relating to the defense of Petrograd and its approaches, would take measures to arm the workers, and thus would assure the revolutionary defense of Petrograd and the safety of the people from the attack which is openly being prepared by military and civilian Kornilovites.

The Bolsheviks were backed by a young Left SR deputy, an eighteen-year-old military clerk named Lazimir. They in turn made

Lazimir chairman of a committee to work out the proposal in detail, "so the demand to create the Military Revolutionary Committee looked like it came from a Left SR, not from us," Trotsky later explained.

Despite Menshevik charges of an insurrectionary plot, the Bolsheviks were still vague about the role this organization might play, beyond the "defense" spelled out in the enabling resolution. Several days were to pass before the committee became an active force. Nevertheless, here was the conception, if not the actual birth, of the body which was to superintend the overthrow of the Provisional Government—the as yet unnamed Military Revolutionary Committee of the Petrograd Soviet.

Late that night, after the soviet had adjourned, a few of the Bolshevik chiefs went to meet Lenin. So as not to call attention to his hiding place, Lenin made it a practice to go out to see his lieutenants; this first meeting of the series took place at the apartment of yet another Finnish Bolshevik, one Kokko, in a dreary wooden building on the Vyborg Chaussée about half a mile north of Serdobolskaya Street. Stalin was among those present, and probably Trotsky. The substance of the conversation, though not recorded, is easy to guess: the armed insurrection, the forces that might accomplish it, and the occasion when it could most quickly be launched.

By the following day, October 10, the Bolshevik Party had finally been goaded to the decisive fork in the road. The Petrograd city conference of Bolsheviks, meeting in the Smolny Institute between sessions of the soviet, finally endorsed Lenin's mood—without any specifics—by urging "the replacement of the government of Kerensky, together with the stacked Council of the Republic, by a workers' and peasants' revolutionary government." Later that evening, as a cold mist rolled in from the Gulf of Finland, Lenin left the Fofanova apartment, disguised with wig and eyeglasses and still clean-shaven. He was headed for his first formal meeting with the Bolshevik Central Committee since the July Days.

Most histories represent this meeting of October 10 as the time when the Bolsheviks actually decided to seize power. The session had been planned five days earlier—before Lenin returned to Petrograd—as a party conference. But because Lenin would now be present to raise the issue of insurrection, the meeting was restricted to the twelve members of the Central Committee present in Petrograd. They gathered in an apartment on the ground floor at 32 Karpovka Street, a drab brick building on the Petrograd Side. Of all places, this was the home of the Menshevik writer Sukhanov, whose sensitive, tubercular wife, Galina Flakserman, was a Bolshevik of a dozen years standing. She persuaded her unsuspecting husband to stay overnight near his newspaper office in the center of town across the Neva, so that the Bolshevik Central Committee might utilize her unwatched premises. And the Central Committee needed the whole night; with occasional respite for tea and sausages, the twelve men argued for all of ten hours, well into the dawn. They sat in the dining room, with its one window opening on the courtyard carefully covered. Across the canal in front, there was enough coming and going at the John-of-Kronstadt nunnery to divert any attention from the Sukhanovs' unusual visitors.

Only the sketchiest minutes of this meeting were kept, but enough to show how Lenin reasoned and raged to get support for insurrection. Sverdlov began with a routine report on the equivocal political mood among the frontline armies. Then he gave the floor to Lenin for a "Report on the Present Situation." Here is the entire record of the meeting from this point on, as translated from the published proceedings of the Central Committee:

> Lenin takes the floor.
>
> He states that since the beginning of September a certain indifference towards the question of uprising has been noted. He says that this is inadmissible, if we earnestly raise the slogan of seizure of power by the soviets. It is, therefore, high time to turn attention to the technical side of the question. Much time has obviously been lost.
>
> Nevertheless the question is very urgent and the decisive moment is near.
>
> The international situation is such that we must take the initiative.
>
> What is being planned, surrendering as far as Narva and even as far as Petrograd, compels us still more to take decisive action.
>
> The political situation is also effectively working in this direction. On July 16–18, decisive action on our part would have been defeated because we had no majority with us. Since then, our upsurge has been making gigantic strides.
>
> The absenteeism and the indifference of the masses can be

explained by the fact that the masses are tired of words and resolutions.

The majority is now with us. Politically, the situation has become entirely ripe for the transfer of power.

The agrarian movement also goes in this direction, for it is clear that enormous efforts are needed to subdue this movement. The slogan of transferring the entire land has become the general slogan of the peasants. The political background is thus ready. It is necessary to speak of the technical side. This is the whole matter. Meanwhile we, together with the defensists, are inclined to consider a systematic preparation for an uprising as something like a political sin.

To wait for the Constituent Assembly, which will obviously not be for us, is senseless, because it would make our task more complex.

We must utilize the regional congress [of the Northern Soviets] and the proposal from Minsk to begin decisive action.

Comrade Lomov takes the floor, giving information concerning the attitude of the Moscow regional bureau and the Moscow Committee, as well as about the situation in Moscow in general.

Comrade Uritsky states that we are weak not only in a technical sense but also in all other spheres of our work. We have carried a mass of resolutions. Actions, none whatever. The Petrograd Soviet is disorganized, few meetings, etc.

On what forces do we base ourselves?

The workers in Petrograd have forty thousand rifles, but this will not decide the issue; this is nothing.

The garrison after the July Days cannot inspire great hopes. However, in any case, if the course is held for an uprising, then it is really necessary to do something in that direction. We must make up our mind with regard to definite action.

Comrade Sverdlov gives information concerning what he knows about the state of affairs throughout Russia.

Comrade Dzerzhinsky proposes that for the purpose of political guidance during the immediate future, a Political Bureau be created, composed of members of the C.C.*

---

* This "Politburo" never functioned—it never even met (the fate of more than one revolutionary committee). It should not be confused with the Politburo created in 1919, the direct ancestor of the present ruling group in the USSR.

After an exchange of opinion, the proposal is carried. A Political Bureau of seven is created (the editors plus two plus Bubnov).

A resolution was accepted, reading as follows:

RESOLUTION

The Central Committee recognizes that the international situation of the Russian Revolution (the mutiny in the navy in Germany as extreme manifestation of the growth in all of Europe of the worldwide socialist revolution; the threat of a peace between the imperialists with the aim of crushing the revolution in Russia) as well as the military situation (the undoubted decision of the Russian bourgeoisie and of Kerensky and Co. to surrender Petrograd to the Germans) and the fact that the proletarian parties have gained a majority in the soviets; all this, coupled with the peasant uprising and with a shift of the people's confidence towards our party (elections in Moscow); finally, the obvious preparation for a second Kornilov affair (the withdrawal of troops from Petrograd; the bringing of Cossacks to Petrograd; the surrounding of Minsk by Cossacks, etc.)—places the armed uprising on the order of the day.

Recognizing thus that an armed uprising is inevitable and the time perfectly ripe, the Central Committee proposes to all the organizations of the party to act accordingly and to discuss and decide from this point of view all the practical questions (the Congress of Soviets of the Northern Region, the withdrawal of troops from Petrograd, the actions in Moscow and in Minsk, etc.).

Ten express themselves for it, and two against.

The question is then raised of establishing a Political Bureau of the C. C. It is decided to form a bureau of seven: Lenin, Zinoviev, Kamenev, Trotsky, Stalin, Sokolnikov, Bubnov.

As day broke on the 11th of October Lenin finally had reached the objective he had been fighting for for an entire month: the Bolshevik Central Committee had yielded in principle and acknowledged the aim of armed uprising.* It did nothing more in the direction of deliberate

---

* Trotsky, in his book on Lenin and in other recollections, recounts an exchange with Lenin that supposedly took place at this meeting but is not in the published minutes. Conceivably it was the night before. Trotsky says that he brought up the new project of the soviet military committee and urged the Congress of Soviets

plans, and even its theoretical submission to Lenin was won at the cost of a bitter majority-minority division. Everyone soon knew who the two were who voted against the resolution that Lenin had scribbled out on a piece of notebook paper. They were his oldest and truest lieutenants, Zinoviev and Kamenev. The opposition of these two kept the party leadership in turmoil and gave Lenin his main political worry right up to the eve of the uprising. It is significant that Zinoviev and Kamenev still figured in the proposed Politburo (though this body never functioned). They had more strength than the vote showed, including at least four of the ten Central Committee members who were not present. In a complete vote the opposition would have had better than 25 per cent of the Central Committee, with particular strength in Moscow, where Bolshevik opinion on the insurrection was more clearly polarized pro and con.

It was cold and raining when the twelve Bolshevik leaders filed out of the Sukhanov apartment. Lenin had no overcoat; Dzerzhinsky offered his own, and when Lenin protested, said, "It's an order of the Central Committee, Comrade!" For once, Vladimir Ilyich submitted to party discipline. He went back to his Serdobolskaya Street hideout and busied himself with the preparation of his rejoinder to Zinoviev and Kamenev, when he was not revisiting the agrarian problem with Mme. Fofanova. For the next five days, from October 11 to October 15, Lenin left no preserved writings whatsoever, although Fofanova recalled that this was when he began a "personal correspondence with Zinoviev" that quickly brought him to red-hot anger. He left the apartment twice during this period, once to attend a meeting with some of his lieutenants at the apartment of Mikhail Kalinin (future Chief of State of the USSR) in a log house a mile north on the Vyborg Chaussée near the Udelnaya station, and again on October 14 to meet some of the Bolsheviks from Moscow, who had gathered at the nearby

---

as the occasion for the uprising. "Vladimir Ilyich inveighed against this date horribly. The question of the Second Congress of Soviets, he said, was of no interest to him; what meaning did the congress have? . . . The rising must be begun absolutely before and independent of the congress." Trotsky appears to have stuck by his sense of the political appeal of the soviets. "In the end," he noted, "three groups were formed in the Central Committee: the opponents of the seizure of power by the party. . . ; Lenin, who demanded the immediate organization of the rising, independent of the soviets; and the last group who considered it necessary to bind the rising closely with the Second Congress of Soviets and in consequence wished to postpone it until the latter took place."

apartment of Yalava, the locomotive engineer. The proceedings of these meetings were not recorded.

In the meantime, the exact import of the Central Committee decision of October 10 remained unclear. It is remembered in Communist and anti-Communist history alike as the decision to seize power. Actually all that Lenin's resolution said—and it was a secret document that could put the matter bluntly—was that the uprising was "inevitable" and should be placed "on the agenda." There was no decision as to time or tactics, and indeed no decision whether to strike deliberately or wait for events to produce a crisis. There was no reference to the step taken by the Petrograd Soviet the day before that was to lead to the formation of the Military Revolutionary Committee. There was no reference even to the Congress of Soviets scheduled for the 20th. Lenin mentioned only the northern regional Congress of Soviets, due to open in a few hours, as the body he would presumably ask to initiate an uprising.

Trotsky concedes in his history of the revolution that "no practical plan of insurrection, even tentative, was sketched out in the session of the 10th." But, he alleges, "It was agreed that the insurrection should precede the Congress of Soviets and begin, if possible, not later than October 15." There is no such timetable in the minutes of the meeting; Trotsky is the only writer who records it. "Not all eagerly agreed to that date," he noted. "It was obviously too short for the takeoff planned in Petrograd." Then what *was* the date for? "To insist on a delay would have been to support the right wing and mix the cards. Besides, it is never too late to postpone." Strange reasoning—Zinoviev and Kamenev were correct about the need for delay, but don't admit that you're giving in to them. According to Trotsky, power was to be seized in any event before the Congress of Soviets—though the record makes no mention of it. "About the actual date," Trotsky wrote in 1924, "there was, as I remember, almost no dispute. All understood that the date was approximate, and set, as you might say, merely for purposes of orientation, and that it might be advanced or retarded at the dictation of events. But this could be a question of days only, and not more. The necessity of a date, and that too a near one, was completely obvious." If the necessity of a date was obvious to Trotsky after the fact, there was no corroboration of it at the time. There is no explanation of the party's failure to do anything on or around the 15th and no record of a decision before the 15th to postpone the uprising. There was no reference to a plan for the 15th at the Central Committee meeting on the 16th that went through the debate on insurrection all over again. Trotsky's very literate reasoning fails to conceal the suspicious inventiveness of his memory.

CHAPTER SIX

Offense or Defense?

SINGLEHANDEDLY Lenin polarized Russian political life in the fall of 1917. Everyone had to be for or against Lenin—and all of the non-Bolshevik politicians, even the most ardent socialists among the Menshevik-Internationalists—were against him. (The only exception was the Left SRs, who were emotionally Bolsheviks themselves.) Among Lenin's supporters there were great and growing differences, whether to support or oppose his path to revolution through violent conspiracy, or to seek some middle road. And among the enemies of Bolshevism the question of how to deal with the extremists had opened an unbridgeable gulf between the conservative advocates of force and the socialist advocates of negotiation, with the Provisional Government sinking haplessly between these two antagonistic forces.

When the Bolshevik Central Committee agreed to put armed uprising "on the agenda" with no date specified, there were ten days remaining until Lenin's deadline of the Congress of Soviets. It is difficult to imagine how the Bolsheviks, even with complete agreement, could accomplish Lenin's objective within this limited period of time. So far no specific preparations had been made for insurrection. There was no plan, except for the notes Lenin had jotted down. There was no command structure for military operations, apart from the agitators of the Bolshevik Military Organization; the Red Guards did not even have a city-wide organization as yet. The troops and workers were not prepared psychologically to do anything but defend the Congress of Soviets against "counterrevolution." In fact, most of the party leadership still preferred to give Lenin's insurrectionary directives a defensive interpretation. A member of the Bolshevik Petrograd Committee, Latsis, recalled,

> Hardly any of us thought of the beginning of the uprising as an armed seizure of all the institutions of government at a specified hour. For this we did not have the necessary forces at hand. No count had been made of the available forces. . . .
>
> We thought of the beginning of the uprising as the simple seizure of power by the Petrograd Soviet. The soviet would cease complying with the orders of the Provisional Government, declare itself to be the power, and remove anyone who tried to prevent it from doing this.

Others, higher up, who realized that Lenin was demanding the violent seizure of power prior to the Congress of Soviets, viewed this idea with the utmost alarm. Zinoviev and Kamenev were only the most vocal of this group.

The morning after the meeting in Sukhanov's apartment, Zinoviev and Kamenev prepared to fight Lenin on a broader stage. They prepared a lengthy statement of their objections to the insurrection line, addressed to all the principal committees of the party. A handwritten copy was soon circulating among their fellow Bolsheviks. To the question of an uprising, "already being discussed in one form or another by the entire press and at workers' meetings," Zinoviev and Kamenev frankly urged a negative answer:

> We are deeply convinced that to call at present for an armed uprising means to stake on one card not only the fate of our party, but also the fate of the Russian and international revolution. There is no doubt that there are historical situations when an oppressed class must recognize that it is better to go forward to defeat than to give up without a battle. Does the Russian working class find itself at present in such a situation? *No,* a thousand times no!!!

They would rely instead on the Constituent Assembly, where the Bolsheviks would perhaps win a third of the seats. "The Constituent Assembly plus the soviets" would be "that combined type of state institution towards which we are going." In defense of this modest settlement, they noted, "We have never said that the Russian working class *alone,* by its own forces, would be able to bring the present revolution to a victorious conclusion." Hasty violence would alienate the troops and the peasants, and play into the hands of the counterrevolution.

Like many revolutionaries and most supporters of the government, Zinoviev and Kamenev were awed by the apparent military preponderance of Kerensky's regime.

> It would be most harmful to underestimate the forces of our opponent and overestimate our own forces. The forces of the opponent are greater than they appear. Petrograd is decisive, and in Petrograd the enemies of the proletarian party have accumulated substantial forces: five thousand military cadets, *excellently* armed, *organized, anxious* (because of their class position) and able to fight, also the staff, shock troops, Cossacks, a substantial part of the garrison, and very considerable artillery.

There were corresponding doubts about the fighting spirit on the side of the revolution:

> The decisive question is, is the sentiment among the workers and soldiers of the capital really such that they are impatient to go into the streets? No. There is no such sentiment. Even those in favor of the uprising state that the sentiment of the masses of workers and soldiers is not at all even like their sentiments on the eve of July 3.

The answer for Zinoviev and Kamenev was the Congress of Soviets as a defensive rallying point for the working class. "All Power to the Soviets" meant only "resistance to the slightest encroachment" by the government. Then history would deliver success to the Bolshevik Party, unless it "takes upon itself to initiate an uprising and thus expose the proletariat to the blows of the entire consolidated counterrevolution, supported by the petty-bourgeois democracy. Against this perilous policy we raise our voice in warning."

❀   ❀   ❀

The group that Lenin now hoped to use as the vehicle of insurrection was the Bolshevik-dominated Congress of Soviets of the Northern Region. On the 11th it was finally called to order by Antonov in the Smolny Institute, after it had been postponed twice and changed from Helsingfors. There was a preliminary caucus of the Bolshevik delegates, at which Lenin's feverish message of the 8th was read aloud and discussed. One of the members of the Bolshevik Central Committee—probably it was Trotsky—reported on the decision of the night before and declared that the time had come to set the date for the transfer of power to the soviets. Speaking to the full congress, Trotsky tore into Kerensky on the issue of moving the seat of government out of Petrograd. He denounced the idea as part of a plot to suppress the soviet, but pledged that the soviet and people of Petrograd would continue to hold out against the approaching Germans even if the government fled. Since he was speaking in an open multi-party forum Trotsky made no direct mention this time of the Central Committee's vote for an uprising. But his charge to the delegates of the Northern Region was strong enough: "to pose practically and effectively the question of the transfer of all power to the soviets."

The next day Trotsky addressed the congress again and stepped up the pitch of his revolutionary exhortation, perhaps because the opposition of Zinoviev and Kamenev was so widely rumored by this time. "The revolution is turning into a duel to the death between the revolution and the counterrevolution and its agent, Kerensky," Trotsky shouted. The delegates overwhelmingly endorsed his bold but not very specific resolution:

> The nation can be saved only by the immediate transfer of all power into the hands of the organs of revolution—the soviets of workers', soldiers' and peasants' deputies—at the center and in the provinces. . . . The hour has struck when only by a decisive and unanimous move of all the soviets can the country and the revolution be saved and the question of the central power be solved.

Trotsky in his history called this the "summons to insurrection" —though the action it called for was by no means clear to all. In the end, the meeting of the Northern Soviets did nothing of substance in this direction; it dispersed on October 13th with a feebly routine appeal that the national Congress of Soviets not be disrupted.

In answer to the specter of counterrevolution, a modest step toward protecting the system of soviets was taken the night of the 12th at a session of the Executive Committee of the Petrograd Soviet. Following up the decision of October 9th to organize a revolutionary defense committee, the subcommittee headed by Lazimir had prepared a draft proposal. An endorsement had been added by the Bolshevik and Left SR leadership of the Soldiers' Section of the soviet meeting separately on the 11th, along with a suggestion to convene a special conference of representatives of the regiments of the garrison. Now on the 12th, against an opposition of two Mensheviks, the full Executive Committee voted to proceed with the organization of what was now definitely named the Military Revolutionary Committee, and worked out the specifics of representation and responsibilities. The group would include the presidium of the full soviet and the presidium of the Soldiers' Section, plus representatives from the fleet, from Finland, the trade unions (including specifically the strategic railroad and postal-telegraph unions), the factory committees, the military organizations of each party, the union of socialist officers, the military department of the Central Executive Committee, and the workers' militia.

Traditionally the Military Revolutionary Committee has been regarded as the executive headquarters for insurrection. But as far as the plan of the 12th went, it was only another heterogeneous and unwieldy committee depending on the same people who were already overworked with the business of the soviet. The Military Revolutionary Committee was nonetheless charged with a wide range of military details—assessment of troops and supplies, defense plans, preservation of order in the city, and maintenance of "revolutionary discipline" among the workers and soldiers (evidently to avoid the chaos of the July Days). The idea of a garrison conference of representatives of all the military units was tacked on as another responsibility of the Military Revolutionary Committee. Finally, a special department of the soviet was authorized to give central direction to the Workers' Guard units. Meanwhile the lack of coordination among the revolutionary forces was underscored when a conference of the district soviets in Petrograd proclaimed Sunday, October 22, as the "Day of the Petrograd Soviet," oblivious of the fact that the decisive national congress was opening on the 20th and equally that Lenin had insisted on insurrection even sooner.

The next day the project of the Military Revolutionary Committee had begun to move through the labyrinthine channels of the Petrograd Soviet. The full Soldiers' Section heard Lazimir present the Executive Committee's plan and approved it without debate, though one lone Menshevik protested and voted no. A Bolshevik sailor, Dybenko, head of the revolutionary organization in the Baltic Fleet at Helsingfors, made a fiery speech threatening mutiny if the government should consider scuttling the fleet in the course of a retreat. The forces of revolution were mobilizing rapidly, though they still needed the psychological rallying point of defense against a counterrevolutionary conspiracy.

*   *   *

The suggestion of evacuating Petrograd had done Kerensky so much political damage by the 12th that he tried to repudiate the idea altogether. He told the defense committee of the Pre-Parliament that he would hold Petrograd to the last, and assuredly convene the Constituent Assembly in the city. The papers were full of rumors that the Bolsheviks planned some sort of "move" for the 20th, when the national Congress of Soviets was to convene. And a conservative "Congress of Public Men," opening the same day under the chairmanship of Rodzianko, hinted at a new Kornilov-type movement to eliminate Kerensky's "party of anarchy" and come to grips with the Bolsheviks. "Bolshevism," said the historian Kiesewetter, "is filled with the poison of the old regime; this regime, destroyed legally, still lives in the soul of the Bolshevik, in his habits, in his methods of fighting."

There is a good deal of evidence that the conservatives desired, if they did not actually plan, an authoritarian solution to Russia's revolutionary crisis. Both Milyukov outside the cabinet and Tereshchenko within it told representatives of the Allied governments that they favored a conservative coup. There was talk of enlisting the former Commander in Chief General Brusilov to lead such a move. Minister of Welfare Kishkin told the Kadet party congress on October 14 that the government—i.e., Kerensky—had "hypnotized" itself into a state of passivity, and the congress adopted Milyukov's principle of "a strong power, resorting when necessary to the apparatus of coercion."

For all their belligerence, the men of the Right did not take the

Bolshevik challenge seriously. "The best way to free ourselves from Bolshevism," said the Kadet Party paper, "would be to entrust its leaders with the fate of the country. . . .The first day of their final triumph would also be the first day of their quick collapse." It is altogether likely, as Kerensky contends, that the conservatives welcomed the prospect of a Bolshevik blow at the government that would, they calculated, pave the way for their own take-over.

Kerensky saw his own position as "the struggle of the revolutionary Provisional Government with the Bolsheviks of the Right and of the Left. . . . We struggled on two fronts at the same time, and no one will ever be able to deny the undoubted connection between the Bolshevik uprising and the efforts of Reaction to overthrow the Provisional Government and drive the ship of state right onto the shore of social reaction." In his most recent book Kerensky went so far as to assert, "In mid-October, all Kornilov supporters, both military and civilian, were instructed to sabotage government measures to suppress the Bolshevik uprising."

On Friday the 13th of October, Kerensky felt compelled to appear before the full Pre-Parliament to hear its protests about the removal of the capital from Petrograd, and to deny that the government had any such intention—except in the case of direct military danger. The political extremes of Bolshevism and the Right had met, he charged, not only in their ends of seizing power but in their tactics of slander and provocation. Then Kerensky met with his cabinet to discuss steps to deal with the expected Bolshevik "move." While some of his colleagues wanted strong action against "anarchy," Kerensky professed optimism and cautioned against any use of force that might undermine his moral authority. The cabinet could only agree to issue a proclamation requesting the populace not to participate in the Bolshevik move, but not to fight it either, because "the government itself completely undertakes the liquidation of the move."

The next day sharp disagreement over security measures broke out in government circles. Confidence that the garrison could easily stop any Bolshevik move was expressed by Colonel G. P. Polkovnikov, whom Kerensky had recently appointed Commander of the Petrograd military district on the recommendation of War Minister Verkhovsky. Destined to play a critical role in the events of October, Polkovnikov was a mediocre but arrogant young officer "with a rather old-looking long yellow face, a senseless artificial smile, and a contemptuous calm at the most critical moments," according to a conservative memoirist. Vice-Premier Konovalov, sceptical of Polkovnikov's optimism, demanded a report from the district Chief of Staff, General Yakov Bagratuni. Bagratuni disagreed with his junior but more authoritative colleague and complained that the government had no plan to avoid being taken by surprise in an uprising. Three deputy ministers in the Ministry of Justice handed in their resignations because the Menshevik minister, Maliantovich, had released several arrested Bolsheviks on bail. Kerensky contented himself with a reprimand to Maliantovich, and, hoping for the best in the capital city, departed for General Headquarters at Mogilev to inspect the front. He was so little concerned about the danger of an uprising that he chose this time to remain away for three days.

Anxiety was more general in the Central Executive Committee of the Soviets, which met on the evening of the 14th to debate the whole question of defense and insurrection. The Menshevik leader Dan warned equally of the Bolshevik move and a "counter-revolutionary pogrom." Riazanov, now a Zinoviev sympathizer, replied indignantly for the Bolsheviks:

> The move is not being prepared by the Bolsheviks; the move is being prepared by that policy which in the course of seven months of the revolution had done so much for the bourgeoisie and nothing for the masses. . . . We don't know the day and hour for the move, but we say to the mass of the people: prepare for the decisive struggle for land and peace, for bread and freedom. If as a result of this policy a government of the worker and peasant masses arises, we will be in the first ranks of the insurgents.

B. O. Bogdanov, replying for the Mensheviks, rejected this equivocation and charged bluntly: "The Bolsheviks are preparing an armed uprising and will be at the head of the insurgents. But any attempt at the move will be put down by the government." Martov expressed the quandary of the Menshevik left wing who agreed that the government was to blame for mass revolutionary feeling, but pleaded against any "adventure" to try to "reconstruct the government" at the moment. Dan's resolution, adopted by the CEC, was more or less in the same vein: the evil in a Bolshevik move now was that it would be "ruinous to the defense of the country and will lead to counterrevolution." This last fear was so pervasive that it hamstrung democratic opposition to the Bolshevik seizure of power.

On Sunday the 15th all of the newspapers were full of speculation about the Bolshevik move. The cabinet, in Kerensky's absence, received a jittery report that the Bolsheviks were going to move not on the 20th, "as everybody believed," but on the 19th. Colonel Polkovnikov, less sanguine perhaps after reading the newspapers, issued an order to his troops to forbid them to participate in "irresponsible armed demonstrations on the streets of Petrograd." He repeated the same order, ever more urgently, every single day until the revolution was upon him—as though a few words could stay the rising tide of events.

* * *

Within the Bolshevik leadership at this point there was still far less confidence than the outside world ascribed to them. The men of the Bolshevik Military Organization were so busy either in their headquarters in an apartment on the Liteiny Prospekt or going from one regiment to another, "organizing fighting centers," that they "hardly had time to sleep," their deputy chief Nevsky recalled. "We had to spend nights in the barracks, go from gathering to gathering, arrange meetings, organize the pilferage of rifles, set up new contacts, meet delegates from the front, teach the classes we had arranged for the workers and soldiers, attend the military club, and write articles for the newspaper." The Military Organization, according to Nevsky, had learned well the penalty for rashness in the July Days. In October, "We had to throw cold water on all those flaming comrades who would throw themselves into battle with no conception of all the difficulties of a move."

Under the influence, evidently, of the Central Committee vote of the 10th, the Bolsheviks' Petrograd City Committee produced a radical-sounding resolution hailing "a new upsurge of the revolution" and warning that "continuation of the policy of 'accumulating forces'. . . is equivalent to abandoning the masses." But the group in fact envisaged not a deliberate uprising but rather a governmental provocation, "on an early occasion, as for example, blocking the Congress of Soviets, postponing the convening of the Constituent Assembly, a new betrayal of the army, etc." The Moscow Regional Bureau of the party, dominated by Bukharin and the radicals, voted on the 14th to endorse the uprising, but haggling with the cautious leadership of the Moscow City Committee blocked the establishment of anything corresponding to the Military Revolutionary Committee until the very day of the revolution.

To inform themselves more accurately the Petrograd Committee met again on October 15 to hear reports from the Central Committee (by Bubnov), from the Bolshevik Military Organization (by Nevsky), and from its own district leaders. Bubnov, a hothead, defended the Lenin line of insurrection to forestall the surrender of Petrograd and capitalize on the masses' hostility to the existing regime:

> In order to organize these elements, in order to save the revolution we must take the power into our own hands. . . . When we are in power we will have to carry on mass terror. The general situation is such that an armed insurrection is inevitable, and the question is only to make preparations for it.

But, said Bubnov, "It is impossible to set a date for the insurrection, it will flow forth of its own accord, if there are appropriate conditions for it." He did want to step up planned agitational work; the power would have to be seized before the Constituent Assembly met, or else the "elemental wave" would recede and deprive the Bolsheviks of their chance.

But the reply to Bubnov was a series of doubts. Nevsky was particularly pessimistic: "The Military Organization suddenly moved to the Right," he observed, when it confronted the task of converting the insurrectionary resolution of October 10 into practical steps. The provinces and the peasants could not be reached in time; "Absolutely nothing has been done in the direction of stirring up the village . . . . How do you know that the Fifth Army will not be moved against us?. . . We need a tremendous preponderance of force on which we can count in the first days, in the first hours. And there is no assurance of this either in the Military Organization or in the Central Committee." Nevsky concluded with the remark that the Central Committee resolution had been a little rash in "putting the question so sharply" without considering "the organization of the masses" first.

Then came the reports of the district leaders. On the Vasilevsky Island, towards the harbor, "There is not much desire to take part in the insurrection." In the "Moscow" district to the south, "The masses will rise only at the call of the soviet, but very few will respond to the call of our party." In the industrial Narva district to the southwest, "In general there is no desire to rise up." Only eight of the nineteen districts reported readiness to move, and these, significantly, included the non-Russian party branches (Finnish, Estonian, and Latvian workers who were ardently revolutionary). Kalinin made the comment,

> The resolution of the Central Committee . . . summons our organization to political action. We have practically come right up to the point of armed insurrection. But when this insurrection will be possible—perhaps in a year—we don't know.

Another Vyborg district member countered, "If we don't accomplish the armed insurrection right now, the revolution will plant a cross over us."

While the Bolsheviks debated, the vital question of control over the Petrograd garrison grew more pressing. General Cheremisov, the enigmatic commander of the Northern Front, invited delegates from the Petrograd Soviet and garrison to come to a conference in Pskov to hear his reasons why troops had to be moved out of the city. The Petrograd Soviet, in session Monday evening, October 16, to discuss the defense of Petrograd, appointed a delegation of fifty-six men, headed by Sadovsky, chairman of the Soldiers' Section of the Soviet, and stiffened with several other members of the Bolshevik Military Organization. They set off for Cheremisov's conference armed with a defiant statement drafted by Sverdlov.

At the same session of the soviet Lazimir read his proposal for a Military Revolutionary Committee, already approved by the Executive Committee four days before. Trotsky moved adoption: "We ought to create our special organization to march to battle, and if necessary to die." The Military Revolutionary Committee was overwhelmingly endorsed.

In the Winter Palace, Konovalov took advantage of Kerensky's absence to order some serious defensive preparations. Orders went out during the afternoon to the Peterhof and Oranienbaum officer training schools to send cadets and to the artillery schools to send guns. In the evening a bicycle batallion was ordered to set up checkpoints around the Winter Palace, "in case of the movement of crowds of demonstrators or armed persons toward the Winter Palace." Colonel Polkovnikov assured the cabinet that the garrison was "in general" on the side of the government. Konovalov phoned Kerensky to report the situation to him; Kerensky replied that he would return the next day or the day after to direct measures against the Bolshevik uprising, "if" it began.

❖   ❖   ❖

At this moment the Bolshevik Central Committee was assembling for its second meeting with Lenin to decide the question of insurrection. This time, less conspiratorily, they met in a public building—the council hall of the Lesnoye-Udelnaya district where Lenin was hiding. They were in safe Bolshevik territory—Mikhail Kalinin was the chairman of the district council. The building was a wooden house in the fairy-tale *dacha* style characteristic of this suburb, standing alone in a grove of barren larch trees about a mile to the northeast of Serdobolskaya Street.

The session was one of the so-called "expanded" meetings of the Central Committee, including other party leaders who were invited to participate and vote. There were four leaders of the Petrograd city organization (including Kalinin and Latsis) and a representative of the Bolsheviks of the surrounding province; Krylenko (a long-time Bolshevik and lieutenant in the army) from the Bolshevik Military Organization; Volodarsky representing the Petrograd Soviet; and Shlyapnikov and two others representing the trade unions. Rakhia and Shotman, another Finnish Bolshevik, were Lenin's liaison men. (The affiliation of two others is not clear, and one man was not identified in the record.) Of actual Central Committee members there were only eight, plus two candidates. (Most conspicuously absent was Trotsky, apparently still tied up at the Smolny Institute in the soviet debate over the Military Revolutionary Committee.) Altogether twenty-five men were crowded into Kalinin's second-floor office and the room adjoining it. Sverdlov presided as usual. A woman member of Kalinin's district council stood guard downstairs and made tea. The kitchen window was left open as an emergency exit in the unlikely event that government forces should investigate this deserted area of summer homes and discover the meeting.

Lenin arrived at the council building about 7 P.M., as the winds were whipping up, for what again proved to be an all-night session. He stuffed his wig in his pocket, sat down on a stool, and began reading a "report on the previous session of the Central Committee," to reiterate his demand that the party launch an armed uprising. His exhortation lasted for two hours. But the reports by the various Bolshevik leaders that followed were far from giving a consistent picture of mass readiness to answer the Bolshevik call. Boki, representing the Petrograd city organization, summarized the uneven picture of preparedness that had been reported to the City Committee the day before. Krylenko reported that even the Bolshevik Military Organization was divided in its counsels and inclined to caution: "The majority of the organization feels that it is not necessary to sharpen the question in a practical way, though the minority thinks that we can assume the initiative." Volodarsky, speaking for the Petrograd Soviet, noted "No one is very anxious to go out on the street, but at the call of the soviets all will appear." Milyutin expressed the mirror image of Kerensky's strategy by suggesting that the Bolsheviks should wait for a clash rather than try to strike the first blow. Shotman reported that the Petrograd city leadership was pessimistic, and concluded, "We cannot move out yet—we have to get ready."

Lenin tried to counter this mood by arguing that in the present chaotic situation the forces of the Bolsheviks were adequate. Krylenko attempted to compromise the differences between Lenin and his critics by observing that mass revolt was brewing and suggesting that the Bolsheviks could simply prepare to "support the uprising with armed force if it breaks out somewhere." He was against setting a date: the controversy over ordering part of the garrison out of Petrograd would likely lead to an attack by the government on the Bolsheviks, who could then exploit their opportunity. Trotsky in his history maintained that this was actually the policy of the Military Revolutionary Committee and that Lenin suffered from exaggerated fears of delay. In any case, this unsung strategy was close to the way events actually turned out.

Taking advantage of the mood of uncertainty, Zinoviev spoke out to reiterate his doubts about the wisdom of insurrection and the danger of the party's being isolated if it did not bank on the Congress of Soviets and the Constituent Assembly. "We must definitely tell ourselves," he cautioned, "that we do not plan an uprising within the next five days"—which would of course have postponed any action until after the opening of the congress (still expected on the 20th).

Kamenev spoke candidly of the party's failure to implement the revolutionary line of October 10: "A week has passed since the resolution was adopted, and this resolution therefore shows how not to carry out an uprising: during this week nothing has been done. . . . We have no apparatus for an uprising; our enemies have a much stronger apparatus." He warned that an insurrectionary action would needlessly alienate the popular support which the Bolsheviks were otherwise gaining. "It has not been demonstrated at all," he insisted, "that we must give battle before the twentieth. . . . There is a struggle between two tactics here—the tactic of a plot, and the tactic of faith in the dynamic forces of the Russian Revolution."

Among the other leaders there was a wide range of opinion. One reasonably close to Lenin was Joseph Stalin, though he hedged a little: "The day of the uprising must be convenient. Only thus need we understand the resolution [of October 10]." But waiting too long would play into the hands of the counterrevolutionaries. "There are two lines here: one line steers a course toward the victory of the revolution and relies on Europe [an emphasis Stalin later abandoned]; the second does not believe in the revolution and counts on our being only an opposition." To the Petrograd Soviet—and implicitly Trotsky—he gave credit for already starting the line of insurrection.

Stalin was followed by Kalinin, who again expressed himself for preparedness but against precipitate action. Sverdlov made a tempered concession to Lenin's critics—"We don't have to say that the majority is against us—it is merely not yet for us." The trade-unionist Skrypnik wanted to act before the situation should turn less favorable, even though there was no guarantee of victory. Volodarsky recognized that the leadership had been dilatory: "If the resolution is an order, then it has not been fulfilled. If the question of a move is posed as a question for tomorrow, then we must frankly say that we have done nothing about it. . . . If there were not a tendency in the Central Committee that wants to turn the class struggle into a parliamentary one, then we would be ready now for an uprising, though not at this moment. . . . The resolution must be understood as a course toward an uprising—we must not stop our technical preparations."

Dzerzhinsky and Sokolnikov tried to brush aside such concern about preparing an uprising. After all, Sokolnikov pointed out, the February Revolution had needed none. The party had sufficient forces, but it was wrong to understand the resolution as an order; the party should wait for events to give it the expected opportunity. If the Congress of Soviets decided to assume power, that would be the time to judge whether a mass move was necessary. Such reasoning was close to the dominant sentiment of the party leadership, echoed by several other speakers—and clearly inconsistent with Lenin's demand to seize power before the Congress of Soviets.

The session came to a climax with another direct confrontation between Lenin and the two lieutenants who were brave enough to defy him openly. Lenin repeated his contention that the time was ripe to apply the art of insurrection. Zinoviev countered that while it was all right to regard an uprising as a long run possibility, any immediate attempt would be "adventurism." Kamenev added that the mood of the meeting was one of retrenchment: "The present interpretation of the resolution is a retreat, for it was said earlier that the move must be before the 20th, and now they talk only of a course toward revolution." This seems to reflect Lenin's insistence on a move prior to the Congress of Soviets, rather than any definite planning. Kamenev went on, "Deciding on an uprising is adventurism. We are obliged to explain to the masses that we are not calling on them to move in the next three days [before the expected Congress of Soviets], though we feel that an uprising is inevitable." He proposed endorsing the resolution with the proviso that there would be no move before the Congress of Soviets. Lenin retorted with the draft of a resolution that demanded a vote of confidence:

> The meeting heartily greets and fully supports the resolution of the Central Committee [of October 10]. It calls upon all the organizations and all the workers and soldiers to prepare the armed uprising most energetically, in every way, to support the organ which the Central Committee is creating for this purpose [the Military Revo-

lutionary Committee], and expresses full confidence that the Central Committee and the soviet will in due time indicate the favorable moment and the most expedient methods for an offensive.

This proposition, still without any definite date, was adopted by a vote of 19 to 2 (presumably Zinoviev and Kamenev), with 4 abstentions.

The extent of opposition to Lenin was perhaps more accurately shown by the vote on Volodarsky's proposal to adopt as a supplement Zinoviev's resolution "to take no action before a conference with the Bolsheviks arriving October 20 for the Congress of Soviets." This was rejected by a closer vote, 15 to 6, with 3 abstentions. Zinoviev and Kamenev immediately demanded a "telegraphic summons" for a new and full meeting of the Central Committee. Kamenev in his alarm protested that the resolution would "lead the party and the proletariat to defeat," and went on to "beg the Central Committee to consider me no longer a member of the Central Committee."

Finally the Central Committee took a step, after the nonmembers left the session, which figured prominently in Stalinist historiography. It voted to establish a "military revolutionary center," consisting of Sverdlov, Stalin, Bubnov, Uritsky, and Dzerzhinsky, who would join the as yet unformed "revolutionary Soviet committee." This decision served Stalin's purpose later on to represent himself as the executor of the revolution, although in point of fact the "center" was one of those innumerable committees, not only in Bolshevik experience, that once appointed never meet.

❊　　❊　　❊

The weather was foul again when the Bolshevik leaders dispersed in the early hours of October 17 after their second vote for an uprising. Eino Rakhia accompanied Lenin back to Serdobolskaya Street; "It was pouring hopelessly and blowing hard," he recalled. "The wind tore Lenin's hat from his head, but he didn't even notice because he was so upset by Zinoviev's and Kamenev's stand against him." Rakhia undertook a personal mission of reconciliation: leaving Lenin, he went to see Zinoviev at the Kalske apartment. Zinoviev was worried about Lenin's feelings, and gave Rakhia a letter to take back to the party chief. Rakhia did so, but to his consternation, Lenin literally refused to accept the letter. Rakhia began to open the envelope himself, but this was another offense. "Why are you reading my letter?" Lenin exploded. He finally took it himself, read it angrily, and fired off a reply.

The tension between Lenin and his old lieutenants was pushed to the breaking point a couple of hours later when news of the Zinoviev-Kamenev opposition appeared in the public press. Gorky's paper *Novaya Zhizn* carried an article by the Menshevik Bazarov denouncing the rumored Bolshevik insurrection as un-Marxist. In passing Bazarov mentioned a "handwritten leaflet by two leading Bolsheviks"—the protest letter of October 11 which the two holdouts had been circulating.

To make his position clear, Kamenev gave the *Novaya Zhizn* people a special statement, which the paper published the following day, the 18th:

> In view of the aggravated discussion of the question of a move, Comrade Zinoviev and I addressed the main organizations of our party in Petrograd, Moscow and Finland with a letter in which we emphatically expressed ourselves against our party taking the initiative in any armed move in the immediate future. I must say that no decision of our party is known to me that contains the setting of one date or another for any move.
>
> Such decisions of the party do not exist. Everyone understands that in the present state of the revolution there can be no talk of any such "armed demonstration." There can only be talk of the seizure of power with arms in hand, and people who are responsible to the proletariat cannot fail to understand that it is possible to undertake such a mass "move" only after clearly and definitely posing the task of armed uprising. Not only Comrade Zinoviev and I but also a number of practical comrades feel that to assume the initiative of an armed uprising at the present moment, under the existing relationship of social forces, independently of and just a few days before the Congress of Soviets, would be an intolerable, ruinous step for the proletariat and the revolution.

Any revolutionary party, Kamenev conceded, should be prepared for insurrection if the interests of the masses required it.

> But insurrection, as Marx expressed it [It was really Engels], is an art. And just because of this we assert that our obligation now, in the present circumstances, is to express ourselves against any at-

97

tempt to assume the initiative of an armed uprising, which would be doomed to defeat and would bring on the most ruinous consequences for the party, for the proletariat, for the fate of the revolution. To stake all this on the card of a move in the next few days would mean taking a step of desperation. And our party is too strong, it has too great a future ahead of it, to take such steps of desperation.

Sukhanov immediately took Kamenev's letter to show it to the leaders of the Menshevik Party. With this evidence of Bolshevik dissension, they persuaded the Central Executive Committee to postpone the opening of the Congress of Soviets from October 20 to October 25, in the hope of building an anti-Lenin majority. The notice of postponement was published in *Izvestiya* on the 18th, along with dire warnings that only the Kornilovites and Black Hundreds (the monarchist, anti-Semitic gangs of prerevolutionary times) would profit from the "criminal foolhardiness" of any revolutionary move against the Provisional Government.

In fact, as of October 17th, the Bolsheviks were in no way prepared to stage an uprising within the three days remaining before the original date set for the Congress of Soviets. Lenin had failed to get the party to make enough real preparations in time to give him the seizure of power he wanted before the congress convened. Now his revolutionary chances got a short new lease on life—thanks indirectly to the same two Bolsheviks who were trying to forestall such a risky resort to force.

Following the Central Committee meeting of the 16th Lenin decided to publicize his arguments against Zinoviev and Kamenev in a "Letter to Comrades," a rambling polemic of more than a dozen pages in print. While the published version names no names, it was obviously a counterattack against the stand taken by Zinoviev and Kamenev at the two Central Committee meetings. (At the time of writing Lenin did not appear to have knowledge of the follow-up letter written by his two opponents.) The letter incorporated Lenin's analysis of all the factors assuring the success of an insurrection—the shift of a majority of the workers and soldiers to the Bolsheviks; the spread of revolt among the peasants; and especially the supposedly incipient revolution in Germany. Haste was imperative to capitalize on the mood of the masses, avert famine, and forestall the government's plot to surrender Petrograd. Only an immediate armed uprising would stop the bourgeoisie from stifling the Congress of Soviets and the Constituent Assembly (an institution in which Lenin never ceased to profess belief until it got in his own way). The opposition was contemptible—"an insignificant minority" marked by "an astounding confusion, timidity, and collapse of all the fundamental ideas of Bolshevism and revolutionary-proletarian internationalism." One wonders why Lenin devoted 90 per cent of his efforts in the ten days before the revolution to his polemic with Zinoviev and Kamenev. His only explanation was that "this little pair of comrades, who have scattered their principles to the winds, might cause a certain confusion of mind."

Lenin had finished the letter, intending it as a nonpublic communication to the Bolshevik Party, when at eight o'clock in the evening someone brought him the day's newspapers including *Novaya Zhizn* with its report on Zinoviev's and Kamenev's opposition to an uprising. He immediately added a postscript to the letter with instructions for the whole document to be published as soon as possible. It was more verbal aggression, typical of Lenin, dismissing "the contemptible little fools" of *Novaya Zhizn* and threatening Zinoviev and Kamenev with exposure: "Let the anonymous individuals finally appear in the light of day, and let them bear the punishment they deserve for their shameful vacillations—even if it be only the ridicule of all class-conscious workers."

While Lenin was inveighing against his opponents in the party ranks, the Bolshevik Petrograd City Committee and the Military Organization held a conference in one of the classrooms at Smolny with representatives of the district organizations of the party, to communicate the decision of the Central Committee to the lower echelons. Among the 150-odd Bolsheviks present the debate on insurrection broke out all over again. G. I. Chudnovsky, a friend of Trotsky's who had returned with him from New York by way of the Canadian prison camp and then became a frontline agitator, spoke heatedly against any armed move before the Congress of Soviets. He was seconded by Volodarsky, Riazanov and Larin, all former Mensheviks like himself. Podvoisky and Nevsky, speaking for the Military Organization but, as Nevsky wrote, "schooled in the bitter experience of the July Days," could not bring themselves to support Lenin's line of immediate uprising. Dzerzhinsky was present to defend the Central Committee's decision, but the decisive intervention was Sverdlov's. Appearing suddenly in the room, his wife recounted, "He went up to the table covered with a red cloth that stood at the end of the aisle leading from the door. There were no chairs at the table, and Yakov Mikhailovich [Sverdlov], stepping around the table, stood facing the room, resting his hands on the table, and attentively listened to the next speaker. When Riazanov finished and was followed by a speaker from the Military Organization who also came out against the uprising, the noise in the room increased. Suddenly Yakov Mikhailovich interrupted the speaker. His deep, unusually strong bass voice stopped the noise instantly. 'The decision of the Central Committee on the uprising has been made. I am speaking here in the name of the Central Committee and I will allow no one to reconsider a decision that has been made. We have not gathered to set aside a decision of the Central Committee, but to consider how we ought to carry it out. I ask the comrades to express themselves on the substance of the practical preparation of the uprising.'" Thus brought to heel by the admonitions of "democratic centralism," the assembled party activists voted their endorsement of insurrection.

Sverdlov had still more business in mind for that evening. As the meeting was breaking up, he came over to Podvoisky and whispered, "Now you are going to see Ilyich. He is calling you to report on our preparations."

Sverdlov, Podvoisky, Nevsky, and Antonov (just back from a speaking tour of the front) all got in a car and started off into a rainy night, "dark, muddy and cold," Nevsky recalled. First they went to see Zinoviev, probably in the hope of getting some message of reconciliation to take to Lenin. Over on the Vyborg side they took a streetcar that carried them up to the Vyborg Chaussée. They got off and walked along the street, "swimming in mud," to Kalinin's apartment. There they found Zinoviev, looking a little strange with his hair trimmed.

Zinoviev reaffirmed his skepticism and challenged his visitors: "I will join you in favoring the armed uprising if you can show me that we will keep ourselves in power even for just two weeks." He was not against revolution, but pleaded for caution: "It is necessary to prepare carefully and thoughtfully for the blow which we are getting ready to launch against our enemy, so that we will not get ourselves in an even more serious position than we were in in July, 1917."

Antonov replied laconically for the visitors, "It's pointless to argue. There's no way out. We're already in battle. We must conquer or die!"

After leaving Zinoviev, the Bolshevik military group was conducted on foot for another mile by a Bolshevik worker, Dmitri Pavlov, to his apartment on Serdobolskaya Street, number 35. Along the way they felt they were being followed by a man on a bicycle; one of them whispered, "A spy!" But in the dark they managed to shake him off their trail. At Pavlov's apartment, a few blocks west of Lenin's hideout, they found the party chief waiting for them. So well was the secret of Lenin's own residence kept that the visitors were unaware that this second-floor apartment in a grimy old brick apartment block where Lenin came to meet them was not his actual hideout.

Lenin called on each member of the Military Organization to give his impressions of the revolutionary situation. Antonov said he could not judge the Petrograd garrison, and reported that the sailors in Finland were afraid to leave their posts and expose the Baltic approaches to the Germans. Lenin was chagrined to hear this about the people he had imagined as the shock troops of the revolution: "Shouldn't they understand that the revolution is in greater danger in Petrograd than on the Baltic?" Antonov had to reply in the negative and report that only three thousand sailors were available to move on Petrograd. Nevsky interjected that without officers the sailors of the Helsingfors base could not handle their ships well enough to get them through the minefields into the Neva; they would have to come by train to participate in the insurrection. Podvoisky told Lenin that he needed time—ten days to two weeks—to get his agitators out to all the units of the army and give them an opportunity to have some effect. The regiments that demonstrated most enthusiastically in July had been partially broken up, and lacked their former fire: "They would join a move only if they believed other units would move." With more time the Bolshevik ranks would gain more adherents, whereas at the moment Kerensky still had strong reliable forces that he could bring from the front.

But Lenin immediately rejected the idea of delay: the government would have more time, and above all, "An insurrection before the Congress of Soviets is especially important, so that this congress, whatever it is like, will confront the established fact of the seizure of power by the working class and will immediately confirm the latter."

Podvoisky later recounted how he was "overwhelmed" by Lenin's detailed questioning. Lenin scolded Podvoisky for not having checked up on the military qualifications of his unit commanders in the Red Guard. Podvoisky confessed in his memoir that he only then realized that the Red Guard should become a military force as well as a political one. "What a way to snatch at revolution," Lenin retorted. "Now the most important thing is to run it so as to win, and without applying military science it is impossible to win." He ran through a list of suggestions which no one else seemed to have thought of as yet—form special units of bold young workers, arrange to get arms from the arsenals, prepare to seize the bridges and communications. Podvoisky tried to salvage some pride by reporting that the projected Military Revolutionary Committee of the soviet was going to be completely dominated by the Bolshevik Military Organization. Lenin criticized this too, insisting that the MRC be clearly a nonparty organ to mobilize the masses, without any hint of the "dictatorship of the Military Organization," but steered firmly along the Bolshevik line. In more modern parlance, he intended the MRC to be a front organization.

Nevsky recounted how Lenin overpowered him with "the iron logic of his Marxist method, his unwavering firmness." He felt "a great surge of faith in our cause. . . . Of my doubts not a trace was left." With Antonov encouraged, Nevsky won over, and Podvoisky still dubious, the Military Organization left to put Lenin's directives into effect. They did not yet know that the Congress of Soviets had been postponed, and still believed that it would open on the 20th. Somehow they hoped that they could launch a coup before then. How? Presumably they fell back on Lenin's strategy of an attack from Finland. Antonov and Nevsky left at once for Helsingfors to concert their plans with Smilga and Dybenko for the dispatch of the troops and sailors when the call came.

❈　　❈　　❈

On Wednesday evening the 18th there was a dramatic plenary meeting of the Petrograd Soviet, a crowded session as the delegates to the national Congress of Factory Committees jammed into the Smolny assembly hall along with the members of the soviet. All the talk was about the Kamenev statement that had just come out in *Novaya Zhizn* and the plans of insurrection that it implied (underscored by Trotsky's warning that morning at the Congress of Factory Committees that "civil war is inevitable"). Martov questioned Trotsky point-blank about the Bolshevik plans. "Who gave Martov the right to ask such questions?" Trotsky shot back. Knowing that Kamenev intended if necessary to introduce a resolution against the uprising, Trotsky decided to deny all the "reports, rumors and articles relating to the supposed uprising," and particularly the newspaper story that the Bolsheviks planned to move on October 22. "We are hiding nothing. I declare in the name of the soviet: no armed move has been scheduled by us. But if in the course of things the soviet should be compelled to schedule an uprising, the workers and soldiers would go out at its call as one man." The transfer of power could be accomplished more simply. "It is understood," Trotsky asserted, "that the Congress [of Soviets] will certainly pass a resolution that the power should be handed over to the All-Russian Congress of Soviets." The bourgeoisie feared this and might take counteraction, Trotsky warned, but the government would not be permitted to withdraw the Petrograd garrison or to interfere with the Congress of Soviets: "At the first attempt of the counterrevolution to disrupt the congress, all revolutionary Russia will answer with a determined counteroffensive which will be merciless and which we will carry through to the end." Kamenev willingly agreed with all this.

Trotsky's role in the days before the revolution, distorted as it has been by Stalinist calumnies and his own overwrought defense, is one of the hardest points about this period to establish. That he was the most active, popular, and influential of all the Bolshevik leaders at large in Petrograd is beyond serious dispute. His goal, like Lenin's, was revolution by the Bolshevik Party. But the strategy through which he proposed to accomplish the goal is less certain; the evidence of the time and Trotsky's later rationale for his conduct are in conflict.

Trotsky admitted readily—as in his account of the meeting of October 10—that there was a substantial difference between Lenin and himself, in tying the Bolshevik take-over to the Congress of Soviets. Trotsky's own statements of the time went further, to make it very plain that he wanted to wait for the Congress of Soviets to vote itself the power while the Bolshevik Party prepared with relish for the resistance he expected the Provisional Government to offer. "It is the *lutte-finale*," he told John Reed on the 17th. "The bourgeois counterrevolution organizes all its forces and waits for the moment to attack us. Our answer will be decisive." This is what the Bolsheviks were saying to their followers; Sukhanov wrote, "They were being told: 'Let's wait for what the congress decides on October 20 or 25.'"

After the events of October 24 and 25, Trotsky felt compelled to stiffen the explanation of his leadership beforehand. In his book on Lenin, published in 1924, he suggested that he had deliberately provoked the government: "Our strategy was aggressive in its nature; we were beginning an attack on the power, but our agitation was so arranged that the enemy should set about breaking up the Congress of Soviets, and it would in consequence be necessary to oppose them with the most ruthless resistance." Three years later, trying to make himself look more Leninist than his enemy Stalin, Trotsky contended,

> The plan conducted and realized by me consisted in this: that in the process of mobilizing the masses under the slogan of the Congress of the Soviets as the supreme organ in the country, *and under the cover of this legal campaign,* we prepare the insurrection and strike the blow at a propitious moment, proximate to the Congress of Soviets but by no means necessarily *after* the opening of the congress.

In later writings Trotsky contended that all his talk of waiting for the congress was a deliberate sham to deceive the party's enemies. The official soviet story takes the same stand, while accusing Trotsky of meaning his peaceful statements. In this case Trotsky's critics are probably right; he was prevaricating after the fact rather than before.

It appears, though the recollections are sketchy, that later in the evening of the 18th there was another meeting of the Bolshevik leaders with Lenin, probably in another apartment near his hideout. Trotsky, Sverdlov, Stalin, and Lashevich are mentioned as participants. Despite

Lenin's agitation about Zinoviev and Kamenev, Trotsky found him at this, their only face-to-face meeting between the 10th and the 25th, unusually "calm and confident . . . , less suspicious. . . . All the same, now and again he shook his head and asked, 'and will they not forestall us? Will they not catch us napping?' I argued that from now on everything would develop almost automatically." The group decided to designate Podvoisky, Sadovsky, and Lazimir as the "organizing bureau" of the Military Revolutionary Committee, to have plans of action ready as soon as the full membership of the MRC convened.

Trotsky apparently satisfied Lenin about his disavowal of insurrection at the meeting of the soviet. In a note the next day Lenin absolved Trotsky of any misconduct: "Kamenev's subterfuge used at the meeting of the Petrograd Soviet is downright mean. He is, don't you see, in full agreement with Trotsky. But is it so difficult to understand that Trotsky *could not* talk, that he had no right to, that it was his duty not to talk in face of the enemies more than he did."

Some time on the 18th Lenin received a message giving him the text of the Kamenev statement in *Novaya Zhizn*. This was the worst yet. Lenin dashed off an indignant letter "to the members of the Bolshevik Party" condemning Zinoviev and Kamenev for the crime of "strikebreaking":

> On the eve of the critical day of October 20 [Lenin still thought the Congress of Soviets was to meet then and somehow hoped for an insurrection in the meantime] *after* the center has made a decision, to dispute this *unpublished* decision before the Rodziankos and Kerenskys in a nonparty paper—can one imagine an action more treacherous, more strikebreaking? I would consider it a shame if, in consequence of my former closeness to those former comrades, I were to hesitate to condemn them. I say outright that I do not consider them comrades any longer, and that I will fight with all my power . . . to expel them both from the party.

Before another twenty-four hours had passed Lenin received a letter from Zinoviev hitting back at Lenin for his pressure to secure the insurrectionary decision. The letter made Lenin so angry, according to his landlady, that he didn't even read to the end. He threw it on the table and exclaimed, "Zinoviev has burst out crying like a slobbering old woman. If we have to, we really will expel him from the party." He wrote out a still more violent letter to the Central Committee:

> All the elements of strikebreaking are present here. After a decision was made, no disputing it is permissible, once the matter concerns immediate and *secret* preparations for a strike. Now Zinoviev has the insolence to blame us for "warning the enemy." Is there any limit to shamelessness? Who in fact has done the damage, who has broken the strike by "warning the enemy," if not the men who made their appearance in the *nonparty* press?

Lenin was particularly enraged by the frustration of being unable to attack Zinoviev and Kamenev in public: "We cannot refute the gossipy lie of Zinoviev and Kamenev [that the insurrection was not definitely set] *without doing the cause still more harm.* Therein lies the boundless meanness, the absolute treacherousness of these two persons." There was only one answer—immediate expulsion of Zinoviev and Kamenev from the party. This task came ahead of the uprising, which because of the leak had been "put off for a long while." "I will, at *whatever cost,* brand the strikebreaker Zinoviev as a strikebreaker."

This message of the 19th, climaxing three days of almost exclusive concern with the defiance of Zinoviev and Kamenev, was the last thing of any substance that Lenin wrote (or the last that has been preserved) until the evening of the 24th. There was a short article of the 20th denouncing the SRs for their promises to the peasants, and a terse note of the 22nd or 23rd to Sverdlov about Zinoviev and Kamenev, but otherwise nothing—no more attacks on Zinoviev and Kamenev, no more warnings about counterrevolution, no more urgent appeals for insurrection (except for a couple of lines of encouragement in the note to Sverdlov), no tactical directives. By all appearances Lenin had lost hope that an insurrection could still be launched before the Congress of Soviets (even though it had been put off until the 25th). He did not leave the Fofanova apartment after the 17th; as far as the record shows, none of the Central Committee came to see him after Trotsky's reported visit on the 18th. Feeling politically and physically isolated, Lenin seems to have lapsed into a state of a real depression. He was not to be heard from again until the revolution was actually underway.

CHAPTER SEVEN

The Contest
for the Garrison

By the third week of October everybody in Petrograd expected the Bolsheviks to try to seize power—everybody but the Bolsheviks themselves. However, few believed they could succeed, especially if they moved without the cover of the Soviet Congress. On the main streets of Petrograd the well-to-do public made no effort to conceal their hatred and contempt for the Bolsheviks. One party agitator recalled,

> It was enough for a Bolshevik to appear and say a word, and at once they arrested him and took him to a police station, and told the citizens he was a German spy. . . . I was even arrested on a train, between Tsarskoe Selo and Petrograd. Some businessmen on the train started to throw me out of the window of the moving car. Some soldiers in the car came to my defense and prevented a lynching.

The same Bolshevik heard a professor say at a public meeting on the Petrograd Side, "The Bolshevik is a worm, infecting and eating away the healthy wood that is the foundation of the people's state. We need a hard, *merciless struggle* with them, to save what we now have."

Uppermost in the mind of almost every Bolshevik was not insurrection but the fear of counterrevolution. They knew the hostility of the conservatives and feared renewed repression by the government, whose strength they vastly overestimated. They easily believed every rumor that Petrograd and its soviet would at almost any time be turned over to the Cossacks or the Germans. In the middle of October the Bolsheviks were working with all the desperate energy they had to meet the expected onslaught and turn it to their own account.

From any standpoint, whether it was deliberate insurrection or defense of the soviets while they took over by proclamation, armed force was the key to Bolshevik hopes. Three sources of military support were available to the party—the regiments of the Petrograd garrison, the navy, and the workers' Red Guard. All have been romanticized in the official history. Trotsky, for one, appraised each group candidly: "The numerous garrisons lacked the will to fight. The sailors' detachments lacked numbers. The Red Guard lacked skill. The workers together with the sailors contributed energy, daring and enthusiasm. The regiments of the garrison constituted a rather inert reserve, imposing in its numbers and overwhelming in its mass."

Numerically the garrison was the potentially decisive force, and the Bolsheviks had to win it over or at least neutralize it. Altogether there were about 150,000 men in the Petrograd garrison, mostly overage, very young, or recuperating from wounds. Politically the troops leaned toward the SRs, to the extent that party preferences were clear, but their real loyalty was to the soviet and to anyone who would keep them from being sent to the front. In the wake of the Kornilov affair, several Petrograd regiments voted for "power to the soviets." When the government and the commander of the Northern Front, General Cheremisov, suggested sending them out to battle, most of the regiments were ready to rebel against the authorities and support whatever the soviet did. However, political militancy and fighting spirit varied considerably from one unit to the next, and the Bolsheviks had no assurance as to which regiments they could rely on in actual fighting. The three regiments of Don Cossack cavalry were still expected to be the mainstay of the government.

The conference called by General Cheremisov to explain his need to move reinforcements from the capital met in Pskov on October 17th. Cheremisov and his commissar, the ex-Bolshevik Voytinsky, declared to the delegates that the Petrograd garrison was part of the general defense force of the region and had to move out if so ordered. The mainly Bolshevik delegation led by Sadovsky and Krylenko suspected the political motive of weakening the forces of the soviet. They issued a declaration that had been prepared by Sverdlov insisting that the Petrograd Soviet had the final word on the transfer of garrison units. The conference quickly deadlocked, and ended the day it began with a Bolshevik walkout. Five days later, while this rupture was still fresh in everyone's memory, Cheremisov's Fifth Army elected a soldiers' committee with a Bolshevik majority.

On October 18 the conference of garrison delegates authorized by the Executive Committee of the Petrograd Soviet six days before was finally convoked at Smolny by Sadovsky, chairman of the Soldiers' Section of the Soviet and also a member of the Bolshevik Military Organization. Representatives of one regiment after another rose to state their units' nonconfidence in the government and their willingness to move at the call of the Petrograd Soviet. Trotsky made his usual rousing speech in conclusion, while the spokesmen of the All-Russian Central Executive Committee walked out after being denied the floor.

At the same time, the Bolsheviks were taking steps to organize the sentiment of the soldiers into a reliable political instrument. They had extensive links with the troops through the party Military Organization but could not rely on any of the units to respond to orders in the name of the Bolshevik Party as such. They had to use the authority of the Petrograd Soviet, which they controlled but which lacked the organization to handle troops and defend itself militarily. The solution was worked out by Lenin and Podvoisky at their meeting on October 17th: the Bolshevik Military Organization would move into the paper framework provided by the plan of the Military Revolutionary Committee, and proceed with its work in the guise of an organ of the soviet. Podvoisky and his associates went to work the very next day as an "organizational bureau" for the still embryonic MRC.

Much less effort was needed to make the navy an effective fighting force for the soviet. The sailors were more commonly of working-class origin, and the crews of the battleships and cruisers particularly had a revolutionary tradition going back to 1905. In July, 1917, the sailors from Kronstadt had already shown their readiness to fight against the Provisional Government, and the men at Helsingfors, led by the "Tsentrobalt" (the Central Committee of the Baltic Fleet), were just as eager. They had access to arms and were ready to come into Petrograd. Especially important were two military formations of sailors, the Fleet Guard Crew and the Second Baltic Fleet Crew, quartered in Petrograd itself not far from the Nikolaevsky Bridge and the Marinsky Palace. These men repeatedly affirmed their readiness to move any time the soviet called them.

Among the Petrograd workers, there was no lack of Bolshevik enthusiasm. The vicious circle of shortages, inflation, strikes, and further economic disruption was driving the working class overwhelmingly to vote for the Bolsheviks in the soviets and the factory committees. However, it was easier to find voters than activists, and among the workers willing to take up arms there were serious limitations of organization, equipment, and training. Military formations of workers had grown by fits and starts, beginning with the workers' militia set up after the February Revolution under the aegis of the soviet to help the city government keep order. By the end of March, certain Bolsheviks—Nevsky and Bonch-Bruevich—were urging the creation of a separate body, a Red Guard of workers organized to "defend the revolution." In April they held a couple of organizational meetings, but the effort was blocked by the moderate leaders of the soviet after the alarm of the April Days. Red Guards were organized in a number of factories, particularly in the Vyborg district, but nothing more in the direction of city-wide organization was accomplished until a conference held early in August as an adjunct of the Bolshevik Party Congress elected a planning committee. The great quantitative spurt in the Red Guard came with its legalization at the time of the Kornilov affair. The rolls increased to perhaps 15,000 men (a quarter of them in the Vyborg district). The Red Guard units lined up under the soviet's "Committee for the Defense of the Revolution," and were issued considerable quantities of rifles and ammunition. At the same time, the Bolshevik Military Organization expanded its activity to cover the nominally nonpartisan Red Guards and give them military training as well as the Bolshevik political line.

By October the militancy of most of the workers, expressed in strikes, anti-government meetings, the Red Guard movement, and attempts to implement "workers' control," had reached its peak. On October 7 the Vyborg district Red Guards held a formal conference to set up their headquarters and adopt regulations. They were given a room in the apartment where the district Bolshevik Committee met. Other districts copied the Vyborg setup, while resolutions for power to the soviets rolled into Smolny from one factory after another, including one from the giant Putilov works reported "unanimously." But the creation of a centralized Red Guard organization was still a matter of debate and resolutions; the Bolshevik City conference made it definite only on October 10 when it urged the Petrograd Soviet to "take the matter of creating a Red Guard into its own hands."

On the 12th, simultaneously with its approval of the project of the Military Revolutionary Committee, the Executive Committee of the Petrograd Soviet responded by setting up a "Department of the Workers' Guard." It was provided with a "temporary secretariat" to supervise the development of the Red Guard and call a city-wide organizational conference of Red Guards, "in the second half of the current month." There was no insurrectionary haste in mind here—in fact, the Department of the Workers' Guard did not get around to calling the conference for several days and then set it for October 22.

The Red Guard units had been growing in numbers faster than arms could be found, but in the middle of October there was a breakthrough at the Sestroretsk arms factory out on the shore of the Gulf of Finland. Workers had been hounding Trotsky in the soviet with appeals for arms and impatiently asking, "When is the thing going to begin?"

"Well, we don't hold the arsenals," Trotsky explained.

"We've been up to the Sestroretsk plant," one group exclaimed.

"Well, what about it?"

"They said that if the soviet orders it, they will issue arms."

Trotsky casually wrote out an order for five thousand rifles. They were delivered the same day.

With this, a steady run on the Sestroretsk warehouse began. As soon as they heard of the bonanza, the Red Guards of several factories on their own initiative sent teams up to Sestroretsk in trucks to help themselves to rifles. Not until the 18th did Colonel Polkovnikov receive a request to post a guard and stop the losses, and not until the evening of the 19th did the guard get there. By this time, thousands of Petrograd workers were ready for some excitement, if not for disciplined combat.

*   *   *

Kerensky had been away from Petrograd, touring the battlefront, from October 14 to 17. In his absence the Winter Palace was growing more apprehensive about the danger of a Bolshevik uprising. Acting Prime Minister Konovalov conferred with the military command, and orders went out to strengthen the guard at various key points around the city. The Pre-Parliament's "Committee on the Struggle with the Counterrevolution" heard reports by several security officials, among them Colonel Polkovnikov, who asserted again that all necessary steps had been taken to prepare against a Bolshevik move. A press conference followed, at which the same readiness was expressed. The assistant garrison commander, a Captain Kuzmin, told the reporters, "The uprising conceived by the Bolsheviks won't succeed." So sensitive was the public to the ebb and flow of rumor that one newspaper claimed the next day that these reports had caused the Bolsheviks to call off a move supposedly planned for the 17th.

In the evening Kerensky returned from the front. He intended to go back again immediately, but Konovalov dissuaded him. A meeting of the cabinet was held to review the preparations taken against the Bolsheviks. War Minister Verkhovsky and Interior Minister Nikitin reported their confidence that any street demonstrations could be put down promptly. Kerensky declared that he hoped the Bolsheviks would move so that he would have the opportunity to smash them.

Kamenev's note in *Novaya Zhizn* the next morning disturbed the government no less than Lenin. Everyone in government circles was convinced that the Bolsheviks planned some kind of armed coup for the 20th, two days hence—even though the Congress of Soviets had been put off. Colonel Polkovnikov issued an order warning his troops, "In Petrograd irresponsible appeals for armed moves and pogroms are continuing." He directed the military units to cooperate with the civil authorities in maintaining public order. Kerensky, evidently convinced that the Bolsheviks were about to take the initiative he had hoped for, met with his cabinet in the evening to hear further reports by Verkhovsky and Nikitin. The cabinet gave its assent to firm measures against the anticipated uprising. Kerensky spent the rest of the night working out the military details with Colonel Polkovnikov, General Bagratuni, and the brigade commanders.

The next day Headquarters quickly began to put the agreed-on disposition of troops into effect. As the Menshevik paper *Rabochaya Gazeta* reported on the 20th,

> In spite of the fact that the rumors of the move by the Bolsheviks on the 20th of October have obviously not been borne out, yesterday all the measures for the preservation of the security of the capital were taken that had been decided on at the conference of the Minister-President [Kerensky], the Minister of War, the Minister of Internal Affairs, and the Commander in Chief of the District.

In certain parts of the city Cossack patrols were out all night. "The guarding of the city," the Mensheviks thought, "has been entrusted to the most reliable military units, who beyond any doubt will undeviatingly obey the directives of the Provisional Government." The colonel in command of the Winter Palace guard counted up his forces—some seven hundred officer cadets, including a machine-gun unit with six guns; six field artillery pieces; ample ammunition; and half a dozen armored cars, each armed with two machine guns. He issued detailed instructions for his men to occupy the various approaches to the Winter Palace if an emergency were signalled.

Kerensky was perfectly confident. He had a talk with the British Ambassador Buchanan and told him that he was ready to crush the Bolsheviks as soon as they appeared in the streets. In the same spirit he reported to the Pre-Parliament that he knew the Bolsheviks' intentions and had sufficient forces to take care of them. Outside of Petrograd he was even prepared to take the initiative: in the city of Kaluga, near Moscow, the Cossacks were ordered out and broke up the local soviet. (This development accentuated the fears of the Bolsheviks, as an example of what might happen to the whole Congress of Soviets.) The standing order to arrest Lenin was renewed by Minister of Justice Maliantovich (Trotsky's defense attorney in 1905), and the Petrograd prosecutor asked the army for troops to carry out the order. Ominously, Colonel Polkovnikov replied that he hadn't enough reliable men to spare for a search.

The Mensheviks and SRs of the All-Russian Central Executive Committee gave their full support to the government's defensive preparations. They appointed a new commissar, the SR Malevsky, to represent them at the Headquarters of the Military District, and tried to forbid the unauthorized issue of arms to workers without approval. To offset the effect of the Bolsheviks' garrison conference of the 18th, the CEC got Polkovnikov to summon a new garrison conference at Headquarters.

Most of the units sent representatives to Polkovnikov's conference, but they turned out to have a majority against the government. Dan addressed the group with a warning that a Bolshevik move would provoke counterrevolution and cited Zinoviev and Kamenev in support of his argument. As the soldier delegates debated late into the night, Lazimir challenged the authority of the session. Following his lead, the delegates voted their readiness to join in any "move" ordered by the Petrograd Soviet, declared the conference invalid, and dispersed. Nevertheless the CEC endorsed the government's steps to suppress any demonstration and announced "full coordination of action of the Committee with the Headquarters of the District."

On the 20th the government authorities put the finishing touches on their defensive preparations—a little late, to be sure, if the Bolshevik move had actually come on that day. A bicycle company of forty men was added to the garrison of the Winter Palace. Headquarters at the front was wired to send fresh Cossack units to replace those which were beginning to be affected by Bolshevik propaganda. The Brigade of Infantry Guard Reserves was given detailed instructions about the positions to take "in case of a move by anarchist elements."

This last order is particularly interesting because it shows the thoroughness of the government's military plans and the degree to which they anticipated the actual moves by the Bolsheviks that came on the 24th and the 25th. The "chief objectives of an attack" were listed—the Winter Palace, Smolny (did the government expect to occupy it in the meantime?), the Marinsky Palace where the Pre-Parliament sat, the Tauride Palace, the District Headquarters, the State Bank, the Central Post Office, the telegraph office, and the telephone exchange. "Every effort must be aimed at keeping these institutions in our hands." The government would concentrate on keeping the center of the city (south of the Neva and north of the Fontanka canal) clear of rebels, and holding the strategic Neva bridges. Ironically, the government's plan was almost the exact counterpart, only more thorough, of the strategy

1.

Vladimir Ilyich Lenin. The photograph captures some of the leader's magnetic qualities.

2. A crowd gathers on the Field of Mars in Petrograd during the February Revolution, 1917.

3.

A demonstration before the Winter Palace, Petrograd, February, 1917.

Ruins of the State Prison which was burned and its prisoners freed during the February Revolution.

4.

5.

Prince Georgi Lvov, first Prime
Minister of the Provisional
Government.

Mikhail Tereshchenko, Finance
Minister in the Provisional
Government.

6.

Alexander Konovalov, Minister of
Trade and Industry in the
Provisional Government.

The Provisional Government's first Foreign Minister
(and the leader of the Kadets), Pavel Milyukov,
with his family.

7.

8.

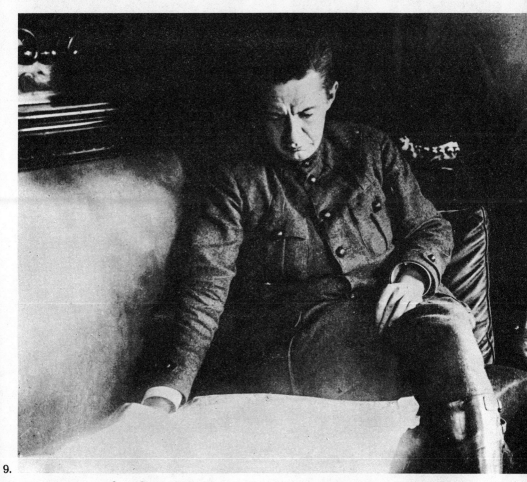

9.

Alexander Kerensky, first appointed Minister of Justice in the Provisional Government, later Prime Minister and the Bolsheviks' chief opponent.

10.

Georgi V. Plekhanov, Marxist theorist and
a leader of the Menshevik faction.

11.

Julius Martov, leader of the left-wing
Menshevik-Internationalists.

12.

Grigori Zinoviev, Lenin's closest
associate but an opponent of
insurrection during October, 1917.

13.

Leon Trotsky, on-the-spot leader of
the Bolshevik Revolution.

14.

Alexei I. Rykov, a cautious Bolshevik in 1917, but Lenin's successor as Premier in 1924.

15.

Vladimir A. Antonov-Ovseyenko, formerly a Menshevik, who led the Bolshevik attack on the Winter Palace.

Moisei S. Uritsky, eldest of the Menshevik revolutionaries in exile who joined Lenin in 1917.

16.

17.

Lev M. Kamenev, the Bolshevik who led the
opposition to Lenin's hard line in 1917.

18.

Joseph Stalin, in 1917 chief editor of *Pravda*,
in an uncharacteristically cheerful photograph
of the period.

The Ksheshinskaya mansion, Bolshevik headquarters between February and July, 1917, and
now the Museum of the October Revolution.

19.

20

Nadezhda Krupskaya, Lenin's wife and an active revolutionary.

Alexandra Kollontai, the most prominent woman Bolshevik, as she appeared in 1908.

21.

Stalin's police record from the files of the Imperial Secret Police.

The forged passport with the portrait taken in disguise that Lenin used to escape to Finland after a warrant for his arrest had been issued in July, 1917.

23.

24.

Lenin announces his April Theses at a meeting of the Bolsheviks and Mensheviks in the Tauride Palace, April 4, 1917.

25.

The May 1 (April 18, old style) demonstrations in the Winter Palace Square.

General Lavr Kornilov reviewing his troops.

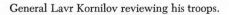

26.

Политическая манифестацiя 18-го iюня 1917 г. въ Петроградѣ.

27.

28.

The Soviet demonstration of June 18, 1917, taken over by the Bolsheviks. The banners read, "Peace to the Whole World," "All Power to the People," "All the Land to the People," and "Down with the Capitalist Ministers."

Demonstrators being shot down on the Nevsky Prospekt during the riot of the July Days.

29.

Yakov M. Sverdlov, Bolshevik party secretary and one of Lenin's most devoted and disciplined followers.

30.

Andrei Bubnov, a militant member of the Bolshevik Central Committee.

31.

Grigori Sokolnikov, co-editor, with Stalin, of *Pravda*.

32.

Felix Dzerzhinsky, liaison man between headquarters, the Bolshevik Central Committee and the Party's Military Organization.

Lenin had outlined. All important points were placed under guard; in the case of the telephone exchange orders were to maintain the guard "until the return of calm in the city, through the 24th of October [sic!]."

While the government was belatedly providing for these police measures, its internal coherence and resolve were wracked again by a new political crisis over the familiar but insoluble issue of war and peace. The one hope for the Provisional Government, the Stockholm Conference proposed by neutral socialists for the summer of 1917, had been torpedoed by the Allied governments. The Allied ambassadors, abetted by Foreign Minister Tereshchenko, had been putting unremitting pressure on Kerensky to restore military discipline and step up the Russian war effort. War Minister Verkhovsky came to the conclusion that morale could never be rebuilt in the army without the definite prospect of an early peace, and on October 20, without consulting the cabinet, he said so at a meeting of the defense and foreign affairs committees of the Pre-Parliament. Tereshchenko was furious, and rushed to report this stab in the back to Kerensky; the cabinet at once endorsed the suspension of Verkhovsky from his ministerial post and sent him off on "leave." This summary move enraged the socialists in the Pre-Parliament, who were prepared to carry on their battle with Kerensky even in the teeth of the coming revolutionary storm.

Kerensky says that he received an Austrian feeler for a separate peace about this time, and alleges that the Bolsheviks struck when they did on German orders to forestall the political gain that a peace move would bring to the Provisional Government. This is sheer speculation about a move that is much more fully explained by events in Petrograd itself. It was the Bolsheviks who were profiting more and more from Kerensky's unwillingness to consider peace, as the French military representative Jacques Sadoul observed:

> The desire for an immediate peace, at any price, is general.
>
> On this point, all the Russians whom I have seen, without exception, are agreed with the Bolsheviks, and the only thing that divides people is a difference of clarity, or to be frank, of honesty in the expression of this view: an end to the war, cost what it may. . . .
> Anarchy reigns in the rear. For six months the government has not governed any more. The Milyukovs, the Kerenskys are chatter-

ing ideologues, without energy, without method, incapable of accomplishment.

✳   ✳   ✳

The Bolshevik leadership was still involved on the 20th with the reverberations of the Zinoviev-Kamenev problem. *Rabochi Put* carried the second installment of the condemnation Lenin had written on the 17th, along with a note of protest from Zinoviev: his views were far from what Lenin represented then to be, and the party could still close ranks. Stalin added the editorial comment, "For our part we express the hope that with the declaration Comrade Zinoviev has made (and also the declaration of Comrade Kamenev in the soviet) the question can be considered exhausted. The sharpness of tone of Comrade Lenin's article does not change the fact that fundamentally we remain of like mind."

The Bolshevik Central Committee met with eight members and one candidate present to talk about Lenin's break with Zinoviev and Kamenev. Sverdlov read Lenin's most recent and violent letter demanding that they be expelled from the party, a step that none of the Committee were ready to take except the candidate member Ioffe. Dzerzhinsky suggested as a compromise that Kamenev be ordered simply to quit political work; he added that Zinoviev (who, like Lenin, was under order of arrest) had gone back into hiding and was not doing anything anyway. Stalin favored waiting for a full plenum of the Central Committee to decide the matter. Uritsky reported that the Moscow Bolsheviks favored this course, and moreover opposed the armed insurrection themselves. Sverdlov said that the present meeting lacked the authority to expell Kamenev and Zinoviev from the party, but that it might accept Kamenev's tendered resignation from the Central Committee. Debate then swirled around this proposal. Trotsky was in favor of accepting the resignation. Stalin was against it, but thought that Kamenev and Zinoviev should be forced to submit to the majority in the name of unity. Sokolnikov, an editor of *Rabochi Put* along with Stalin, pointed out that he was against the editorial statement conciliatory to Zinoviev. Milyutin offered a resolution that no member of the CC should speak against a decision of the body, and this reaffirmation of "democratic centralism" was adopted unanimously. Finally the

Committee voted 5 to 3 (probably Stalin, Milyutin, and Dzerzhinsky) with 1 abstention to accept Kamenev's resignation. Stalin thereupon offered his resignation as an editor of *Rabochi Put;* this was rejected.

Turning to preparations for a showdown with the government, the Central Committee heard a report from the Bolshevik Military Organization (the text of which has been lost), which evidently raised the question of the group's status in relation to the projected Military Revolutionary Committee of the soviet. Trotsky suggested, "All our organizations can enter the revolutionary center [the MRC], and in our [Bolshevik] group there discuss all questions of interest." This formulation served as the authority for the leaders of the Bolshevik Military Organization to become in fact the core of the Military Revolutionary Committee.

It was also on the 20th that the Military Revolutionary Committee finally became a reality and held its first plenary session, in a classroom on the third floor of the Smolny Institute. The makeup of the committee followed the plan voted by the Executive Committee of the Petrograd Soviet on the 12th, with several dozen members, including the whole presidium of the soviet; representatives of the trade unions, factory committees, and the army; and members of the military organizations of the parties—i.e., of the Bolsheviks and Left SRs, the only people who took part in the MRC. No record was ever made of the exact number of members, let alone a list of names, which constantly fluctuated.

The first plenum of the MRC did nothing more than listen to reports on behalf of the "organizing bureau," by Podvoisky and Antonov (just back from Finland and the front). The same two announced that they were starting to dispatch commissars to various buildings and military units (though no actual assignments were recorded), and they warned against possible clashes that might accompany the Cossack parade scheduled for Sunday the 22nd. A second plenum of the MRC was held on the 21st to chose a bureau of five men, and conceivably it was a plenary meeting that heard the report on negotiations with Headquarters that night. Otherwise there is no record of any further meeting of the full committee, certainly not before the uprising. According to Trotsky, "The committee hardly met once in plenary session. . . . The work was carried on through the bureau under the guidance of the president [presumably himself as chairman of the soviet], with Sverdlov brought in upon all important matters."

The bureau of the MRC selected on the 21st consisted of Lazimir, another Left SR named Sukharkov, Podvoisky and Antonov from the Bolshevik Military Organization, and Sadovsky, the Bolshevik chairman of the Soldiers' Section of the Petrograd Soviet. Lazimir was officially the chairman of the bureau and of the full MRC. (Trotsky claims that he was not only an ex officio member but chairman as well, though no available documentation supports this; he was, of course, chairman of the entire soviet). Podvoisky was Lazimir's deputy and Antonov the secretary. But the practice of the committee was highly informal: any member of the bureau signed documents in the name of the chairman or the secretary. The real leader was Podvoisky; by October 24 he was signing most of the papers "for the chairman." A day or two after the Bolshevik seizure of power Lazimir had ceased to play any active part. (Left SR participation in the MRC ended quickly.) All of the other active members up to the seizure of power were members of the Bolshevik Military Organization: Nevsky, Yeremeyev, Lashevich, and Mekhanoshin, a Bolshevik soldier. Sverdlov and Dzerzhinsky were the liaison men of the Bolshevik Central Committee. After the crisis broke on the 24th, practically all the members of the Central Committee, including Lenin, participated in the frantic meetings of the MRC at one time or another. But fundamentally the MRC operation was the work of the Bolshevik Military Organization, and in unguarded moments it was still referred to as such. After two meetings, the Military Revolutionary Committee had served its essential purpose of giving the label of the soviet to the efforts of the Bolshevik Military Organization to get control of the Petrograd garrison.

Otherwise the preparations of the Petrograd Soviet gave little satisfaction to the Bolshevik leadership. The Central Committee met on the 21st (with eight members present) and heard a report by Dzerzhinsky on the "complete disorganization in the Executive Committee"; he had to propose that the Bolshevik members of the body do their work or get out, and a group of new people (including Stalin, Milyutin, and Dzerzhinsky himself) were assigned to the Executive Committee to stiffen it. The Zinoviev-Kamenev affair had its final echo in a proposal to print as a brochure the three installments of Lenin's "Letter to

Comrades" that *Rabochi Put* had just finished publishing that morning. Presumably still hoping for unity, the Central Committee rejected the proposal. Finally the Central Committee took up the impending Congress of Soviets and discussed possible rules and agenda. Sverdlov mentioned the need for a preparatory meeting of the Bolshevik delegates and suggested that Lenin be brought into a meeting again to help prepare theses for such a meeting. Nothing in the minutes as recorded implied any talk about an uprising prior to the congress, and no recorded meeting of the Central Committee was held again on this or any other question until the storm had broken on the 24th. All of Lenin's imprecations to the contrary notwithstanding, the Bolshevik Central Committee had acquiesced in the policy of waiting for the Congress of Soviets to initiate a take-over peacefully.

A legend about this meeting or a later one the same day originated with John Reed, author of the world-renowned eyewitness account, *Ten Days That Shook the World*. He reported,

> On the 3rd [of November; October 21st, old style] the leaders of the Bolsheviki had another historic meeting behind closed doors. . . . I waited in the corridor outside the door; and Volodarsky as he came out told me what was going on.
> Lenin spoke: "November 6 will be too early. We must have an all-Russian basis for the rising; and on the 6th all the delegates to the congress will not have arrived. . . . On the other hand, November 8th will be too late. By that time the congress will be organized, and it is difficult for a large organized body of people to take swift, decisive action. We must act on the 7th, the day the congress meets, so that we may say to it, 'Here is the power! What are you going to do with it?'"

There is no documentary or memoir evidence that such a meeting on that date ever occurred. As Reed describes it, it would have been in Smolny; it is certain that Lenin never went to Smolny before the 24th (although there is one report that Lenin went out of his hideout on the 22nd to an undisclosed meeting place). Furthermore, the notion that an uprising could be "too early" because the delegates had not arrived never appears in Lenin's published writings, and seems rather the wording of a compromise speaker. In the confusion of those days Reed probably mixed up the secondhand verbal reports he got of several Bolshevik meetings, up to the day of the revolution itself.

＊   ＊   ＊

While the Bolshevik Central Committee marked time, the Military Revolutionary Committee—or the Bolshevik Military Organization acting under that name—was beginning to establish some strength. Another Bolshevik-sponsored conference of regimental committee members met at Smolny to hear Trotsky propose three resolutions, all of which passed: (1) to endorse the creation of the MRC and promise it "full support in all its steps toward more closely connecting the front and the rear in the interests of the revolution"; (2) to urge avoidance of violence and "provocation" on the part of both the pro-soviet forces and the Cossacks when meetings took place the next day, the "Day of the Petrograd Soviet"; (3) to demand that "the All-Russian Congress of Soviets must take power in its own hands and guarantee peace, land, and bread to the people," to which end the conference pledged the congress "to put at its disposal all our forces, to the last man." Again, nothing was said about insurrection before the congress, and someone actually spoke up to note that the resolution did not square with the articles by Lenin that had just appeared in *Rabochi Put*. "The MRC calculated," Podvoisky wrote afterwards, "that the enemy himself would be the first to take the offensive."

To tighten its ties with the garrison the MRC began in earnest to dispatch commissars to the various military units and key buildings. "The majority of these commissars," recalled one of the group, "were young Bolshevik officers who were active workers in the Military Organization of the Central Committee and had only just been released from prison (on bail posted by the party) where they had been held on charges of active participation in the events of July 3–5." A number of Bolshevik delegates arriving from the provinces for the Congress of Soviets were pressed into service as commissars. But in some cases, for lack of staff, the MRC merely confirmed commissars chosen by the units themselves from their own ranks. Only a couple of the appointments of the 21st were recorded, though presumably a fair number were made. Chudnovsky went to the Preobrazhensky Regiment, strategically quartered just east of the Hermitage, and persuaded them to support the soviet or at least remain neutral. In a bold attempt to get control of the garrison from the top, eight men (including Lazimir, Sadovsky, and Mekhanoshin) were delegated to go to the Headquarters of the Military District and demand that it submit to their authority. The Left SRs in the MRC were a little unhappy over this boldness, and preferred to "infiltrate" the Headquarters without venturing to countermand its orders, but they finally agreed on the formula that the commissars should demand that Headquarters submit all military orders to them for endorsement.

At the same time, the MRC commanded the arsenals and arms depots not to issue arms or ammunition without written permission of the MRC, and commissars were sent out to enforce these orders. Oddly enough, the Headquarters of the military district was formally notified of this assertion of power by the MRC. A particularly important move was the appointment of M. K. Ter-Arutiuniants as commissar of the Kronverk Arsenal, behind the Peter-Paul fortress, to forestall a reported government plan to distribute its stock of arms to the cadets and Cossacks.

Perhaps influenced by knowledge of these steps, the government became convinced that the Bolshevik "move" which it had expected on the 20th was now due to be launched on the 22nd. The Kadet paper asserted confidently that if the Bolsheviks moved, the masses would refuse to follow them and they would easily be suppressed. Nevertheless the authorities were afraid to assert themselves firmly. It was reported that the government would not enforce its ban on street meetings as long as they were peaceful. Colonel Polkovnikov ordered the scheduled religious procession of the Cossacks cancelled, so as not to provoke any clash that might serve as the excuse for an insurrection. But with some strange inspiration the government picked this critical day to cut the Petrograd bread ration by one-third.

The delegates of the MRC met Colonel Polkovnikov at his headquarters towards eleven o'clock that evening. Sadovsky, in his phlegmatic way, stated the claims of the committee, but Polkovnikov firmly refused to submit to their demands. "We only recognize the Central Executive Committee, we don't recognize your commissars; if they break the law, we will arrest them," the delegates were told. All they could do was take a taxi back to Smolny and report to a special session of the MRC (or more probably of its bureau) that Headquarters had "broken with the soviet." Thereupon the MRC called an emergency conference of the regimental representatives who had first convened on the 18th. Sparked by Trotsky and Sverdlov, the conference gave its assent early in the morning of Sunday the 22nd to a proclamation that was telephoned to the entire garrison. In retrospect this statement stands out as the beginning of the soviet take-over:

> At its meeting of the 21st of October the revolutionary garrison of Petrograd rallied around the Military Revolutionary Committee of the Petrograd Soviet of Workers' and Soldiers' Deputies as its leading organ.
>
> In spite of this, on the night of October 21–22 the headquarters of the Petrograd Military District failed to recognize the Military Revolutionary Committee and refused to conduct its work in co-operation with the representatives of the soldiers' section of the soviet.
>
> By this act the headquarters breaks with the revolutionary garrison and the Petrograd Soviet of Workers' and Soldiers' Deputies.
>
> By breaking with the organized garrison of the capital, the headquarters is becoming a direct instrument of the counterrevolutionary forces.
>
> The Military Revolutionary Committee disclaims all responsibility for the actions of the headquarters of the Petrograd Military District.
>
> Soldiers of Petrograd!
>
> 1) The protection of the revolutionary order from counter-revolutionary incursions rests on you, under the direction of the Military Revolutionary Committee.
>
> 2) Any directives for the garrison that are not signed by the Military Revolutionary Committee are invalid.
>
> 3) All directives for today—the Day of the Petrograd Soviet of Workers' and Soldiers' Deputies—remain in full force.
>
> 4) Every soldier in the garrison has the obligation of vigilance, restraint, and undeviating discipline.
>
> 5) The revolution is in danger. Long live the revolutionary garrison!

At an early hour in the morning Vice-Premier Konovalov was informed of the MRC's proclamation. He hastened to the Winter Palace to discuss the situation with Kerensky, only to find to his surprise that no one had told the Prime Minister about it yet. The two men resolved to suppress any attempt to create a "dual power" and agreed that Colonel Polkovnikov was not acting decisively enough to accomplish this. Kerensky decided to work directly through the garrison commander, General Bagratuni, and instructed him to send the Petrograd Soviet an ultimatum to retract its statement to the troops.

Polkovnikov (on whose initiative it is not clear) convoked another garrison conference of his own. Few people came; most of the regimental representatives went instead to a meeting at Smolny to discuss Polkovnikov's call. Polkovnikov had to request Smolny to send a delegation, which it did, led by the Bolshevik lieutenant Dashkevich. There was a heated exchange. The headquarters spokesmen insisted that the actions of the MRC were illegal. The Bolsheviks reaffirmed their demand to pass on all orders and departed with an invitation to return next day for further negotiations. General Cheremisov, consulted by the Petrograd Headquarters, insisted on his right to move the garrison to the front and threatened to use his whole army against the Military Revolutionary Committee if need be. By the end of the day the government had orders out to start loyal troops on their way toward Petrograd from all up and down the front, from the Baltic provinces to Rumania. With this support in view, Kerensky wired Chief of Staff Dukhonin that it would be easy to handle the Bolsheviks. However, the French Ambassador Noulens, after talking with Kerensky about his security measures, left disturbed; "By his words and his vague gestures, I understood that nothing had been organized. He still undoubtedly relied on good luck."

The "Day of the Petrograd Soviet" came off without serious incident. Meetings and demonstrations were held all over the city. "Our best orators, including Trotsky, Volodarsky, Kollontai, and others," the Bolshevik Lashevich recalled, spoke at one gathering after another, and were heard by 25,000 people—a considerable number in the days before radio and loudspeakers. In the evening Trotsky made an impassioned speech at the House of the People on the Petrograd Side: "The Soviet Government will give everything the country contains to the poor and the men in the trenches. You, bourgeois, have two fur caps!—give one of them to the soldier, who is freezing in the trenches.

Do you have warm boots? Stay at home. The worker needs your boots.
. . ." He won a great ovation with his eulogy of "the soviet, which is
taking on the great burden of carrying to a conclusion the victory of
the revolution, and of giving you bread, land, and peace."

Judgments of the success of the day's demonstrations depended on
the politics of the observer. Milyukov wrote, "The frightened population remained at home or stood aside." Abramovich, a leader of the
Menshevik-oriented Jewish Bund, concurred on the passivity of the
masses. But according to Trotsky,

> All Petrograd, with the exception of its upper strata, was one solid
> meeting. . . . The people of the slums, of the attics and basements,
> stood still by the hour in threadbare coat or gray uniform, with
> caps or heavy shawls still on their heads, the mud of the streets
> soaked through their shoes, an autumn cough catching at their
> throat. They stood there packed shoulder to shoulder, and crowding
> ever closer to make room for more, to make room for all, listening
> tirelessly, hungrily, passionately, demandingly, fearing lest they
> miss a word of what it is so necessary to understand, to assimilate,
> and to do.

Sukhanov, witnessing Trotsky's speech, reported "a mood bordering on
ecstasy. . . . Throughout Petersburg more or less the same thing was
going on. Everywhere there were final reviews and final vows. Thousands, tens of thousands and hundreds of thousands of people. . . .
This, actually, was already an insurrection. Things had started. . . ."

Along with all the speechmaking of the 22nd the conference of Red
Guards finally convened at the premises of the Bolshevik Military Organization on the Liteiny Prospekt near the bridge to the Vyborg Side.
Sverdlov and Dzerzhinsky represented the party leadership. The conference adopted a set of "Rules of the Workers' Red Guard" providing
for a quasi-military organization of squads, platoons, companies, and
battalions. In the spirit of the revolution, "The whole commanding staff
. . . is elected"; at the top there would be a representative "Central
Command" directly subordinated to the Petrograd Soviet. But like the
Military Revolutionary Committee, the key men in the Central Command of the Red Guards were the same Bolsheviks who had been
doing the planning for a Workers' Guard ever since August.

In some quarters there was noticeable relief that the Bolsheviks had not started an actual uprising on the 22nd after all. Kerensky, meeting his cabinet in the evening as usual, insisted that the time had come to liquidate the Military Revolutionary Committee. Foreign Minister Tereshchenko felt that he had momentarily persuaded Kerensky to issue an order for the arrest of the leaders of the soviet. But Colonel Polkovnikov reported that he had reopened negotiations with the MRC, and the cabinet decided to confine its demands to the retraction of the MRC claim to countersign orders. The Menshevik and SR representatives of the Central Executive Committee expressed their hope for a peaceful settlement through their negotiations with the Petrograd Soviet. Finally it was decided to propose terms to allow more representatives of the "revolutionary democracy" at Headquarters (presumably including the men from the MRC) and to leave the MRC commissars with the regiments as long as they were subordinate to the commissars of the CEC—a rather unrealistic thing to expect of the Bolsheviks. On the 23rd Konovalov, Tereshchenko, and S.N. Tretyakov, chairman of the Economic Council, had lunch with the British Ambassador Buchanan and complained that Kerensky was too much of a socialist to deal effectively with the forces of anarchy.

*   *   *

Monday the 23rd of October was an ominously overcast day. The church spire in the Peter-Paul fortress was lost in the low clouds, and a biting wind was whipping up the grey waters of the Neva. The Bolsheviks, seriously alarmed about a possible government strike, began organizing some defenses around Smolny. Up to this point Smolny still had a military guard appointed by the government before the Bolsheviks took over the Petrograd Soviet, and it was hardly secure from the standpoint of the soviet's new leaders. Trotsky later recalled some of the difficulties they were having:

> The machine-gun unit, which had been given this assignment under Kerensky, seemed ill-suited, though the machine gunners became Bolsheviks at the moment of the coup. The commandant of Smolny at the time was Grekov. He considered himself an SR-Syndicalist and under the Bolsheviks spent a long time in prison. At that moment he was very hostile to us. . . . Grekov . . . said, "Well, of

course, you can perhaps accomplish a coup, but this, of course, won't be for long—they will strangle you"—and he didn't want to be linked with us. But the commander of the machine-gun unit came up to me and said that we, if you please, are for you.

When they began to check the machine guns, they turned out to be in completely useless condition. The soldiers were lying around and also appeared to be completely unfit for the struggle. We decided to bring in some other machine-gun unit, I don't remember which; but only at dawn on the 25th did they appear there with their machine guns.

Red Guards and armored cars gave a little more substance to the Smolny garrison. More appointments of commissars to the garrison units were made by the leaders of the Military Revolutionary Committee (though only a couple are documented), and the committee proclaimed very boldly "to the Population of Petrograd," in the first of a steady flow of fiery leaflets,

> In the interests of the defense of the revolution and its conquests against attempts on the part of the counterrevolution, we have appointed commissars to the military units and especially important points in the capital and its environs. Orders and directives pertaining to these points will be executed only after confirmation by the commissars whom we have authorized.

Simultaneously the committee issued an order to the garrison to be ready for any trouble and to prevent the entry of any "Kornilovite" forces into the city, with arms if necessary. "The revolution is in danger! But nevertheless its forces are incomparably greater than the forces of the counterrevolution! Victory is ours! Long live the people!"

A young Bolshevik lieutenant by the name of Blagonravov got back from a mission to Moscow on the 11 A.M. train, and walked from the Nikolaevsky station to Smolny to get his next assignment. He found the heads of the Military Revolutionary Committee busy in their office on the third floor. Podvoisky told Blagonravov that the workers and soldiers could no longer be restrained from revolution, but that the Central Committee of the party had decided to conduct its struggle against the government in such a way as to minimize losses. Podvoisky was referring particularly to a debate in the MRC the day before about control of the Peter-Paul fortress, which had so far eluded their grasp. Ter-Arutiuniants, commissar of the Kronverk Arsenal, had been directed to take over the nearby fortress as well. He came back to Smolny to report to the MRC that the fortress commander refused to recognize him and had almost arrested him. Antonov proposed direct action: to send some reliable troops of the Pavlov Regiment to seize control of the fortress. "Trotsky was called in to consider this question," Antonov recalled. "Trotsky was then playing the decisive role. The advice he gave us was a product of his revolutionary intuition: that we capture the fortress from within. 'It cannot be that the troops there are not sympathetic,' he said." A majority of the MRC supported Trotsky, and Antonov was "extremely annoyed." He wrote a report to Lenin about the "indecisiveness" of the MRC:

> I understand the tactic of utilizing soviet legality; I understand the necessity of not being cut off too far ahead of the basic reserves, and of remaining in contact with the masses of workers and soldiers. But when reaction attacks, it is necessary to act quickly and decisively. In this tendency to put off the decisive battle until the Congress of Soviets, on which Trotsky insists, we can lose the initiative, we can let the masses cool off, we can lose everything.

The MRC still needed a commissar to initiate the peaceful penetration of the fortress. As often happened, Podvoisky turned to the nearest available man—Lieutenant Blagonravov—to toss him the assignment. With considerable anxiety, as he confessed in his recollections, Blagonravov covered the half-hour walk from Smolny to the fortress, went through the outer and inner gates, and asked a soldier for the local Bolshevik leader, a certain Pavlov. Pavlov was nearby, haranguing a group of his comrades. Blagonravov had Pavlov call a meeting of the Bolshevik Party members in the garrison clubhouse, so he could gather details on the mood of the garrison, which turned out to be very uneven. The machine-gun battalion of a thousand men under a Left SR officer was the most reliable; Blagonravov told them to be ready for any trouble. The permanent garrison and the bicycle battalion were more dubious, especially the latter, which had been brought into the fortress by the government because of its loyalty.

Commissar Ter-Arutiuniants, flustered again, came over from the Kronverk Arsenal to report that the lieutenant in command of the arsenal would not agree to release any arms. Blagonravov went back to the arsenal with Ter-Arutiuniants, and after an argument with the guards, got in to see the conscientious but effete lieutenant. They threatened to arrest him; this secured his honor, and he submitted. They let him go home to his apartment, on his word of honor that he would stay there. Then they put some of the reliable machine gunners on guard at the arsenal.

Late in the afternoon meetings to convince the garrison were held, first in the fortress courtyard and then in the Circus Modern, with debates and exhortations by both sides. The colonel in command of the fortress, "an old Tsarist bully with a typical resounding military voice and confident metallic movements," spoke in support of the government. The climax came when Trotsky and Lashevich appeared to address the troops. "Brilliant speeches by Trotsky, Lashevich, and myself," according to Blagonrovov, carried the day for the Bolsheviks. Lashevich recounted how a division was called for at the close of the meeting in the Circus Modern: "The overwhelming majority with cries of hurrah rushed to the Left" to show their support for the soviet against the government. "The soldiers listened to us," said Trotsky, "and they came with us. . . . It became clear to me that we would not only win, but win almost without resistance." The fortress was secured, and the issue of arms to the workers began by the truckload.

❋   ❋   ❋

All this time the Military Revolutionary Committee was still burning the candle at both ends, by continuing to negotiate with the military headquarters while at the same time doing everything it could to solidify its control over the troops and the stocks of weapons. Pursuant to the Headquarters invitation of the day before, the MRC emissaries returned to parley. The two sides wrangled over the authority and responsibility of the regimental commissars. Colonel Polkovnikov demanded acceptance of his own authority over them and refused to negotiate further. Thereupon the MRC representatives walked out, only to be called back immediately. Now Polkovnikov told them that he would allow representatives of the Soldiers' Section of the soviet to work at Headquarters and to approve or complain about his orders, provided that the soviet people retracted their claim to countersign or countermand them. This concession no doubt reflected the show of Bolshevik strength on the 22nd, as well as awareness by the military that they simply could not enforce their orders. Some members of the Central Executive Committee who were present urged the MRC men to accept the offer, but they left without making any commitments and went back to Smolny to report.

During the day the government hastened to shore up its own shaky position. Orders went out to strengthen the guard over stocks of arms —even as these arms were being pilfered by the Red Guards. The city militia was put on alert. Calls went to General Headquarters at the front to hasten the dispatch of the reliable troops that had been promised. General Cheremisov came into Petrograd for a long conference with Kerensky, but he still seemed more concerned with his authority to move the garrison to the front than with the plight of the Provisional Government. The leaders of the All-Russian Central Executive Committee saw Kerensky and pledged their support, but they asked him not to undertake any forceful measures against the Bolsheviks that would upset the possibility for a peaceful negotiated settlement with the Petrograd Soviet.

Kerensky went before the Pre-Parliament to explain to them that he had withheld direct action against the MRC because it had not done anything during the twenty-four hours since issuing its demand to countersign orders. Either he did not yet know or failed to appreciate what the Bolsheviks were accomplishing through their commissars in the garrison, including the Peter-Paul fortress. The Pre-Parliament lapsed into one of its characteristically violent Left-Right debates on foreign policy.

By nightfall of the 23rd the MRC was meeting with success almost everywhere in its moves to get control of the garrison. At an evening session of the Petrograd Soviet Antonov gave a detailed report on the accomplishments of the MRC, including the take-over of the Peter-Paul fortress: "Commissars have been assigned to all the military units. Everywhere they are willingly received. No orders or directives will be carried out without the approval of the commissars." Through its commissars the MRC was in fact accomplishing its demand to countersign orders, despite the deadlock in negotiations with Headquarters.

The authority of Headquarters over the garrison was dissolving rapidly. A special meeting of the regimental representatives at Smolny just before the soviet session was told that the majority of the garrison "will carry out only the orders of the MRC" and that "at the first call of the All-Russian Congress of Soviets of Workers' and Soldiers' Deputies the military units are ready, with weapons in hand, to demonstrate their full support for carrying out the decision of the Congress." In other words, they expected the decisive clash with the Provisional Government to come when the Congress of Soviets voted itself into governmental power. They did not feel that it was urgent to discuss the state of negotiations with Headquarters; this question was postponed to the next session . . . which never took place.

In the soviet, someone asked Antonov, "Does the Committee know about the movement of government troops from the front. What measures have been taken against this?" "They will not dare lay hands on the MRC," Antonov replied. He listed the forces known to be moving against the city, but professed confidence in the "revolutionary ring that surrounds Petrograd." He concluded his report with a confident statement on the line of waiting for the soviets to vote themselves power:

> We are keeping revolutionary order, we are taking the necessary steps so that the Congress of Soviets will not be overthrown, so that the Constituent Assembly will not be overthrown.
> We are fulfilling the will of the revolutionary soviet, we are going forward, consolidating revolutionary order and approaching the moment when the soviet power, having disarmed the counter-revolution, will suppress its resistance and complete the triumph of the forces of the revolution.

Trotsky led the discussion to approve Antonov's report, and the soviet resolved to support all the efforts of the MRC to "guarantee the possibility of free and unobstructed work of the All-Russian Congress of Soviets which is about to open." A Menshevik challenged Trotsky about the insurrectionary implications of the MRC; in reply, according to *Izvestiya* the next morning, "Trotsky did not deny that the creation of the MRC provided the political headquarters for the seizure of power and transfer of it into the hands of the soviets." Bold remarks, yet how did Trotsky actually conceive the "seizure of power"?

"As Antonov read his report," Trotsky wrote in his history,

> one had the impression that the headquarters of the insurrection was working with wide open doors. As a matter of fact Smolny had almost nothing to hide. The political setup of the revolution was so favorable that frankness itself became a kind of camouflage: Surely this isn't the way they make an insurrection? That word "insurrection," however, was not spoken by any one of the leaders. This was not wholly a formal measure of caution, for the term did not fit the actual situation.

This was a remarkable concession from the man who supposedly directed the uprising, that the line of waiting was still in effect. Trotsky's next admission is startling, but undoubtedly true:

> It was being left to the government of Kerensky, as you might say, to insurrect. . . . On the 23rd the talk was still not about insurrection, but about the "defense" of the coming Congress of Soviets—with armed forces if necessary. It was still in this spirit that the resolution was adopted on the report of Antonov.

Towards midnight on October 23rd occurred the last and strangest installment in the negotiations between the MRC and Headquarters. The MRC received an ultimatum from General Bagratuni to withdraw their countersigning order, or the soviet commissars would be removed and prosecuted by the military courts for their illegal actions. The SR leader Gotz and the Menshevik Bogdanov came along to see the MRC leaders and try to persuade them to renounce their presumed intention of seizing power. These representations, no doubt supplemented by growing anxiety about the state of the defenses of Smolny, determined the MRC response. Having *de facto* control of the garrison, the MRC was evidently prepared to retract its most provocative claims of the past two days in order to avoid the risk of an open conflict before the Congress of Soviets. They sent word back to Headquarters that the ultimatum was "acceptable in principle."

CHAPTER EIGHT

The "Art" of Insurrection

THREE o'clock in the morning, October 24. The lights were still burning in the cabinet room, the resplendent Malachite Hall on the river side of the Winter Palace. Prime Minister Kerensky, meeting with his cabinet, had finally decided that the time had come to settle with the Bolsheviks. Since no reply to General Bagratuni's ultimatum had come in, the cabinet authorized the arrest of the leaders of the Military Revolutionary Committee. Now the ministers had gone home, leaving Kerensky with General Bagratuni and Colonel Polkovnikov to set in motion the forces they hoped would decapitate the Bolshevik movement.

A messenger brought a note in. It was the news that no one had expected, nor scarcely desired—the Bolsheviks had, after all, accepted the ultimatum. At this late hour, Kerensky was in no mood to suspend his preparations for a preemptive attack. Taking satisfaction in the implication that "the organizers of the uprising were compelled to announce officially that they had committed an unlawful act which they now wished to retract," Kerensky nonetheless reasoned that "this was but another case of the usual delaying tactics and a deliberate deception." General Bagratuni continued to send out telephone and telegraph messages to call reliable troops into Petrograd. Colonel Polkovnikov ordered all the commissars appointed by the MRC removed from their units and prosecuted for any "illegal actions" they had committed. A detachment of cadets was ordered to close down the

Bolshevik newspapers *Rabochi Put* and *Soldat,* on the ground that they were inciting insurrection. To preserve political balance, the government simultaneously ordered two right-wing papers shut down.

At five thirty in the morning the cadets arrived at the printing plant where *Rabochi Put* and *Soldat* were rolling off the presses, near the river on Konnogvardeiskaya Street, less than half a mile from Smolny. They stopped the presses, broke up the plates, confiscated the papers already printed, closed the shop and left it under seal, with a few policemen on guard. Ironically, the feature item in the suspended edition of *Rabochi Put* was an editorial by Stalin assuring the masses that everything they wanted would be delivered by the Congress of Soviets the next day, and that the Provisional Government would give way peacefully if the populace showed their firmness. Along with Stalin's article, and perhaps more pertinent, were reports "on the eve of the second Kornilov movement" of government troop movements and the machinations of Headquarters. The MRC's defiant proclamation of the 22nd was included, having apparently missed publication on the 23rd. Otherwise, save by considerable stretch of the historical imagination, there was nothing in *Rabochi Put* that pointed to a deliberate and imminent Bolshevik coup.

It was still before the dawn of another grimly overcast day when employees of the printing plant ran breathlessly into the Smolny Institute to report what had happened. Trotsky and the leaders of the Military Revolutionary Committee had been on the alert there all night, and had already received alarming reports of the approach of new troops toward Petrograd. A proclamation was just coming off the Smolny printing press to warn all of Petrograd, "The counterrevolution has raised its criminal head. The Kornilovists are mobilizing their forces to suppress the All-Russian Congress of Soviets and break up the Constituent Assembly." Everyone was alerted to possible pogroms, and a list of the regiments and their phone numbers was appended so that people could contact them in the event of disorders.

The report of the cadets' seizure of the printing plant, recalling the fate of *Pravda* in July, seemed to confirm all the Bolsheviks' fears and warnings about a counterrevolutionary strike, and catapulted them into a frenzy of activity. By phone and leaflet the alarm was spread for all the pro-soviet forces in the capital, and a stream of orders began to flow to the commissars of the military units and the leaders of the Red Guard to alert their forces for any eventuality. "The counterrevolutionary plotters have taken the offensive," announced one leaflet after another, without the slightest distinction between Kerensky and the rightists. "The campaign of the counterrevolutionary plotters is directed against the All-Russian Congress of Soviets on the eve of its opening, against the Constituent Assembly, against the people. . . . The Military Revolutionary Committee will direct resistance against the attack of the plotters. The whole garrison and the whole proletariat of Petrograd are ready to deliver a crushing blow to the enemies of the people." Garrisons in the outskirts of Petrograd were ordered to block the movement of any hostile forces into the city, "by force if necessary." Specific orders to reopen the Bolshevik printing plant went to the nearest reliable troops, the Litovsky Regiment and an engineer battalion quartered in an imposing neoclassical barracks near the Tauride Palace. The troops responded in something less than company strength and got to the press towards midmorning. They easily thrust the police guard aside and opened the premises. By eleven o'clock the workers had *Rabochi Put* rolling off the presses again.

The vigor of the MRC response unsettled its SR contingent and the cautious Bolsheviks as well. Speaking for the Left SRs, Kamkov warned, "We did not enter the MRC for an uprising. The power must be created by the Congress of Soviets." Yielding to these misgivings, the MRC adopted a statement for the press: "Contrary to all kinds of rumors and reports, the MRC declares that it exists not at all to prepare and carry out the seizure of power, but exclusively for the defense of the interests of the Petrograd garrison and the democracy from counterrevolutionary encroachments."

While the MRC was handling the emergency, the Bolshevik Central Committee met to consider the expected attempt to suppress the party and the soviet. Nine members and two candidate members assembled for their first meeting as a party body in the Smolny Institute, hitherto strictly soviet territory. Kamenev was among them; he had felt no reason to go through with his threatened resignation. Under the pressure of the morning's events, the Central Committee abandoned its prepared agenda; its first steps were to approve the dispatch of forces to reopen the newspapers and to forbid its own members to leave Smolny (probably for fear of arrest). The main policy question was relations with the All-Russian Central Executive Committee. Trotsky wanted the Bolsheviks to go to the CEC session scheduled later in the day and denounce the CEC for "undermining the cause of revolutionary democracy." Because of the closing of the newspapers Kamenev was prepared to repudiate the negotiations they had been conducting with the CEC, though he wanted to pursue talks with the Left SRs. Trotsky proposed a set of emergency assignments for the Central Committee members—Bubnov to keep in touch with the railroad workers, Dzerzhinsky to be responsible for the post office and telegraph, Milyutin to work on the food supply problem, Sverdlov to keep watch on the movements of the government. (How Sverdlov was expected to handle this broad assignment in addition to all the rest of his responsibilities was not explained.) Kamenev was assigned to negotiate with the Left SRs, and Lomov and Nogin were directed to leave for Moscow to inform the Bolsheviks there of the new turn of events. There was some discussion of the location of an auxiliary party headquarters in the event that government forces captured Smolny; Trotsky's suggestion to designate the Peter-Paul fortress was adopted. With this, the total recorded substance of the Central Committee's last meeting before the revolution was completed. This was the meeting which the official historiography represents as the occasion of the final decision to launch the insurrection, but there is no evidence that the Committee had anything in mind yet except to stave off the blows of the government until the Congress of Soviets convened.*

❊ ❊ ❊

* In line with the more objective recent Soviet writing on the revolution, the historian Yerykalov wrote in 1966 in *Problems of the History of the Communist Party of the Soviet Union*,

> In the morning and during the day of October 24 there were still no such moves of revolutionary troops. At the morning session of the Central Committee a decision about a move was not taken, and the activity of the MRC was directed toward the summoning of revolutionary forces for battle readiness. The orders and directives of the MRC, as a rule, ended with the instruction, "await further directions." In the directing organs of the uprising there was vacillation in regard to its timing.

One of the many factual puzzles of this confusing day is a reported meeting of the Bolshevik Petrograd City Committee early in the morning of the 24th, that supposedly resolved in favor of a revolutionary offensive at this point. The occurrence of the meeting and the substance of the resolution are known only through the recollections of one of the Petrograd activists, a certain Belov; no minutes exist and the meeting is not mentioned in any other document or memoir. In all likelihood Belov has recalled what was argued at a meeting on an earlier date, and confused it with the events of the 24th.

At ten o'clock in the morning Kerensky called his weary cabinet back into session to inform them of the steps he had taken to suppress the Bolsheviks and to get their endorsement of the speech he was about to make to the Pre-Parliament. His chief military commissar V. B. Stankevich arrived from the front, and Kerensky asked him, "Well, how do you like Petrograd?" The city appeared normal and Stankevich did not know what he meant. "Maybe you don't know that we are having an armed insurrection?" Stankevich laughed.

The meaning of this somber joke lies in Kerensky's understanding of "insurrection"—not anything new that the Bolsheviks were doing that day, but their efforts of the past three of four days to usurp authority over the garrison. When Kerensky assured Stankevich that he was taking firm measures to settle with the Bolsheviks, he seemed unaware that the joke was on himself; the real insurrection had not yet begun.

Foreign Minister Tereshchenko had more foresight. He met Ambassador Buchanan and told him that the Bolsheviks had lost their courage and called off their planned demonstration. "But after the closing of the newspapers," Buchanan noted, "Tereshchenko expects that this will provoke a Bolshevik rising. He is urging Kerensky to arrest the members of the revolutionary military committee."

In fact no action was taken to accomplish the arrests or break up the Bolshevik forces. The chief of the city militia ignored the government's directives because he considered himself responsible only to the City Duma; throughout the uprising the militia went about their normal police duties and took no part at all in the defense of the government. The sub-minister Palchinsky, soon to find himself responsible for the Winter Palace, jotted down some candid criticisms: "Incompetence of Polkovnikov and absence of any plan at all. Hope that the crazy step would not be made. No idea of what to do if it were. " Apart from the newspaper affair, most of Kerensky's steps were defensive. Cadets replaced the regular guard at the railroad stations, and the garrison of the Winter Palace was strengthened by a bicycle battalion and, of all things, the "Women's Battalion of Death."

This curious unit of bourgeois girls was recruited by Kerensky after the Russian rout in July with the idea of shaming the Russian men into fighting better. They had done nothing but sit in a Petrograd suburb, however, until they were called in to help defend the government on the morning of October 24. "I saw these unfortunates when they passed under the windows of the French Embassy," wrote Ambassador Noulens, "on the way to take up their position. They marched in step, affecting a martial spirit which was obviously contradicted by their plump figures and their feminine waddle."

At midday the Pre-Parliament convened for a regular session with its chairman, the SR Avksentiev, presiding. Kerensky appeared and asked Avksentiev for permission to make a special statement. It was about 12:30 when Kerensky began what turned out to be nearly an hour-long speech, delivered, wrote Fyodor Dan, "with the great pathos characteristic of him." The democratic achievements of the great Russian Revolution, Kerensky warned, were under attack by both political extremes, most recently "by those open appeals for insurrection which come from an irresponsible section of the democracy—I would not say extremist in the sense of its trends, but extremist in the sense of absence of reason—which has split off from the revolutionary democracy." He cited the frank words about an uprising in Lenin's letter "To Comrades" published in *Rabochi Put* a few days before. He denounced Trotsky and the rest of the Bolsheviks for their inflammatory pronouncements, particularly as they were directed toward the army. He equated the Bolsheviks and the Ultra-Right, warned of pogroms, and charged that "by organizing an uprising . . . , by disorganizing the defensive capacity of the country—intentionally or unintentionally," the Bolsheviks were playing into the hands of Kaiser Wilhelm and committing "treason and betrayal of the Russian state." They who attempted an uprising a scant three weeks before the scheduled elections to the Constituent Assembly were "the real enemies of the people and of Russian freedom."

Kerensky recounted in detail the negotiations that had transpired between Headquarters and the Military Revolutionary Committee, the MRC claim to countersign orders, his own extension of time for the MRC to reconsider, and the failure of the Bolsheviks to reply—until 3 A.M. of this very day, when Kerensky judged it too late to talk terms. "At this moment," he declared, "the period of grace has expired, and we do not as yet have the declaration that was supposed to have been issued to the regiments." He failed to mention at all the suppression of the newspapers, which had obviously made the negotiations a dead issue for the Bolsheviks, and expressed offended surprise that "the obvious, definite, overall condition of a certain part of the population of Petersburg is a state of insurrection."

At this point, Konovalov came into the hall and handed Kerensky a message. Kerensky read it and announced, "I have been given a copy of the document that is now being sent to the regiments: 'The Petrograd Soviet is in danger. I hereby order the regiments to be in complete readiness for action and to await further instructions. Any delay or failure to execute the order will be considered a betrayal of the revolution. Signed for the Chairman, Podvoisky. Secretary, Antonov.'"

This was, of course, only one of the many messages that the MRC was sending out, and a relatively innocuous one at that. But the rightist members of the Pre-Parliament shouted, "Traitors," and Kerensky charged, "This is an attempt to incite the rabble against the existing order. . . . I use the word 'rabble' deliberately, because all the responsible elements of the democracy and its Central Executive Committee, all the army organizations, and all that Free Russia can and must be proud of—the reason, the conscience, and the honor of the great Russian democracy—all protest against this"—mainly, in Kerensky's presentation, because the effect of the trouble would be to open the country wide to the German army. Concluding his valedictory address, Kerensky affirmed his reluctance to curtail anyone's liberty, but warned that he was now ready to liquidate all the enemies of Russian freedom. He demanded a vote of confidence and left the hall amidst a standing ovation from everyone except Martov's small group of left-wing Mensheviks and a few Ultra-rightists. "It would have been funny if it were not so sad," Dan commented. Kerensky had no assessment of his own strength and that of his enemies. "Kerensky, with all his good intentions and sincere devotion to the cause of freedom, was so obviously heading for the abyss with his eyes closed."

From the Marinsky Palace Kerensky went to the Military District Headquarters next door to the Winter Palace, where he spent most of the afternoon directing military measures to forestall any action by the Bolsheviks. His strategy, following Polkovnikov's earlier order to the military commanders, was to guard the key government institutions and utilities against a revolutionary attack and cut off the main areas of

Bolshevik support by raising the Neva drawbridges. Cadets—the only large reliable force in the city—were dispatched everywhere to put the plan into effect and maintain street patrols. Automobiles were commandeered to provide extra transportation. Sensing official alarm, some government offices and stores began to close and send their employees home. At three o'clock, the Smolny telephones were cut off at the central switchboard.

The bridges were the key to strategic control of the city, and it was here that the first decisive turn of events occurred. Between two and three o'clock cadets occupied the approaches to the Nikolaevsky Bridge (furthest toward the harbor) and the Palace Bridge, both connecting the center of the city with Vasilevsky Island, and stopped traffic over them. Their orders were to raise the bridges if necessary. The MRC immediately issued a statement that it had not authorized the raising of the bridges and would not allow it, but about four o'clock cadets actually raised the Nikolaevsky Bridge—an event immortalized in Eisenstein's film *October* (or *Ten Days That Shook the World*), with its scene of the wagon and dead horse sliding down the slanting roadway as the bridge rose into the sky. Some cadets from the Mikhailovsky Artillery School tried to raise the easternmost of the main bridges, the Liteiny Bridge connecting the heavily Bolshevik Vyborg district with the area near the Tauride Palace, but a crowd stopped them, and Vyborg Red Guards occupied the bridge. Around 6:30 a cadet patrol approached the Troitsky Bridge, spanning the river from the Field of Mars to the Petrograd Side near the Peter-Paul fortress. They were spotted by a patrol from the strongly pro-Bolshevik Pavlov Regiment, whose barracks were nearby. Lieutenant Oswald Dzenis, confirmed as commissar of the regiment only the day before, ordered one of his companies to occupy the bridge, which it did without incident. Likewise the commissar of the Grenadier Regiment on the Petrograd Side acted on his own initiative when he heard that the bridges crossing the Nevka to the Vyborg district had been raised. The patrols he sent out closed the bridges with no resistance apart from the protests of the bridge-keepers, and brought the heavy iron bridge keys to the barracks for safekeeping. Orders from the MRC only arrived after the fact.

Shivers of alarm swept the city, governmental and revolutionary camps alike, when the news of the raising of the bridges was heard.

Until then the average citizen had no idea that violent revolutionary clashes were in the offing. "Just before October 25 was when I least expected any significant events," recalled a minor literary figure with the *nom de plume* "Knizhnik."

> On the 24th of October, about 2 P.M., I took a streetcar to the center of the city to one of the bookstores, and then I went to Zagorodny Prospekt to visit a lady writer with whom, before the revolution, I had a great friendship that had cooled somewhat as a consequence of our different views about political events. Our conversation had an ordinary character. We touched on politics only on the theoretical and superficial plane, so as not to uncover the sore spots. We talked mostly about mutual acquaintances. Suddenly her husband, who worked on the editorial staff of *Russkaya Volya*, came in and reported that the city was uneasy, the bridges were raised, and that we could expect more agitation. Judging by the morning papers, I didn't expect anything special, but nevertheless I now hurried to my home on the Petrograd Side. This was about 5 P.M.
>
> Fortunately the streetcars were running, the Troitsky Bridge had not been lifted, and I only saw units of cadets on the Neva embankment, headed for the Winter Palace, along with a large unit of women. Most of the passengers in the streetcar looked at these units with curiosity. On the Petrograd Side on the Karpovka I saw a unit of armed workers, silently, but it seemed to me, knowingly looking at the citizens passing by.

❁   ❁   ❁

All afternoon the Military Revolutionary Committee was mobilizing its forces for the expected government drive. The garrison units and factory committees were everywhere responding to the appeals of the MRC by passing resolutions to support the assumption of power by the Congress of Soviets. The Vyborg district Red Guards assembled with rifles in hand on Sampsonievsky Prospekt outside their headquarters.

The fighting qualities of these forces remained an unknown factor. The French journalist Claude Anet, who lived near the Pavlov barracks, commented, "It would take only three thousand resolute men to rout the whole garrison of Petrograd. I would pay well if anyone showed me the phenomenon, unknown here, of the hero, the demigod of Bolshevism—a man ready to give his life for his faith in Lenin, for the triumph of the extremists' ideas. The soldiers are rebelling only so they will not have to go to the front." But morale on the government side was worse. Around 4 P.M., in the first of a fatal series of defections, the bicycle company stationed at the Winter Palace abandoned their posts.

A dependable machine-gun unit finally arrived at Smolny and set up its guns. As they dragged their equipment, clanking and rumbling, through the corridors, the last Mensheviks and SRs of the All-Russian Central Executive Committee, who had maintained their offices in Smolny right up to the last minute, finally abandoned the building. The government had set aside quarters for them in the District Headquarters. Trotsky wrote, "We were now in full command of the building that was preparing to rear a Bolshevik head over the city and the country"—but it was a strange revolution that did not control its own headquarters until the armed struggle was almost underway.

By afternoon a special subcommittee of the MRC was finally appointed, according to Antonov's account, consisting of "Podvoisky, Lashevich, and myself, to work out a plan of struggle with the Provisional Government." The plan, if there was one, was simply to close the bridges and assert control over as many strategic buildings as possible —the railroad stations, the bridges, electric power plants, the telegraph, the telephone exchange, the news wire service, and the State Bank. The idea initially was simply to dispatch commissars to each point to proclaim the authority of the MRC, much as had been done in the military units.

The first attempt to do this occurred in the afternoon, when a Bolshevik delegate to the Congress of Soviets, Pestkovsky, was assigned to the Petrograd Telegraph Office. Here is his account:

> Dzerzhinsky ran up to me with a paper in his hand: "You and Comrade Leshchinsky are instructed to take over the main telegraph. Here is the mandate of the MRC that appoints you commissar of the telegraph. Go right away!"
>
> "How do I take over the telegraph?" I asked.
>
> "The Kexholm Regiment is on guard there, and they are on our side," answered Dzerzhinsky.

I didn't question any more. The assignment at first didn't seem very hard to me, since I was the director of our Petrograd postal-telegraph cell and knew almost all our Bolsheviks there. I found Comrade Leshchinsky, and we set off together. Neither of us had a revolver. When we were getting in the car we both had the same strange, tormenting tension in our minds: here it is, the decisive move of the proletariat that we have been waiting for for decades. How will it end?

Could it still be defeated?

The bitter experience of the July Days did not give us complete confidence in victory.

We decided to work this way. The Provisional Government's commander of the telegraph was a personal acquaintance of Leshchinsky—Staff-Captain Longva, at the time a Menshevik-Internationalist, now a Communist. We would have to talk with him and make sure of his cooperation. Then we would talk with our cell and at once proceed with the "seizure."

It turned out somewhat differently. Comrade Longva, "having no directive from his organization," refused to cooperate with us and only promised "not to interfere." And at the conference with the cell we realized that in the whole telegraph office, among three thousand employees, there was not a single Bolshevik, and only one Left SR, Khaurov; he reported to us that the whole mass of employees was very hostilely inclined against the Bolsheviks. [Unknown to Pestkovsky, all the Bolshevik members of the union were Post Office employees.]

The situation was extremely difficult. But at this point Comrade Liubovich arrived from Smolny to help us. The three of us felt stronger and went to talk with the guards.

When the guards, headed by some lieutenant, saw our mandate from the MRC, they promised to cooperate with us. Then, on October 24 about five o'clock, we three, accompanied by the commander of the guard, went into the main hall of the telegraph and up to the President of the union of postal and telegraph workers, Mr. King (a Right SR), and declared that we were taking over the telegraph. King declared that he was going to throw us out. Then Comrade Liubovich called two Kexholm men and stationed them at the transmitter.

The women working in the office began to scream and cry. The representatives of the "committee" deliberated and arrived at a compromise. They would agree that "the commissar could sit in the room" on condition that we withdraw the soldiers from the room.

We agreed. I "held forth" in the telegraph office, Liubovich went out "to strengthen" the guard, and Leshchinsky went off to the room of the union, in a neighboring building, as a "reserve."

At 8 P.M. of the same day a guard of cadets, specially ordered by the Petrograd Military District, arrived to "replace" the Kexholm men. The Kexholm guard, "cultivated" by Liubovich, declared they wanted to go on guarding the telegraph.

The cadets left.

As the two sides were sparring for control of the bridges, Trotsky addressed a meeting in Smolny of Bolshevik delegates arriving in Petrograd for the Congress of Soviets. He began by hailing the political momentum gained by the party's moves of the past few days, even though some Bolsheviks did not feel ready for provocative action: "A clash was inevitable, and it developed out of the order to summon the garrison to the front." What he meant by "clash," evidently, was the same "insurrection" Kerensky referred to, not anything new that had happened on the 24th, but simply the MRC's assertion of military authority.

At this point Trotsky was interrupted by a message that a delegation from the City Duma had come to Smolny to learn the soviet's intentions regarding public order and safety. He left the assembly hall and conferred with the visitors for half an hour or so. "I told them," he reported, "that if the government starts the iron going, naturally we will answer with steel," though the soviet would welcome any cooperation from the old city authorities in maintaining order. But basically the question of violence depended on whether the government would lie down and die quietly: "All Power to the Soviets—this is our slogan. In the days ahead, while the All-Russian Congress of Soviets is in session, this slogan must be put into effect. Whether this will lead to an uprising or a move will depend not only or so much on the soviets as it will on those who in spite of the unanimous [sic!] will of the people may try to keep governmental power in their own hands."

Returning to the assembly hall, Trotsky told the delegates what had transpired and went on to describe the precautionary military movements that the MRC had ordered. "The military situation for us is favorable in the highest degree. Now everything depends on the congress." He did not want to preempt the responsibility of the delegates, certainly not openly, yet he made it clear what the party expected of them when they convened formally the following day: "The only salvation is a firm policy of the congress. The arrest of the Provisional Government is not on the agenda as an independent task. If the congress sets up a power and Kerensky does not submit to it, then it would be a policing question rather than a political one." If Trotsky is to be believed by what he said before the revolution rather than after, the Bolsheviks were still waiting for the Congress of Soviets, and did not yet suppose that they could destroy the government beforehand.

Following Trotsky, the Bolshevik delegates heard a report on the Pre-Parliament and its vote against Kerensky on the land and peace issues. Then Stalin came on, to say that the Bolshevik papers were being printed again after the attempt to close them. He did mention that there was some dissension in the leadership—"In the Military Revolutionary Committee there are two tendencies: one, immediate uprising; two, to concentrate our forces at first"—but, he assured the delegates, "The Central Committee of the Bolshevik Party adheres to the second." He said the Left SRs had demanded to know whether the aim of the MRC was to maintain order or launch an insurrection; if the latter, they would pull out. "Of course," Stalin reported, "we answered, order, defense. And they left their men in." After the meeting Trotsky talked with the delegates from Kronstadt. He sent them off to the base with instructions to return at dawn with the whole Kronstadt force, "for the defense of the Congress of Soviets."

By this time everyone in Smolny felt the grim tension of impending battle and uncertain outcome. One of the Bolshevik women assigned secretarial duty for the evening found time to write to a friend, on the letterhead of the Executive Committee of the Petrograd Soviet:

Dear Tanya!

I am writing you at an exceptional time and for that reason on special paper. I hope you will keep this letter as an historical document. In the city now things are alarming. I will sit all night on duty in the office of the Petrograd Executive Committee. All possible rumors are going around. Our telephone has been cut off by order of Kerensky. With some effort I persuaded my sick friend to go home, though she wanted to stay with me on duty today, and now I am worried about her because the bridges have been raised, according to rumor there are guards at them, there may be a sharp conflict at any minute, and I don't know whether she will be able to reach home safely.

In the room next to me there are guards; downstairs there is a gathering of the faction [probably of the Bolshevik Congress delegates, where Trotsky was speaking], where the debates have become extremely sharp. They are waiting tensely to see whether today's session of the Petrograd Soviet will take place. Tomorrow is the Congress of Soviets. To wait longer has become impossible, unthinkable. The country stands on the verge of complete ruin if we go on in the old way. The hand of Reaction has been raised over the Constituent Assembly, over the soviets, over all the conquests of the revolution. It is felt that with a little more time all this will be crushed. Will it succeed?

In the city now things are alarming. The streets have not been lighted. It's dark. And in Smolny people will be on duty all night, and I among them.

I don't know whether you will get this letter. I will write again some time.

Anything can be expected at this alarming time. There are machine guns on the roof; if they move against the soviet, they won't come with their bare hands. But I have a conviction that everything will end happily and that we will survive not only this pivotal week, but many more too, and that we will finally come out into the light.

I will write as soon as the situation has cleared up. I am writing so little about everyday things because the time and the circumstances are special. My health has now improved and I'm serving again in the soviet in a true hot spot. Therefore I can't think about going on leave for the time being—there is no time for it, though I have the right to take it. Somehow I will take the time to write you a long letter—I have so much interesting material that I have to stick to one thing at a time.

Good-bye for now.
Ludmilla

At 7 P.M. the Petrograd Soviet did in fact convene and Trotsky repeated his affirmation that the Bolsheviks planned no move before the Congress. "The MRC," he said, "arose not as an organ of insurrection, but on the basis of the self-defense of the revolution." He described all the steps of the MRC in the past day as defensive responses to the government's initiatives, the net effect of which was to prepare the ground for a take-over by the Congress of Soviets. The government, according to Trotsky, had become "a semi-power which the people don't believe in and which doesn't believe in itself, for it is dead on the inside. This semi-power is waiting for the sweep of the broom of history, to clear a place for a genuine power of the revolutionary people." The adherents of the soviet had demonstrated their ability to control the garrison and the fleet in defiance of the government's orders. "Tomorrow the Congress of Soviets opens. The task of the garrison and the proletariat is to place at the disposal of the congress the accumulated force against which the governmental provocation may smash itself. Our task is to deliver this force to the congress unsplit and unimpaired. When the congress says that it is organizing the power, it will be completing the work that has been going on all over the country. This will mean that, freeing themselves from the power of the counterrevolutionary government, the people are convoking their congress and setting up their power." This was Trotsky's fullest and most direct statement of his strategy of using the Congress of Soviets to vote power into the hands of the Bolsheviks with a minimum of military risk and a maximum of popular support. The government was playing into his hands perfectly with its ineffective attacks. "If the pseudo-power makes the risky attempt to revive its own corpse, then the popular masses, organized and armed, will give it a decisive rebuff, and the rebuff will be the stronger, the stronger is the offensive of reaction. If the government tries to use the twenty-four or forty-eight hours that are left to it to stick a knife in the back of the revolution, then we declare that the forward units of the revolution will answer blow for blow, steel for iron." The blows were beginning already, and would soon prove so successful for the revolutionaries that there would be little left for the Congress of Soviets to do as the elected representatives of Russia. Trotsky's strategy was about to be invalidated by its own success.

*   *   *

In the Petrograd harbor there was one large warship, the cruiser *Aurora*, a veteran of the Russo-Japanese War. It had been undergoing repairs at the Franco-Russian Shipyard, but the work was finally finished, and orders had been given to put to sea on the 24th to test the engines. According to the revolutionary custom, the crew's committee referred the order to the Tsentrobalt in Helsingfors. On the 23rd, Dybenko, chairman of the Tsentrobalt, countermanded the order and told the crew to keep the ship in Petrograd until the 26th. The crewman, Belyshev, who became commissar of the ship recounted what then happened:

> The reason for staying in port was explained to the command on the basis that the cruiser *Aurora* was needed to take active part in supporting the soviet and possibly the impending overturn. The 24th of October I received from the MRC the appointment as commissar of the cruiser *Aurora;* for this a special session of the ship committee was held with the captain and other officers present, where I briefly explained my instructions as commissar, and made it clear that I would apply and carry out all orders and directives coming from places such as the MRC, no matter what the captain or other officers thought.

The MRC regarded the *Aurora* as one of its great hopes. Trotsky dispatched the MRC proclamation on "counterrevolution" to be sent out on the ship's radio, and during the day the MRC instructed the crew of the *Aurora* to guard themselves against possible government boarding parties. In the afternoon, when the crisis broke around the bridges, the MRC looked to the *Aurora* again. Commissar Belyshev continues:

> In the evening a directive was received from the MRC for the Cruiser *Aurora* to restore traffic on the Nikolaevsky Bridge. To comply with the instruction—to take the Nikolaevsky Bridge— it appeared necessary for the ship to move up as near as possible to the bridge, and to do so I gave directions to get steam up, warm up the engines, and prepare to weigh anchor. At the same time we got in touch with the Second Baltic Fleet Crew, who were directed, as soon as the *Aurora* weighed anchor, and under the cover of our guns, to drive away the cadets, occupy the bridge, and restore traffic.

But just as we had finally gotten ready to weigh anchor, the captain refused to navigate the ship, asserting that it was impossible for a cruiser to sail up the Neva. Without delay, I gave the order to make soundings in the channel of the Neva, the depth of which showed that the cruiser could freely proceed. With a chart of the depth of the Neva channel I went again to the captain and asserted that he had to pilot the ship. When he refused again, I gave the order to arrest all the officers, which was carried out. In spite of the refusal of the captain and the other officers, we nevertheless decided to weigh anchor ourselves. I don't know what influenced the captain—either fear for his own hide, or something else, but nevertheless at the last minute of our preparations he agreed to pilot the ship to the bridge. And at 3:30 A.M. the ship dropped anchor at the Nikolaevsky Bridge.

Having ordered the *Aurora* to reopen the Nikolaevsky Bridge, the MRC decided the time had come to call in the main reserve that Lenin had been banking on, the Baltic Fleet at Helsingfors. Around 8 P.M. a telegram went from Antonov to Dybenko—"Send regulations." This was the code signal they had agreed on during one of Antonov's visits to Helsingfors—"Send ships and men." The hour was late to call for such distant support for a deliberate insurrection, but it made sense as part of the preparation for a showdown when the Congress of Soviets opened. Dybenko forced the admiral to release his ships, and four minelayers were on their way the next morning. The main body of the sailors left by train as planned, starting at three the next morning, but it seems that their journey was "sabotaged" by the railroad authorities, and in the end they missed the decisive action.

By evening the Red Guards were out in large numbers. The square in front of the Vyborg district Red Guard Headquarters looked like an army camp, and the building itself "was boiling with armed workers from various plants," to quote one participant. Armed workers headed off by the truckloads for Smolny, to join the crowd in the gardens in front of the Institute. Assignments were not always ready for them; one of the arsenal workers recalled how a truckload of them, just barely brought under Bolshevik influence, was sent back home for the night with nothing to do.

Anxious about the government's chances of mobilizing counter-forces, the MRC undertook further take-overs, aimed at communications. Around 9 P.M. they ventured to extend their authority from the telegraph office to the news wire service next door. A Finnish Bolshevik newspaperman with a woman as his secretary and a guard of sailors took charge to censor all outgoing dispatches. Commissars were also assigned to supervise the telephone, power, and railroad stations. Sometime after nine the designated commissar, a Lieutenant Katz, and a company from the Izmailovsky Regiment arrived at the Baltic Station (the expected point of arrival of the cadet reinforcements who had been ordered in from Oranienbaum and Peterhof) with instructions "to share in guard duty" and check on all arriving and departing trains. A pro-Bolshevik machine-gun regiment in the outskirts of Petrograd was meanwhile ordered to block both rail and road access to the cadets.

Towards 10 P.M. government forces attempted a counterblow, uselessly directed like the first of the day against the Bolshevik press. This time a lieutenant colonel and a squad of cadets from the Mikhailovsky Artillery School in the Vyborg district went to the nearby building that still housed the Bolshevik editorial offices, apparently looking for Lenin. By mistake they stumbled into the "Free Reason" Workers' Club on the second floor, and during the ensuing uproar the Bolsheviks took the labels off their doors upstairs and phoned for Red Guards. Moving upstairs, the cadets found themselves invading a Menshevik office, and before they had located their intended target, the Red Guards arrived to arrest them.

While the MRC was beginning to move into action systematically, the crisis in the Provisional Government was deepening. Kerensky had expected his vote of confidence in an hour or so after the Pre-Parliament gave him its ovation. Instead the deputies broke up into party meetings for four hours, and when they reassembled after 6 P.M., they clashed violently over fundamentals of policy as well as over what to do about the Bolsheviks. Speaking for the Left SRs, Kamkov declared, "It is clear that the Provisional Government, since it does not enjoy the confidence of the country, must finally go. We must create a revolutionary democratic power, responsible to the organs of the revolutionary democracy," i.e., the soviets. The moderate Left—Mensheviks, Menshevik-Internationalists, and Right SRs—agreed to back a resolution proposed by Martov. According to this view, the main danger of

the Bolsheviks was that they would pave the way for the counterrevolutionaries—exactly what the Right hoped of them; the government
was to blame for the Bolshevik problem by failing to act faster to make
peace and distribute land to the peasants. Shattering precedent, the SR
Gotz brought the Menshevik Dan into his party's caucus to argue for
the Martov formula. When the vote came, with less than two-thirds
of the deputies present, it was 123 for the resolution of censure, 102
moderates and conservatives against, and 26 abstaining: hardly the
vote of confidence that Kerensky, in his dire straits, wanted.

It was 9 P.M. or a little later when Dan and Gotz and a reluctant
Avksentiev took their resolution to Kerensky in the Winter Palace. Dan
thought they could get Kerensky to save the day by emergency decrees
on peace, land, and a constitution. Kerensky, with some irritation,
left a session of his cabinet to talk with them. He was outraged at the
document they showed him—"already of no use to anybody . . . , end-
lessly long, complicated, and hardly understandable to ordinary mortals," as he described it. Kerensky said that he might as well resign and
let the authors of the resolution try to govern. Dan in his memoirs
reconstructed the analysis he gave Kerensky in reply. Kerensky was
"being misled by the 'reactionary staff' . . . which in its own self-
deception, was deceiving the government, assuring it that the staff had
'loyal troops' sufficient to overcome the Bolsheviks in an open battle."
(This much Kerensky took to heart himself later in the night, when he
fired Polkovnikov.) Dan told Kerensky that the resolution, though it
might hurt the government's pride, would exploit the cleavage among
the Bolsheviks and steal some of their revolutionary appeal. "We
stressed the fact . . . that there was great hesitation among the Bolsheviks themselves, that the mass of the Bolsheviks were afraid and did
not want an uprising, and that the adoption of our proposal could
strengthen the tendency among the Bolsheviks towards liquidating the
uprising."

During the day Dan and the other moderate socialist leaders had
been in touch with Kamenev, who was evidently going beyond his
instructions to negotiate with the Left SRs. Kamenev suggested that
the test of strength could still be avoided until the Congress of Soviets,
if only the government would not press its provocations further. Dan
contended, according to Kerensky's account, that

The Bolsheviks revealed in their negotiations with the leaders of the majority [of the Central Executive Committee] of the soviets a readiness "to submit to the will of the soviet majority," and said that they were ready "even tomorrow" to take all measures to stop the uprising "which had broken out contrary to their desires, without their approval." In conclusion Dan, asserting that the Bolsheviks would disband their military headquarters tomorrow (always tomorrow!), declared to me that all the measures I had taken to suppress the uprising only "disturbed the masses," and in general by my "interference" I only "prevented the representatives of the soviet majority from successfully conducting negotiations with the Bolsheviks for the liquidation of the uprising."

All this made Kerensky "tremble with anger." He replied to Dan, "The government doesn't need demands and orders. It is time not to talk but to act." Knowing of Kamenev's talks with the socialists, Kerensky saw in the proposal of the latter only the proof of deliberate Bolshevik duplicity. He believed that Kamenev had been given the assignment "to distract the attention of the central organs of the socialist parties from Lenin's real aims, lull their suspicions, and make sure that when Trotsky attacked, the Provisional Government would get no active support from them." But Trotsky later commented,

The way Kerensky represents it, as though specially delegated Bolsheviks undertook to deceive the Mensheviks and SRs about the imminent liquidation of the insurrection, does not square with the facts. In fact the people who took active part in the negotiations were those Bolsheviks who really wanted to liquidate the uprising and believed in the formula of a socialist government made up of a coalition of parties.

Kerensky evidently had no appreciation of the divisions in the Bolshevik ranks and the impulse still strong among many of Lenin's lieutenants to put off the crisis. He accused Dan and his friends of repudiating the government; they in turn refused to cooperate with a government that would not listen to them. "With heavy hearts we left the Palace," Dan wrote. "The die was cast."

From the Winter Palace Dan and his friends turned in the other political direction, to a midnight meeting of the All-Russian Central

Executive Committee at Smolny (the last session of the old CEC before the Second Congress of Soviets put the Bolsheviks in control of it). Here the moderates had even less luck with their resolution as a basis for negotiation, though Dan warned eloquently that Bolshevik violence would be an invitation to counterrevolution: "The counterrevolution is stronger at this moment than it has ever been before." Trotsky went to the speaker's stand to reply, as John Reed watched fascinated: "His thin pointed face was positively Mephistophelian in its expression of malicious irony." Ridiculing the moderates for their contradictory record, Trotsky appealed for all the delegates to the Soviet Congress to back the "headquarters of the revolution" if they meant to speak for the masses. Erlich, the representative of the Jewish Social Democrats, proposed a resolution calling on everyone to stay calm under the leadership of a new "Committee of Public Safety" while the Provisional Government was urged to act on the land and peace questions. Volodarsky replied for the Bolsheviks that these matters were now the business of the Congress of Soviets. The Bolsheviks walked out of what they regarded as a powerless body, leaving the old CEC leaders to vote their totally ineffective resolution and adjourn their business for the last time at 4 A.M.

* * *

After the socialists had left the Winter Palace, Kerensky and his cabinet together with the military began to discuss forceful means of dealing with the Bolshevik defiance. By midnight word was coming in of the take-over of key points—the telegraph, the bridges, the railroad stations—by armed groups of Bolsheviks. Malevsky, the chief military commissar for the CEC, reported that members of the CEC had been visiting the barracks to try to persuade the troops not to cooperate with the Bolsheviks, but to no avail. It was agreed that cadets should be sent with armored cars to retake the telegraph agency and the Baltic Station. Minister of Religions Kartashev called for decisive measures. "What a bloodthirsty Minister of Religions we have!" exclaimed Kerensky. Now the conservatives were alienated. "Certain of the so-called rightist members of the government," Kerensky recalled, "criticized very sharply the 'indecisiveness' and 'passivity' of the higher military authorities, but failed completely to take into account the fact that we had to act all the time between the hammer of the Bolsheviks of the

Right and the anvil of the Left." Here Kerensky was reasoning almost as Dan had, even to the point of representing the Right as the more active threat. He hinted betrayal by his Kadet ministers: "This severe criticism did not manifest itself in the least tendency to take active part in the organization of the struggle with the people who were coming to terms with the insurrection, or even to support me more energetically."

It was probably around 1:00 A.M. when the cabinet meeting broke up in disarray, and a crowd of officials were observed to leave the Winter Palace in their cars. Kerensky turned to his military commanders to review their plans to assemble reliable forces and capture the Smolny Institute. Colonel Polkovnikov was still optimistic, despite the statement of a delegation from the Cossacks that the cavalry would not fight unless they were assured of a complete victory and not a stalemate as in July. Kerensky finally became suspicious of Polkovnikov: "It became more than evident that all his reports of the past ten to twelve days concerning the attitude of the troops and the preparedness of his own staff for a decisive struggle with the Bolsheviki had no basis in fact." Kerensky's representative at the city administration came in to report that the Bolsheviks were moving all over the city without resistance and that "the staff of the Petrograd military district was watching the developments with utter indifference, showing no inclination for activity on its part."

Kerensky and Konovalov rushed over to the District Headquarters, demanded an explanation from Polkovnikov, and then decided, "It was no longer possible to rely on Colonel Polkovnikov and the majority of the officers of his staff. It became urgent in this eleventh hour to take command into one's own hands." In line with his thesis of a right-wing conspiracy to let the Bolsheviks destroy the Provisional Government, Kerensky afterwards accused Polkovnikov of deliberate treason:

> It was very unfortunate that we, the members of the government learned too late that Polkovnikov and his whole staff like him were playing a *double game* during these fateful days and actually joined the group of officers whose plans included the overthrow of the Provisional Government at the hands of messieurs the Bolsheviks.

By this time reports were coming back from cadet patrols. They had met overwhelming Bolshevik forces and failed to retake a single building. At the telegraph office, Commissar Pestkovsky had felt uneasy until the sailors took over the news wire service next door: "It was very comforting to have the sailors as neighbors, because the Kexholm men inspired little confidence. During the night the cadets appeared once more. The sailors ordered them, 'Forward, march!' and they went off again."

In place of Polkovnikov, Kerensky put General Bagratuni in direct command of the garrison and had him issue orders to the three Cossack regiments to prepare for action and "come to the rescue of the CEC, the Provisional Government, and the Revolutionary Democracy." But now even the Cossacks began to doubt whether there was any point in fighting for Kerensky. The Cossack Council was in session the rest of the night. It reported that the Cossacks were "getting ready to saddle their horses," but it found excuses for inaction; there was no infantry to work with the mounted units as was the custom in handling mobs. Finally the Cossacks announced their complete neutrality, and the government lost the force it had counted on most of all.

✱   ✱   ✱

When Kerensky's cabinet meeting broke up, the patrols of the Pavlov Regiment stationed on Millionaya Street—the thoroughfare running eastward from the Winter Palace to the Champs de Mars and the Troitsky Bridge—"had their attention especially drawn by a large number of automobiles leaving the Winter Palace through the Palace Square." So recalled Commissar Dzenis.

> They set up roadblocks, and were given directions henceforth to stop and question all automobiles and people passing through, to check their documents and detain suspicious individuals. Not five minutes had gone by after this order was given when a medium-height grey-haired man in civilian clothes was brought into the regimental club (where I had set up the operational headquarters of the regiment along with the regimental committee). It appeared that he had been detained along with his automobile as he was leaving the square onto Millionaya Street. I asked for his documents. It appeared that he was Lieutenant Colonel Surnin, head of the counterintelligence of the Headquarters of the Petrograd military district. I immediately sent him in his own automobile to Smolny to put him at the disposition of the Revolutionary Committee.

I had just managed to send him off when they brought in two new people, one after the other—the Minister of Religions Kartashev and an associate of the Minister of Finance. Arrest them or not? Up to now the MRC had been stubbornly silent in the face of our insistent inquiries: evidently they didn't have time. I decided—once you have begun you have to keep on.

The regiment moved its patrols forward and captured isolated cadet sentries. A whole crowd of people, officers and civilians, began to fall into the hands of the Pavlov men. They were quartered in a temporary jail—the buffet of the regimental club. Smolny still had no telephone service and the response to the arrests had to come back by courier:

> Finally two notes written by Podvoisky arrived, one after the other. The first: the Revolutionary Committee is highly satisfied by the arrest of the head of counterintelligence Surnin; it appears that they have already put him where he belongs. But the second note is a surprise: the Revolutionary Committee feels that it has been confronted with the fact of a clash too early; it still does not know when operations will begin, but no matter what, not before the next day, i.e., October 25. The arrests, especially of such important figures as ministers of the Provisional Government, it considers premature actions that will evoke alarm and attention on the other side. They propose that we cease the arrests and remove the roadblocks. However, the circumstance that our reconnaissance (though it is weak, we have nonetheless succeeded in organizing some reconnaissance service) has noticed animation among the troops of the Provisional Government, who are also preparing very seriously for a clash, compels us this time to disobey the Revolutionary Committee and execute its orders only in part.

This is how, in a fit of enthusiastic insubordination, the "insurrection" began. Dzenis goes on:

> The apprehension of people leaving the Palace and the government buildings adjacent to it continues. The people we arrest are put in the regimental club; by noon on October 25 up to two hundred people have been collected there. But my comrades do not want to confine themselves just to the arrest of passersby, and ask permission to take the cadet outposts. It appears that the Provisional Government has already set up outposts on its side too. I had to

agree, but without the right to start shooting. The results spoke for themselves.

Here is the picture on Millionaya Street. Not far from our roadblock, twenty-five or thirty paces, stands a guard detail in a sentry box. Three Pavlov men sneak up on them from the rear and suddenly appear from behind. There is a shout, "Hands up. Drop your rifles!" and the cadets are both taken alive, without any noise. During the night we managed in this way to capture a whole series of outposts at various points (including the Pevcheskaya Chapel on the Moika). About three o'clock in the morning a guard detail in a sentry box and along with them the commander of the guard were captured in the same way.

In the meantime, the MRC finally decided to approve what the troops were doing anyway. Dzenis wrote:

> About two o'clock I got a note from the MRC that it was necessary to strengthen the roadblock and organize actual control over passersby and traffic. But it was already too late: in the Palace they had come to, and none of the more influential people decided to leave it.
> So went the whole night of October 24–25.

Despite all the appearances of a systematic take-over, the Military Revolutionary Committee made no recorded decision for a general attack on the government before dawn on October 25. Until Lenin appeared at Smolny each move of the MRC had come in response to a government initiative—the removal of the troops to the front, the strike at the press, the raising of the bridges, the movement of troops from the military schools and the front. The Bolsheviks could still well imagine that the Congress of Soviets and their own party headquarters were prime targets of the military, so much so that they were ready to negotiate and temporize right up to the last minute. The movements of their forces were precautionary and limited. What the Bolsheviks could not calculate was that the government's forces would give way so readily, that the cadet guards would yield everywhere without a fight, that the Cossacks would refuse to come out, that the commander of the military district was perhaps betraying the Prime Minister. In short, the Bolsheviks had naturally but grossly overestimated the strength of the government, almost as much as the government had overestimated itself.

*　　*　　*

All day Lenin had been stewing and fuming in the Fofanova apartment, far removed from where the action was. He knew from Antonov that the Central Committee was planning to wait for the Congress of Soviets. He was incensed to read a newspaper report that the MRC had been negotiating with Headquarters and might agreed to its terms. The day's reports contained nothing but news of the government's troop moves and the soviet's defensive proclamations. Mme. Fofanova came home from work late in the afternoon with the news that the Nikolaevsky Bridge had been lifted and an impression of the confusion at the Vyborg district Bolshevik headquarters. Lenin decided that he must go to Smolny. He sent Fofanova down to the Vyborg district party headquarters to get a message to Smolny for permission for him to leave his hideout. She returned to tell him that permission was refused. Thereupon he sat down to write out an urgent appeal to his Bolshevik followers to launch the uprising he had been demanding:

Comrades:
   As I write these lines on the evening of the 24th, the situation is impossibly critical. It is clearer than clear that now, in truth, a delay in the uprising is equivalent to death.
   With all my power I am striving to persuade the comrades that now everything hangs on a hair, that there are questions on the agenda that are not settled by meetings or congresses (not even by congresses of soviets) but only by the peoples, by the mass, by the struggle of the armed masses.
   The bourgeois onslaught of the Kornilovists, the removal of Verkhovsky, show that we cannot wait. We must, no matter what, this evening, tonight arrest the government, after we disarm the cadets (or defeat them, if they resist), etc.
   We cannot wait!! We may lose everything!!

Power should be seized by the Military Revolutionary Committee or— Lenin was not even sure of the MRC—"by another institution." All the workers and troops, he wrote:

must be mobilized right away and immediately send delegations to the Military Revolutionary Committee, to the Bolshevik Central Committee urgently demanding that in no case should power be left in the hands of Kerensky and Co. until the 25th, by no means; the matter must be decided, without fail, this evening or tonight.

History will not forgive delay by revolutionists who could win today (and certainly will win today) but risk losing much tomorrow, they risk losing everything.

Once again Lenin was going around the Bolshevik leadership when they dragged their feet and trying to mobilize rank and file pressure against them—though how he expected his letter to have the desired effect in the next few hours is impossible to fathom. There is, in fact, some doubt whether anyone received the letter who was in a position to act on it—at any rate, probably not the Central Committee. But the letter is a vivid revelation of Lenin's political premises: "Seizure of power is the point of the uprising; its political aim will be clarified after the seizure." Something like Bonaparte—you plunge into the battle, and then you see what happens. In any case, the decision must not be left to arithmetical democracy: "It would be a disaster or formalism to wait for the vacillating votes of October 25. The people are justified and obliged to decide such questions not by voting but by force." Again, "the proper moment" must be seized. "The government is wavering. We must finish it off no matter what." Why, if the government was collapsing? To create the kind of power that Lenin lived for but rarely admitted. Only with such a mind could he write again, for the last time, "To delay the move is the same as death."

Lenin sent Mme. Fofanova out with his letter and a second request for permission to go to Smolny. Again he was refused. He sent her out a third time, saying that he would wait for her until 11 P.M. When she returned about 10:50, Lenin had departed, leaving a note—"I have gone where you didn't want me to go."

Shortly before, Lenin's bodyguard Rakhia had come by, likewise to tell him that the bridges had been raised. Rakhia wrote in his recollections,

I reported to V. I. He answered me, "Aha, this means it's beginning. The revolution is beginning. We must get to Smolny right away."

I began to protest that this was impossible, that shooting had already begun on the streets in some places, and that when I came the streetcars had already stopped running. He didn't want to listen to me. I just had to agree with him.

I disguised him more or less: I found some impossibly old cap and the very worst clothes, that gave him a very contemptible appearance, and we set off hoping that in this get-up no one would really recognize him on the streets. I only warned him not to talk with anyone, so that he would not give himself away by his voice. We jumped on a streetcar that came along, and found it completely empty. The conductor was a woman. Suddenly V. I. asked her, "Where are you going?" She said, "To the carbarn." I was scared. He had a characteristic voice, and he had often spoken at meetings; I thought she recognized him. But he continued, "Why are you going there?" She looked at him: "Why do you wonder? Don't you know what's happening? What kind of a worker are you that you don't know there's going to be a revolution? We're going to beat the bourgies." I thought that if he talked any more she would recognize him. Lenin talked with her the whole way, and she never knew to this day that it was V. I.

The streetcar went down Lesnoye Prospekt alongside the rail yards of the Finland Station, until it turned right to cross over to the carbarns on the Petrograd Side. Lenin and Rakhia got off after their twenty-minute ride, skirted the Mikhailovsky Artillery School, and headed on foot towards the Liteiny Bridge and Smolny. They passed within two blocks of the Bolshevik editorial office on Finland Prospekt where almost at that very moment the patrol of cadets was trying to find Lenin and put *Rabochi Put* out of business once again. Then, Rakhia recalled,

As we approached the Liteiny Bridge, I saw soldiers and Red Guards standing on it. I told V. I. that it was dangerous to cross. He said, "Where there are soldiers and Red Guards together, there is no danger." He stood in the crowd and then suddenly went on, in spite of the fact that they were not allowing anyone across the bridge. I decided not to leave him alone, and went after him.

Once across the bridge, Lenin and Rakhia turned eastward for the long, cold, and dangerous walk down Shpalernaya Street, nearly two miles, to the Smolny Institute. Then the thing they most feared happened. Rakhia's account goes on,

> Up ahead two cadets of the artillery school, mounted on horses, approached. I noticed that they were talking about something, and I whispered to V. I. to go past them without attracting attention, while I stayed back. We had two falsified passes; we had erased and changed them very unskillfully. I gave him one and kept the other for myself. The cadets approached and asked for our passes. I made it appear that I did not understand, and raised my voice, and at this moment V. I. walked ahead. I had two revolvers in my pockets and I decided to open fire with them if they went after V. I. One of them said to the other, "Well, what are you talking with that drunk for? Chuck it!" They spurred their horses and rode off.

On such chance escapes does the fate of nations and revolutions sometimes depend.

❋   ❋   ❋

It takes a little more than an hour to get from Serdobolskaya Street to Smolny by the combination of streetcar and foot that Lenin and Rakhia followed. They must have arrived at Smolny about midnight. But, as Rakhia related, there was still one more hurdle to pass.

> They would not let us through. It seems that they had changed the credentials of the delegates to the Congress—they had been white, but now they were red. A small crowd gathered around us. We stood there. "Well," I thought, "we've gotten here, and they ought to be able to recognize Vladimir Ilyich." But he was surprisingly calm. Suddenly I thought of a way out of the situation: I decided to carry the offensive to the guards. I began to shout, "What a mess, I'm a delegate and they won't let me through," and so on. I started a racket; the crowd supported me and pushed the two Red Guards aside, and we moved in. V. I. came last, laughing, satisfied with the favorable outcome. We went upstairs. V. I. stopped to sit down by a window, and sent me to get Stalin.* Then

---

* This account was published in 1934, when the Stalin cult had already set in. It is surprising that Trotsky is even mentioned.

Trotsky came, and someone else—I don't remember who. We went into a little room. V. I. sat at the end of the table.

At this point, Lieber, Dan and Gotz [the two Mensheviks and the SR, attending the meeting of the All-Russian Central Executive Committee] came in from the hall. Dan took a bundle out of his overcoat pocket, and addressing Lieber and Gotz by their first names, offered them something to eat. As he was taking out a French roll with sausage and cheese, he cast a casual glance to the side and only then recognized Vladimir Ilyich. This stunned him so that he scraped his bundle up in his arms, and all three sprang out of the room. V. I. and the rest of us roared with laughter.

Trotsky recalled the same scene, though according to him it was Dan and another Menshevik, the former Labor Minister Skobelev, who came in:

Dan, who had an experienced eye, looked to one side and to the other when he saw us, nudged Skobelev with his elbow, winked, and left. Vladimir Ilyich also nudged me: "The scoundrels recognized me!" But this was not dangerous, because by that time we were masters of the situation.

Aside from these anecdotes, the most significant moment of the October Revolution is one of the least documented, for reasons that can only be guessed. The memoirists are unusually vague and contradictory about Lenin's arrival at Smolny and the impact it had on the course of events. Obviously it must have electrified the entire soviet headquarters. There is reason to believe that Lenin, by direct command or perhaps by his mere presence, had a decisive effect in changing the orientation of his lieutenants from the defensive to the offensive.

If the operations of the MRC during the night are carefully followed, it is apparent that a marked change in tone and direction occurred after midnight. A new spirit of bold and systematic attack appeared, exemplified in orders to military units to seize outright the public institutions that were not yet under the control of the MRC. Up to this point the moves of the MRC had all been peaceful or defensive. The committee had twice turned down Lenin's idea of returning to Smolny—because they could not protect him, or feared his presence would provoke the government, or feared that he would upset their expectation of waiting for the Congress of Soviets. But the masses of men they had set in motion to counter the government already had most of the city under their control; it was no longer easy to see the distinction between defense and offense. Lenin, apparently, provided the catalyst to turn the soviets' cautious defenders into the aggressive heroes of insurrection.

One memoirist, Lomov, comes close to the probable truth. Lomov had not yet left on his mission to Moscow, and was busy at Smolny. Before Lenin's arrival, he wrote, "Neither we nor Kerensky risk taking the path of a final engagement. We wait, fearing that our forces are still not sufficiently encouraged and organized. Kerensky is afraid to take the initiative in his own hands.

"Thus things go on until eight or nine o'clock in the evening"— Lomov was off three or four hours on the time. "Suddenly Comrade Lenin appears. He is still in his wig, completely unrecognizable. Everything decisively changes. His point of view triumphs, and from this moment we go over to a determined offensive."

"To work!" said Antonov to himself when he saw Lenin. "Our leader is with us! Full speed ahead!"

Until he arrived at Smolny Lenin had no information that the MRC was responding to his demand to seize power before the Congress of Soviets. In all probability they were not trying to do this up to the moment of his return; they were stumbling into power all over the city thanks only to the total ineffectiveness of the government. But it could very well be that none of them dared confess to Lenin their defensive intentions, nor did they need to, since the state of affairs looked well enough like an offensive. Lenin was still angered by the reports he had read of the MRC's agreement with Headquarters the day before. "His first question as soon as he arrived," Trotsky recalled, "was: 'Could this be true?' 'No, it's to cover up the game,' we reassured him." From that time on every Bolshevik who was in the revolution had to represent the party's hedging tactics as some sort of ruse to fool the opposition and pave the way for a coup.

❖　❖　❖

The first of the new orders apparently prompted by Lenin's return was given to a member of the MRC, Lashevich. He was instructed to get troops from the Kexholm Regiment and seize the telephone exchange, the State Bank, and the Treasury. "For the MRC," Lashevich recalled, "it became clear that the moment had come to act." He drove across town to the Kexholm barracks near the Nikolaevsky Bridge, roused the regimental committee, and demanded two companies. The commander of one of the companies, Lieutenant Zakharov, described his reaction:

> Late in the evening, when I was already asleep in my clothes on a divan in the officers' meeting room, I was waked up by Lieutenant Smirnov of our regiment, a member of the regimental committee, and told that by order of the regimental committee, I must immediately go out with my company and assume the guard at the Petrograd city telephone station, and that as a member of the regimental and brigade committees I must do this without special orders from the regimental staff. I quickly went to my company and found the men already lined up with their weapons. The chairman of the regimental committee, Sergeant Smirnov of the machine-gun unit, informed me that I was being given responsibility to take the telephone station, which was being guarded by cadets of the Vladimirsky military school, and he added that I must do this as quickly as possible and if possible without fighting. Two commissars were assigned to work with me. Of course, I understood that my move was the beginning of a "coup d' état" (the definition I thought of at that moment), but I decided not to refuse the assignment but to carry it out as best I could, especially since the mood of the soldiers was very reliable—I felt this at once with my first glance at them.

Led by Lashevich, the detachment moved out along the embankment of the Moika Canal around 1:00 A.M. They met a few cadet sentries and disarmed them. Nearing the telephone building, Zakharov and his men made a dash to the open entry way and captured the armored car that had been parked there. But it was useless to them: none of the men could handle its machine guns. In the courtyard of the building they met the cadet guards rushing out of the guardroom. There was a moment of tension as the hostile forces confronted each other and shouted deadly threats back and forth. Lashevich parleyed with the guard commander and reached an agreement to avoid bloodshed: the outnumbered cadets could leave with their arms, if they

163

promised not to fight for the government. Without a shot, the Bolsheviks had the telephone office. They promptly reconnected Smolny and cut off the phones of the Winter Palace.

Leaving one company of the Kexholm Regiment to guard the telephone station, Lashevich moved on with his other company and some sailors from the Second Baltic Fleet Crew who had caught up with him. His next objective was the State Bank, on the Catherine Canal. It was about 6 A.M. when they found the back entrance, disarmed the sentry, and occupied the building. Lashevich woke up the detail of soldiers from the Semyonovsky Regiment quartered there and announced to them that he was taking over in the name of the MRC. The men replied that they too were for the MRC and insisted that they be left on duty as representatives of the soviet. Lashevich left a few of his own men with them and proceeded to the Treasury. Here his task was ridiculously easy: "The Treasury was guarded by the soldiers most devoted to us—the Pavlov men."

In the meantime, by the frosty light of the moon, other small forces were occupying the remaining key points. A detachment of Kexholm troops and sailors, with some Putilov Red Guards, occupied the Central Post Office around 1:30 A.M. The Nikolaevsky station, terminus of the Moscow railroad, and the power plants were taken over by similar detachments about the same time; usually the appearance of a soviet commissar was enough to make the employees on duty recognize the new authority. At 3:30, the *Aurora* anchored at the Nikolaevsky Bridge, already closed by Red Guards and then retaken by a platoon of government shock troops. Backed by the "moral effect" of the cruiser, sailors from the shore units easily cleared away the cadet guards and secured the bridge. By now the Provisional Government was practically isolated in the Winter Palace. At last the preemptive insurrection Lenin demanded had become a reality.

CHAPTER NINE

The Winter Palace

AT dawn on Wednesday the 25th of October the rare autumn sun broke through the Baltic overcast, as a cold new day of bright illusion opened for Petrograd and Russia. "All the streets were filled with people. There were swarms around Smolny like a giant anthill. Emissaries, commissars, delegates, automobiles, trucks, armored cars, sailors, Red Guards, soldiers, peasant members of the Congress—all this broad and turbulent stream flowed toward Smolny"—so wrote one of the Bolshevik commissars, Uralov, returning in a horse-drawn cab from his mission to commandeer a conservative newspaper.

Elsewhere in the city, life remained nearly normal. Stores, schools, and government ministries all opened as usual. Most of the streetcars continued to run. For the man in the street it was still hard to tell what was going on. "Knizhnik," the writer, went out early to get a newspaper and learn what had happened:

> I got on a streetcar, deciding to go to the center for newspapers. At the Troitsky Bridge I saw a patrol of sailors. In the Neva a cruiser was visible at the Nikolaevsky Bridge. In the streetcar some elderly citizen, evidently a merchant, was loudly and heatedly telling his neighbor that he was sick of the state of things, that the power of the Provisional Government was not a firm power, and therefore let even the Bolsheviks take power, if only there will be order.

Most of the day, "Knizhnik" recalled, he went from one point to another looking for news, wandering uncomprehendingly through the crowds like Tolstoy's Pierre Bezukhov at the Battle of Borodino. He went to Smolny with his old soviet pass, but they denied him entrance. Back at home he wondered what was meant by the machine-gun fire he heard. Only on the morning of the 26th did this man of the book learn in print what had been transpiring all around him.

The Bolshevik press of the 25th had not caught up with events, and gave little indication of the state of the insurrection. *Rabochi Put* devoted its entire front page to Lenin's recent article on the peasants, and the main item inside was an editorial by Zinoviev, of all people, with the same old appeal for power to be transferred from the bourgeoisie to the representatives of the masses—already out of date. *Izvestiya,* published for the last time by its old Menshevik and SR management, despite a Bolshevik attempt at censoring it, was more nearly *au courant:* "The Bolshevik uprising, which we have warned against as a terrible trial for the country, is being organized and started. . . . The dictatorship of one party, no matter how radical, will be as hateful to the great majority of the people as the autocracy."

Despite the Bolshevik take-over of the telegraph and telephone offices, the government still had a direct wire to General Headquarters in Mogilev that was unknown to the insurrectionists. Colonel Polkovnikov, still in his office despite Kerensky's repudiation, wired his view of things to GHQ:

> I report that the situation in Petrograd is menacing. There are no street demonstrations or disorders, but a systematic seizure of institutions and railroad stations, and arrests are going on. No orders are being carried out. The cadets are abandoning their posts without resistance, and despite a series of orders the Cossacks up to now have not left their barracks. Conscious of my responsibility to the country I must report that the Provisional Government is in danger of losing all power, and there is no guarantee that attempts will not be made to capture the Provisional Government.

At eight in the morning, after an hour's sleep in the Winter Palace, Vice-Premier Konovalov was awakened by a call from the city administration to tell him that the Bolsheviks had occupied the telephone exchange. Konovalov phoned the District Headquarters, only to learn that "Colonel Polkovnikov . . . was writing a report to the Prime Minister to tell him that the situation was critical and that the Provisional Government had no soldiers at its disposition." Konovalov found this hard to believe and called for Bagratuni, who could only confirm the news. The substance of the report was wired to GHQ by Kerensky's military aide General Levitsky at 10 A.M.:

> Against the overwhelming numbers of the Petrograd garrison, there remains not one unit in the full sense of the word on which the government can rely. . . . The units in the Winter Palace are only guarding it as a formality, since they decided not to move out actively. The general impression is as though the Provisional Government were in the capital of a hostile state, which has completed mobilization but not yet begun active operations.

There had been a lull in active soviet operations since the nighttime take-overs, while the leaders of the MRC snatched some sleep on chairs or on the floor of their meeting room. Apparently the Bolshevik leadership had not yet decided whether to attack the government directly; a telegraphic report from the MRC sent to Dybenko in Finland at 8 A.M. still stressed protection of the Congress of Soviets. Levitsky sensed this mood still:

> The indecisiveness of the Bolsheviks, who have actually been able to dispose of all of us for quite a time, gives me reason to feel that they will not dare go counter to the opinion of the army at the front and will not go beyond what they have done, but this optimistic opinion of mine may be baseless if the army does not underscore more firmly the opinion expressed by the Headquarters Committee.

❖　　❖　　❖

At about 9 A.M. Commissar Uralov was at MRC headquarters in Smolny waiting for instructions. In his recollections he wrote,

> I suddenly heard a loud exclamation:
> "Papa, Vladimir Ilyich, our father!"
> Looking around, I saw Comrade Bonch-Bruevich embracing and kissing Lenin in the doorway.
> "I didn't recognize you, native!" Bonch exclaimed.

I was stunned and shocked: "Ilyich! So here he is, the sovereign of our souls." This was the first time I had seen him in person, for I came to Petrograd only after the July Days, when he was already in hiding.

"What a plain ordinary person he is," was the first thought that entered my head. It was hard to believe, and hard to square this real Ilyich with the Lenin whom I had created in my imagination, who had to be of powerful stature, with a loud voice, etc. Under this powerful impact of such an unexpected meeting, I was practically stupified, and froze against the wall.

But then something even more surprising happened. Pulling himself away from Bonch (everything happened unbelievably fast), Lenin quickly went over to a plain little table with nothing on it, and several men followed him. Among them, as far as I remember, were, I believe, Stalin, Kamenev, Sokolnikov [all riding high in 1924 when Uralov wrote!], and others, in all about seven men. Some of them sat on the windowsill, somebody stood behind Lenin, another opposite rested his knee on a chair. The comrades present in the room did not realize that an historic session was going on here.

Going up to the table and quickly sitting down on a plain Viennese chair, Lenin began, as fast as he could, without any introduction or foreword, to lay down a program of action: "To declare the Provisional Government overthrown," "to declare all power transferred to the soviets," "to open the Congress of Soviets this evening," "to take the Winter Palace, arrest the ministers, and put them in Peter-Paul," and something else—I don't remember.

I remember that these decisions were voted on. But the most important thing about this is that it all happened in the course of around ten or fifteen minutes. Unprecedented swiftness, unanimity, and decisiveness.

Lenin's proclamation was published as a leaflet, "To the Citizens of Russia," at ten o'clock in the morning:

The Provisional Government has been overthrown. Governmental power has passed into the hands of the organ of the Petrograd Soviet of Workers' and Peasants' Deputies—the Military Revolutionary Committee, which stands at the head of the Petrograd proletariat and garrison.

The cause for which the people are struggling is the immediate proclamation of a democratic peace, the elimination of landlord property in land, workers' control of industry, the creation of a soviet government. This cause is sure.

Long live the revolution of the workers, soldiers, and peasants!

The immediate challenge to the Bolsheviks was the Winter Palace, in which the Provisional Government held out behind considerable force, far from overthrown. The decision to surround and attack the Palace, Antonov wrote somewhat cryptically, "was based not on the general organizational preparation of the uprising, but proceeded only from the fact that it attributed a vast role to the upsurge and enthusiasm of the masses." In other words, the attack was improvised after the rest of the city fell unexpectedly into the hands of the Bolshevik forces.

The two strong men of the MRC, Podvoisky and Antonov, set themselves up together with Sadovsky as a "troika" to make detailed operational plans. Sadovsky bowed out because of his work as head of the Soldiers' Section of the Soviet, so they promoted Chudnovsky from his position as a regimental commissar to work with them instead. They all alleged that the "troika" was organized on the evening of the 24th, but the specifics of their work refer exclusively to the operations of the 25th. It is much more likely that their efforts were another response to Lenin's return.

"It was in the morning of October 25, about eleven o'clock, in the Revolutionary Committee room in Smolny," wrote Commissar Dzenis, that "the 'operational plan' was laid out in rough outline." Up to this point, no one seemed to know what the MRC intended to do; in fact, Commissar Blagonravov of the Peter-Paul fortress claimed that he thought up the idea all on his own of an attack on the Palace and came over to Smolny about noon to suggest it. He found, of course, that he had been anticipated. "The first person who caught my eye on reaching the second floor was Comrade Antonov-Ovseyenko. He pulled me into the quarters of the MRC where comrades Podvoisky and Chudnovsky were having a lively talk next to a map of Petrograd covered with flags." According to Sadovsky, "Podvoisky and Chudnovsky argued violently about the plan of action against the Winter Palace, about the significance of Peter-Paul, about strategy, and made dispositions of our boats and naval forces on the Neva. What the final plan was I can't recall."

The MRC's actual plan for the capture of the Winter Palace was mostly the work of Antonov, so he claimed. The officer-rebel of 1905 at last had the opportunity to fashion a revolutionary victory. According to Blagonravov, who took part in the proceedings,

> We began quickly to work out a plan of military action and made an approximate count of our forces. The chief support point and base would be the Peter-Paul fortress, which would be in touch with neighboring units and the *Aurora* (Antonov went to the *Aurora*). Military units would be on the side of Millionaya Street, the Nevsky Prospekt, and the other streets leading to the Winter Palace, to isolate the Winter Palace with a solid ring and then at the first signal to gradually tighten this ring around the Palace. To guard against the possible movement of unpredictable Cossack units and cadet schools, screens of nearby Bolshevik military units and factories were set up. These screens would paralyze a possible blow at the rear of our troops attacking the Winter Palace.

An elaborate network of command posts was mapped out—headquarters at Smolny, "field headquarters" at the Peter-Paul fortress, "reserve headquarters" on the *Aurora,* "front headquarters" at the Pavlov barracks for the right wing and at the Baltic Crew barracks for the left wing. But the cumbersome command setup delayed the whole operation considerably. In Trotsky's view the planning was over-thorough: "The plan for capturing the Palace was worked out in the style of a large operation. When civil and semi-civil people undertake the solution of a purely military problem, they are always inclined to excessive strategic ingenuities. . . . Feeling their own weakness in matters of reconnoitering, communications, maneuvering, these Red martials felt obliged to roll up against the Winter Palace such a superiority of forces as removed the very possibility of practical leadership. An incongruous grandeur of plan is almost equivalent to no plan at all."

Two regiments, the Pavlov and the Kexholm, provided the bulk of the attacking force, as they had during the night. By noon or a little after they were moving into position, the Pavlov Regiment taking the eastern sector of the arc from the Neva down to the Nevsky Prospekt, and the Kexholm Regiment the western sector from the Nevsky around to the river below the Admiralty. Podvoisky went out to explain the plan to the regimental commissars: a surrender ultimatum would be sent to the government, and upon expiration of the allotted time the Peter-Paul fortress would display a signal to open fire.

Antonov and Blagonravov went to the fortress to discuss details of the attack on the Palace—the surrender ultimatum they would send the government, the arrangements for artillery fire in the event the government refused to give in, and the signals to order the attack. Antonov then went by launch to the *Aurora* at its mooring near the Nikolaevsky Bridge, to cordinate plans with the crew. Blagonravov recalled the arrangements:

> A red signal would be hoisted on the flagpole at the fortress (a lantern, to indicate our readiness). Then the *Aurora* would open fire with its guns, at first in the air; in case the Provisional Government did not surrender, the fortress would begin to fire live ammunition. And then if the Winter Palace continued to resist after this, the *Aurora* would open real fire with its guns.

The troops waited—but no orders came to move. The Kronstadt sailors, expected to arrive at 2 P.M. to stiffen the fighting spirit of the soldiers, failed to appear. The whole operation had to be postponed.

❋   ❋   ❋

When Kerensky learned of Colonel Polkovnikov's despondent report, his first impulse was to assume personal command of the defense of the government. Konovalov persuaded him to summon a cabinet meeting "to consider everything and work out measures," and the call went out to the ministers. Kerensky went over to Headquarters anyway, and there a delegation of the cadet defenders of the Winter Palace found him. They had just received a surrender-or-die ultimatum, the first direct Bolshevik pressure on the Palace, and they wanted some assurance that help was coming if they tried to stand and fight. Knowing that he could not really give them any, Kerensky resolved to go personally to meet the Cossack divisions supposedly on their way to the capital and hurry them to the relief of the Provisional Government. He called for his car, only to be told that all the Palace cars had been sabotaged. Thereupon two aides, Lieutenants Knirsh and Sobolev, were sent out to find cars. They saw one parked in front of the home of one of the secretaries of the American Embassy, and asked for it. The secretary was reluctant, but drove with the Russian officers to the Headquarters building and yielded the car when Kerensky personally confirmed his need for it. Meanwhile another car, a Russian-owned Pierce-Arrow, had been found, and Kerensky chose to ride in this one when his party set off about 11:30 A.M. Knirsh was instructed to go first in the American car, flying the American flag, but he did not know the way, and let Kerensky's car go ahead. Contrary to a popular story, Kerensky made no attempt to disguise himself as a nurse, but wore his customary uniform, and actually drew salutes from startled insurgent soldiers as his car sped past. The Bolshevik leadership had no idea of Kerensky's flight until they captured the Winter Palace and found him gone. By that time he was in Pskov, 180 miles away, pleading with his generals to put their troops in motion and crush the Bolshevik rebels.

As Kerensky was preparing to leave, Deputy Premier Konovalov convened the emergency cabinet session in the Winter Palace. Most of the ministers still had no difficulty getting through from their homes or ministries—Tereshchenko, Nikitin, Admiral Verderevsky, acting War Minister General Manitovsky (Verkhovsky's replacement); the Kadets Kishkin (Welfare), Kartashev (Religions), and Smirnov (State Comptroller); the Mensheviks Gvozdev (Labor) and Maliantovich (Justice); the SRs Maslov (Agriculture) and Liverovsky (Ways of Communication); and the nonparty ministers Bernatsky (Finance), Salazkin (Education), and Tretyakov (Economic Council). Apart from Kerensky himself, only the Menshevik Prokopovich was missing —he had already been arrested. (Later in the day he was released, but he was still absent from the Palace during the seige.) The cabinet was bitter about Polkovnikov's conduct, and Minister of Agriculture Maslov even wanted to have him arrested. They agreed on the need for a strong man to command the defense; Minister of Justice Maliantovich proposed Minister of Welfare Kishkin for the responsibility. The Menshevik Minister of the Interior demurred, with the comment that Kishkin, an aggressive conservative, would not be effective with the broad democratic circles of Petrograd. The question was left up in the air while Konovalov went out to parley fruitlessly with the Cossacks, and the other ministers took a break for tea and sandwiches. After lunch and more dejected discussion, the ministers finally designated Kishkin as "Governor-General," despite Nikitin's warning, and voted to remain in session until relief arrived from the front or they were arrested. Polkovnikov went home and thus escaped the siege of the Palace. In his place Kishkin appointed the deputy cabinet minister P. I. Palchinsky to command the defenders of the Winter Palace. Otherwise, according to Palchinsky, the cabinet meeting was only "a fruitless discussion." Palchinsky was appalled when he took over his new duties. He noted his reactions at the time: "Absence even of a plan of the Palace. . . . No provisions. No plan. Confusion and delay among the officers, and poor morale among the cadets, to whom no one gave enough concern."

One lone attempt was made by government forces to evict the Bolsheviks from the buildings they had seized. The government's Chief Army Commissar, Stankevich, took it upon himself to organize a detachment of cadets to retake the telephone exchange. They marched off, only to find the building guarded by a large soviet force with an armored car. A few shots were fired and some of the cadets were disarmed. The rest abandoned the enterprise.

Back at the General Staff, across the square from the Palace, Stankevich urgently wired GHQ to speed the relief columns:

> The forces of the Provisional Government are two and a half schools of cadets, a battery from the Mikhailovsky School, and two armored cars. These forces are sufficient for us to hold out forty-eight hours, but not more, and there is no possibility of our taking any active measures without help from outside. On the streets there is outward calm, street traffic is continuing, but the question of provisioning is very serious.

In response GHQ assured Stankevich that the troops were on their way. Stankevich asked that they be instructed to move from the railroad stations directly to the Winter Palace, and be prepared to meet resistance. A few reinforcements from the city—a couple of squadrons of loyal Cossacks, and some more cadets—actually made their way to the Palace without interference, offsetting somewhat the defection of the government's armored cars. Claude Anet watched the cadets march in from the Palace Square: "They were all young recruits. These Russians of the north at eighteen look like twelve. They were beardless kids, tired, who came dragging their feet, volunteers all the same, to put themselves at the service of the government. It was pitiful and moving, this column of youngsters who wanted to be heroic."

Neither side was seriously guarding the Palace Square. Government officials came and went until after dark. Three American correspondents, John Reed, his wife Louise Bryant, and Albert Rhys Williams, walked into the Winter Palace hoping to interview Kerensky. Reed took special note of

> a large, ornate room with gilded cornices and enormous crystal lustres, and beyond it several smaller ones, wainscoted with dark wood. On both sides of the parquetted floor lay rows of dirty mattresses and blankets, upon which occasional soldiers were stretched out; everywhere was a litter of cigarette-butts, bits of bread, cloth, and empty bottles with expensive French labels. More and more soldiers, with the red shoulder-straps of the *yunker*-schools, moved about in a stale atmosphere of tobacco-smoke and unwashed humanity.

Hopes were sagging in the Palace with each passing hour that failed to signal the arrival of the promised relief forces. It turned out that the lead unit, a bicycle battalion coming up by train, had been stopped by pro-Bolshevik forces at a station forty miles south of Petrograd and persuaded not to fight against the soviet. Five Cossack regiments were reported due to arrive only on the 26th. Minister of Justice Maliantovich wrote,

> One thing became more and more certain, that we could not count on any active military support except what we had right there. And could we count on what we had?
>
> How long would we go on here? How would all this end? How would we act? What orders should we give the military units around us?
>
> To resist to the last man, to the last drop of blood? In the name of what?

❁   ❁   ❁

During the day Bolshevik forces extended their control to most of the few remaining points of government authority, without resistance. The warden of the Kresty Prison was handed an order by the Vyborg Red Guards to surrender the building, and his political prisoners—all of six men in jail for agitating among the troops—were released. Shortly after noon pro-Bolshevik soldiers and sailors surrounded the Marinsky Palace, where the Pre-Parliament had once more convened in about one-third of its strength, and demanded that the delegates disperse. A conference of party leaders agreed to submit under protest, only to be resisted on the floor; finally by a vote of 56 to 48 the body agreed to yield in the hope of convening again some better day. In fear of coming trouble the administrative offices of the government closed, and all school children were sent home.

Early in the afternoon, without waiting to dispose of the government's resistance at the Winter Palace, the Bolsheviks opened a triumphal session at Smolny of the Petrograd Soviet and Bolshevik delegates to the Congress of Soviets to celebrate their victory. Their meeting place was now like a fortress, ready for any counterattack: "In front of Smolny, numerous detachments of the Red Guard and the regular army protecting the Revolutionary Committee. Machine guns in the gardens. Between the columns of the entrance, several cannons. The doorway is strictly barred. . . ." So wrote the French military attaché Jacques Sadoul, who talked his way in anyway. Inside, "The vast white and cream corridors are jammed with a militant and triumphant crowd, comrades and soldiers."

Trotsky, alone at the presidium table, opened the proceedings with his characteristic éclat. "Especially etched in my memory is the immortal speech of Comrade Trotsky," recalled a wavering Menshevik delegate to the Congress. "I have heard him before this speech and afterwards, but another such speech I never managed to hear. It was like molten metal, every word burned the soul, it awakened thought and roused adventure, as he spoke of the victory of the proletariat. We listened to him with bated breath, and I saw that many people were clenching their fists as they brought themselves to the final decision to follow him unwaveringly wherever he might call them."

"In the name of the Military Revolutionary Committee I declare that the Provisional Government no longer exists!" Trotsky announced, to the accompaniment of restrained and "thoughtful" applause. "Some of the ministers have been put under arrest. (Bravo!) The rest will be arrested in the next few days or hours." (Applause.) Trotsky announced the end of the Pre-Parliament, denied stories of pogroms, hailed the revolutionary soldiers and workers, and predicted the expeditious capture of the Winter Palace. He promised a new government that would put an end to the slavery of the masses. Then a real sensation for the audience—"In our midst is Vladimir Ilyich Lenin, who because of a whole series of circumstances could not appear in our midst before now. . . . Long live Comrade Lenin, back with us again!"

"These words were met with loud applause," wrote the Menshevik delegate, "and when comrades Lenin and Zinoviev appeared on the tribune they were given such a triumphal ovation that it was clear whose side victory was on."

Lenin's first public appearance since the July Days was brief and to the point: "Comrades: The workers' and peasants' revolution, which the Bolsheviks have been saying all along was unavoidable, has been accomplished.

"What is the significance of this workers' and peasants' revolution? Above all the significance of this coup lies in the fact that we will have a soviet government, our own organs of power, without any participation whatsoever by the bourgeoisie. The downtrodden masses themselves will set up the government"—a rhetorical echo of Lenin's "any cook can run the government" philosophy. "The old state apparatus will be smashed to its foundations and a new apparatus of administration represented by the soviet organizations will be set up. From now on a new era is beginning in the history of Russia, and this third revolution must lead to the victory of socialism as its end result." He promised immediate peace negotiations (though in a passage published only by the non-Bolshevik press he warned that they might not bear fruit immediately). He promised the land to the peasants and workers' control in the factories (both sooner or later retracted by the Soviet Government). "In Russia," Lenin concluded, "we must now undertake the construction of a proletarian socialist state." And as an afterthought, "Long live the world socialist revolution!"

Trotsky came on again to call for the appointment of emissaries to meet the troops advancing from the front and win them over to the side of the revolution. "You are predeciding the will of the All-Russian

Congress of Soviets," a voice in the audience complained. In reply Trotsky for the first time sounded like the kind of revolutionist Lenin had wanted: "The will of the All-Russian Congress of Soviets has been predecided by the tremendous fact of the uprising of the Petrograd workers and soldiers that took place last night." "Uprising" was perhaps a strong word for the changing of the guard at a few public buildings. The real fight lay ahead, but Trotsky assured his listeners, "Now we only have to exploit our victory."

Trotsky was followed by Lunacharsky, who urged the supporters of the soviet to show their political maturity and maintain order, and then Zinoviev spoke. Like Lenin, he was appearing for the first time since July. Despite his opposition to the insurrection, he was given a great ovation. He was now prepared to renounce his doubts: "Comrades, we are in the period of insurrection. I believe there can be no more doubt about the outcome—we will be victorious. I am convinced that the greater part of the peasants will join our side as soon as the peasants have learned about our agrarian program. Long live the social revolution which has just begun! Long live the working class of Peter [familiar slang for the city], which will carry its victory to completion!" Then a little more attention to the outside world, which was and would remain a major concern for Zinoviev: "Today we have paid our debt to the world proletariat and dealt a powerful blow to the war, a direct body blow to all the imperialists and especially to Wilhelm the Butcher. Down with the war! Long live international peace!"

It was time for the resolution, claimed in the collected works of both Lenin and Trotsky as the handiwork of the respective author, but actually introduced by Volodarsky. This document praised again the valor and solidarity of the Petrograd workers and garrison, endorsed in advance the establishment of a soviet government and a course toward socialism and peace, and hinted at the rigors to come: "The Petrograd Soviet of Workers' and Soldiers' Deputies summons all the workers and all the peasants of Russia to support the workers' and peasants' revolution unreservedly and with all their energy. The soviet expresses its conviction that the city workers, in alliance with the poorest peasantry, will manifest inflexible discipline and create the strictest revolutionary order necessary for the victory of socialism." Finally, there was a nod to the doctrine of Marxist internationalism most closely associated with the ideas of Trotsky: "The soviet is convinced that the proletariat of the west-European countries will help us carry through the cause of socialism to a complete and firm victory."

All this proud oratory did not prevent growing anxiety in Smolny. Lenin was determined to be able to announce the fall of the Winter Palace before the Congress of Soviets convened, lest he lose the whole impact of the preemptive revolution on the Congress. The Congress had been set for noon, and then postponed until evening. The delegates were milling around impatiently. The operational chiefs of the MRC conferred fruitlessly. Lenin threatened to have them shot if the Palace was not quickly taken. "Comrade Lenin wrote dozens of notes to me, Antonov, Chudnovsky," recalled Podvoisky, "in which he castigated us for delaying the opening of the Congress and thereby causing agitation among the deputies to the Congress: 'We have to open the meeting of the Congress, and the Winter Palace still isn't taken!'" No one seemed to know why the signal was not given to advance and deliver the planned ultimatum to the government. Kamenev told Jacques Sadoul that the revolutionary forces were moving slowly to avoid violence. Whether this statement represented party policy, a minority hope, or the concealment of mismanagement is hard to say.

Over at "field headquarters" in the Peter-Paul fortress, two bicyclists with the ultimatum were waiting for the word to leave for the Winter Palace. They were to go when the fortress was ready to raise its signal of battle readiness. A considerable problem of readiness had presented itself, however. It was discovered that the fortress, which had always looked out over the river as a menacing hulk of reaction, had in fact no artillery better than museum pieces, except for one gun that was traditionally fired to sound the noon hour each day (as it still does). The fortress was almost devoid of offensive value. Commissar Blagonravov ordered a search of the storerooms, and sure enough, some old three-inch field guns were discovered. But there was no way to hoist them up to the emplacements on the fortress walls, and it was impossible to use indirect fire from behind the walls at the short range of the Palace, just across the river. Blagonravov decided to set his guns up on the open campground that stretched around the back side of the fortress and adjoined the river bank below the downstream end of the fortress. Next he found that the fortress artillerymen had decided to take a position of neutrality in the battle between the soviet and the government, and refused to man the guns. He threatened them with

33.   Revolutionary leaflets being distributed in Moscow in 1917.

Nikolai Bukharin, leader of the radical Bolsheviks in Moscow and
Vyacheslav Skriabin (Molotov), the future foreign minister.

34.

35.   Red Guards and soldiers under General Kornilov mix in friendly fashion after the soldiers refused to support the rightist Kornilov movement in August.

No. 1 Serdobolskaya Street, the apartment of Margarita Fofanova, which Lenin used as a hideout in October, 1917. (The photo shows the building as it appears today, with the tower added.)

36.

37.   The Smolny Institute, seat of the Petrograd Soviet after July, 1917, and headquarters for the Bolshevik uprising.

The Lesnoye-Udelnaya District Council Building, used for the Bolshevik Central Committee meeting on October 16, 1917.

38.

39.

A Bolshevik guard detail on the steps of the Smolny Institute, October, 1917.

Red Guards checking passes at the entrance to the Smolny, October, 1917.

40.

41.

Guards outside Lenin's room in Smolny on the day of the revolution, October 25, 1917.

Lenin's quarters in Smolny from October, 1917, to March, 1918.

42.

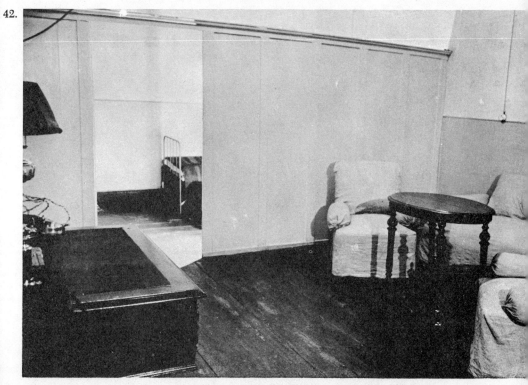

43.

The cruiser *Aurora* with its guns trained on the Winter Palace.

Bolshevik forces guarding the telephone station after seizing it from the Government troops.

44.

45.   The Peter-Paul fortress—a recent view.

Women soldiers in the Provisional Government's "Battalion of Death."

46.

47.

Storming the Winter Palace, a painting commissioned for the Museum of the Great October Socialist Revolution in Leningrad.

48

Къ Гражданамъ Россіи.

Временное Правительство низложено. Государственная власть перешла въ руки органа Петроградскаго Совѣта Рабочихъ и Солдатскихъ Депутатовъ Военно-Революціоннаго Комитета, стоящаго во главѣ Петроградскаго пролетаріата и гарнизона.

Дѣло, за которое боролся народъ: немедленное предложеніе демократическаго мира, отмѣна помѣщичьей собственности на землю, рабочій контроль надъ производствомъ, созданіе Совѣтскаго Правительства — это дѣло обезпечено.

ДА ЗДРАВСТВУЕТЪ РЕВОЛЮЦІЯ РАБОЧИХЪ, СОЛДАТЪ И КРЕСТЬЯНЪ!

Военно-Революціонный Комитетъ
при Петроградскомъ Совѣтѣ
Рабочихъ и Солдатскихъ Депутатовъ.

25 октября 1917 г. 10 ч. утра.

Proclamation of the Petrograd Soviet of Workers' and Soldiers' Deputies announcing the overthrow of the Provisional Government and the transfer of power to the Soviet, October 25, 1917.

50.

49.

The Red Flag is unfurled in Moscow after the revolution.

A conference of Bolshevik officials shortly after the revolution. Trotsky is visible in profile at the left, and Alexandra Kollontai is seated at the right.

51.
Kerensky with some of his followers after he eluded the Bolsheviks and escaped from Petrograd.

52.

Members of the Constituent Assembly. Bolsheviks and Socialist-Revolutionaries are at the left.

Ninth Congress of the Communist Party, meeting in 1920. Bukharin, Stalin, Lashevich, Kamenev, Lenin and Rykov are recognizable.

53.

54.   The three central figures are Anatol Lunacharsky, Lenin and Kamenev.

55.

Stalin and Lenin at the time of the revolution.

Trotsky and his staff inspect troops in Red Square after the revolution.

56.

57.   Lenin, in power in 1918, reads *Pravda* in his Moscow office.

the direst consequences, and they reluctantly moved the guns into the chosen position.

By this time it was getting dark when, Blagonravov recalled, "A small unforeseen circumstance disrupted our plan: there was no lantern for the signal. After a long search we found one, but to get it up on the flagpole so that it could easily be seen presented great difficulties—and Tregubovich, who was trying to take care of this, got terribly rattled by his repeated failures." While his aides struggled with the lantern, Blagonravov went out to the campground again to see how the artillery was. Another blow—the gunners reported that there was no oil in the recoil mechanisms and that the guns might explode if they were fired. "A wave of terrible pain struck me in the head, and my hand reached involuntarily to my holster." Blagonravov threatened to have them all shot if they were lying, but the lieutenant in charge calmly insisted that he was telling the truth.

* * *

In the Winter Palace provisions were not lacking for the cabinet, at least—dinner was served at six o'clock. The ministers had hardly finished their meal when, Maliantovich recounts, a delegation of cadets came up to have a look at the government they were defending. They asked, "What shall we do?" The answer, according to Maliantovich: "We could only say that we couldn't give any military orders."

For safety's sake, the cabinet moved out of the Malachite Hall facing the Neva, the Peter-Paul fortress, and the guns of the *Aurora*. They gathered instead in Tsar Nikolai's private dining room, overlooking the courtyard. The room was half-dark, with the one table lamp shielded from the window with some newspapers. The ministers took their seats at the round dining table for the evening's vigil.

Around the entrances to the Palace cadets and the women's battalion had been piling up firewood barricades all afternoon. Near 6 P.M. this was reported to Chudnovsky, who had taken command of the eastern sector of the Bolshevik arc around the Palace. Chudnovsky decided it was time to get his men into position with machine guns, but he finally realized that the nearby Preobrazhensky Regiment, of which he was personally the commissar, was unreliable. He drove off to the Pavlov barracks to get more of their men up to the line.

Now a few rifle shots rang out around the Winter Palace, as the cadets began to fire at soviet troops who ventured too close to the Palace Square. The besiegers showed more caution than courage—according to Podvoisky, "They dropped into every hollow and seemed glued to the granite walls." Tired of waiting for the ultimatum to come from Peter-Paul, Podvoisky put a telephone call through to the Winter Palace to suggest the defenders lay down their arms. They refused. The soviet troops then began a somewhat ragged rifle fire, and a platoon forced its way into the huge General Staff building that arcs around the south side of the Palace Square.

All this time Smolny kept phoning the Peter-Paul fortress to find out what was happening. Sverdlov got on the phone, and the fortress people asked him to send some reliable artillerymen. Blagonravov finally threw up his hands and dispatched the ultimatum, ready or not. Between 6:30 and 7 the two bicyclists from the fortress arrived at the Headquarters of the Military District and presented the ultimatum. It read as follows:

> By order of the MRC of the Petrograd Soviet of Workers' and Soldiers' Deputies the Provisional Government is declared overthrown. All power is going into the hands of the Petrograd Soviet of Workers' and Soldiers' Deputies. The Winter Palace is surrounded by revolutionary troops. The guns of the Peter-Paul fortress and the ships *Aurora, Amur* and others are trained on the Winter Palace and the building of the General Staff. In the name of the MRC we propose to the members of the Provisional Government and the troops loyal to it that you capitulate. The Provisional Government, the officials of the General Staff and members of the high command will be arrested, the cadets, soldiers and employees will be disarmed and after individual checks will be released.
>
> We give you twenty minutes to answer. Give the answer to our envoy. The period of the ultimatum expires at 7:10, after which we will immediately open fire. Evacuation of the infirmary must be completed in the time allotted for your answer. Evacuation to be made onto Millionaya Street. Give your answer to our envoy.
>
> Chairman of the MRC Antonov
> Commissar of the Peter-Paul fortress
> G. B[lagonravov].

In the somber old Headquarters building on the east side of the Palace Square were Governor-General Kishkin and his assistant Palchinsky, along with General Bagratuni and his adjutant, Colonel Paradelov. Naturally ignorant of the troubles at the fortress, and unable to decide on a response to the twenty-minute ultimatum, the officials went over to the Palace to get a decision, leaving only Paradelov and a small force of cadets in the Headquarters building. Meanwhile they requested one of the cyclists to return to the fortress and ask for a ten-minute extension.

It was a little after seven o'clock when Kishkin read the surrender ultimatum to the cabinet. Since more time had already gone by than the ultimatum allowed, and nothing had happened, the ministers decided that the ultimatum was probably an empty threat. The waiting bicyclist was sent back with the answer that there would be no answer. However, Konovalov was alarmed enough to wire Chief of Staff Dukhonin at Mogilev to hasten the movement of loyal troops. Dukhonin replied, "Measures for the earliest arrival of the troops are being taken," but he added ominously, "I consider it my duty to report that in the region nearest to Petrograd, independently from us, the movement is being hindered."

To stiffen the uncertain defense, Palchinsky went into the great White Hall of the Palace to make a speech of encouragement to the cadets of the Oranienbaum and Peterhof schools. There was silence. He appealed to them to do their duty. They shouted the customary, "We will!," but not with much enthusiasm. Palchinsky repeated his speech to the engineer cadets in the courtyard. The response was about the same.

General Bagratuni had meanwhile got General Cheremisov on the direct wire to report the deteriorating situation in Petrograd. Cheremisov appeared shocked at the news that Polkovnikov had been relieved from command: "Who can report to me further about the state of things? Who replaced Colonel Polkovnikov, and who is running things in Petrograd, the government or you?

"Are you there?"

There was no answer; this was evidently the moment when Bagratuni was called to receive the Bolshevik ultimatum. Then Colonel Paradelov came to the apparatus to wire Cheremisov the explanation that Kishkin had been appointed to direct the defense of Petrograd. Cheremisov inquired, "What is the Governor-General doing? If he was appointed by the government, does this mean that the government can make its power effective?"

Paradelov knew Kishkin's reputation as a critic of Kerensky, and replied, "There is something hard to understand about the appointment, and there is even reason to suppose that they bypassed Kerensky to make it." This set Cheremisov to wondering what regime he might actually be supporting if he allowed units from his army to proceed to the relief of the Winter Palace.

Cheremisov's talk with the District Headquarters was suddenly interrupted by shooting outside the building. Commissar Dzenis of the Pavlov Regiment, knowing that the ultimatum had expired, ordered his men to open fire on the District Headquarters. "We conducted the siege and the attack in a very disorderly way," he confessed. "At the head of twelve or fifteen comrades," he recalled, "I ran into the building. Upstairs we found several cadets trying to remove the telephones. Five minutes later intense firing on the building began." Apparently this was a sortie by the cadets from the Palace. "The cadets hit our soldiers downstairs at the entrance to the building . . . , but they did not have enough of a force to occupy the building again. Besides, this involved great risk of being wiped out by the advancing soldiers and Red Guards who were moving nearer and nearer to the square. The cadets all pulled back into the Winter Palace." General Bagratuni and Colonel Paradelov were captured, amid shouts of triumph on the soviet side.

Podvoisky was asked many times afterward why he did not press the attack and storm the Palace at this point or even before. He explained that he wanted to avoid bloodshed and wait for the results of his political warfare "by our adherents among the cadets and Cossacks, and also by groups of sailors and soldiers in civilian clothes who had been let in through secret entrances by our supporters." Whether deliberately or spontaneously, the defenders' will to fight was indeed dissolving, as the curious behavior of the government's one battery of artillery testified.

The four horse-drawn guns, manned by cadets of the Mikhailovsky Artillery School, were stationed in the Palace courtyard. The governmental commissar at the school, a grounded army pilot named

Akashev, was disturbed when he heard that his cadets might have to fight, and against hopeless odds. "These cadets are children, we have to take care of them, it is the people themselves who ought to fight for the Provisional Government," he told the officers. "I decided to go into the Winter Palace and lead the artillery out," Akashev related. "It was easy enough for me to get by into the Palace Square, and from there I simply walked into the Winter Palace. It was around 7 P.M. There was the usual Petrograd fog; at times, there was a sprinkling of rain."

The captain in command of the battery did not know until the commissar told him, that the whole city was in the hands of the Bolsheviks. Nevertheless Akashev was balked by the higher officers in his direct attempt to argue that "any resistance would lead to nothing, it would only be pointless and superfluous bloodletting." He persuaded the battery commander to cooperate in a ruse: the captain would tell his superiors that the battery was deploying for action, while the commissar ordered the cadets to ride out of the Palace and led them off to the school. Someone was suspicious:

> An officer was being sent by Headquarters to find me. It was already dark, and I hid in the courtyard. Soon the cadets, mounted on their horses, began to ride out onto the Palace Square with their guns. Along with the last gun was the horse that had been prepared for me. Seeing that the battery was moving, I stepped up to the horse that was prepared for me, in order to mount and ride out with the others. But now a cadet saw me and pointed me out to the officer from Headquarters who was looking for me. As he was approaching me I managed to mount my horse. He began to ask me who I was and on what basis I was giving orders. My horse was highstrung and all the while "danced" under me. Now holding back and now letting the horse go, I made it look as though I couldn't handle the horse. I tried not to answer the questions, or answered that I myself poorly understood what was going on, while I was trying to move quickly out to the Palace Square. When I rode out the gate of the Winter Palace I was at the end of the column of the last unit. The artillery headed at a trot across the square to the arch on Morskaya Street.

Passing under the arch and down the short stretch of Morskaya Street to the Nevsky Prospekt, the battery was promptly seized by soldiers of the Pavlov Regiment. "The cadets, seeing that the soldiers were not numerous, began to resist and tried to get away," reported a Pavlov commissar. "At this point our armored car came up and a number of soldiers ran up to the roadblock where the artillery was taken. The cadets were sent to the regimental barracks, and two guns with them. The other two guns were set up on the Nevsky Prospekt, on the Moika Bridge, aimed at the Winter Palace." Commissar Akashev was arrested by the officer who had challenged him, but managed to talk his way free again, and walked toward the besiegers' lines.

"Where are you coming from?" he was challenged.

"From the Winter Palace."

"That's just what we need."

"Are you soviet?"

"Yes, we're for the soviets."

* * *

As the minutes went by and eight o'clock struck, there was no reply by the government to the ultimatum, and no signal from the fortress to attack. Petrograd's customary night life was in full swing: the theaters were full on the Nevsky Prospekt, and in the House of the People on the Petrograd Side Chaliapin was singing "Philip of Spain" in Verdi's *Don Carlos*. Red Guards waiting for orders came into the opera for a few minutes at a time to get warm. On the ring around the Winter Palace, Antonov recalled, "Anxiety rose. They took a shamefully long time with the signal gun. It had gotten pitch dark. It was getting terribly, ominously tense around the Winter Palace, and they were hurrying us from Smolny."

Antonov decided to go to the fortress to learn personally what had gone wrong. He arrived as the fortress garrison was opening loud but not very effective rifle and machine-gun fire at the target across the river. "Thanks to you, the devil knows what may happen," Antonov exclaimed when he met Blagonravov. Blagonravov hastily took Antonov out to the campground to see for himself what was wrong with the artillery. In the dark, the nearsighted Antonov stumbled and fell full length in a mud puddle. Blagonravov helped him wipe the mud off, but by this time they had lost their way in the dark. Finally they saw the kerosene lamp that marked the gun position. Hurrying over, they found two reliable Bolshevik soldiers who confirmed that the guns could not be fired without great risk. Then the whole trouble seemed immaterial. A messenger was running toward them; he fell down in the mud but got up and came on with the news: "The Winter Palace has surrendered and our men are there." Back in the fortress the report was confirmed (wrongly, as it turned out) that the government had accepted the ultimatum—even though small arms fire could still be heard. And now two sailors arrived from Smolny, gunnery men, who advised after all that the fortress fieldpieces could be fired without much danger.

Despite all the delays in the Bolsheviks' siege operations, the garrison of the Winter Palace grew steadily more discouraged, particularly after their artillery was captured. Many of the defenders might have left the Palace at this point, had the surrounding ring of besiegers not made exit so difficult. A messenger from the Cossack Council, on his way to advise the Cossacks in the Palace to quit, was arrested by the besiegers and failed to accomplish his mission.

The cadets of one of the schools, debating whether to fight, sent one of their men out to the soviet lines to try to arrange a safe exit for their group. Podvoisky decided to send Chudnovsky with the cadet back into the Palace to try to persuade the whole defending force to surrender. Chudnovsky went "apprehensively," he confessed, though the men at the barricades promised him safe conduct.

Chudnovsky was ushered into the Palace courtyard, where he was forced to wait twenty minutes while the Palace commander Palchinsky was haranguing his cadets. When Palchinsky saw Chudnovsky, he exclaimed, "Arrest him! Arrest him!" Surrounded by a crowd of cadets, Chudnovsky was taken inside the building, shouting all the time that the defenders had no chance and had better surrender. Palchinsky threatened to have him shot and assured the cadets that reinforcements were on their way. Dissuaded from surrender, but fearful of Bolshevik reprisals, the cadets insisted that Chudnovsky be released. Palchinsky gave in: "All right, I release him. You are free and can go," he told the Bolshevik emissary. Shooting had begun in the square, and Chudnovsky demanded an escort of cadets to get him back to his own lines. The cadets took the opportunity to escape from the Palace altogether.

While Chudnovsky was detained in the Palace the besieging forces grew tense and nervous. Podvoisky ordered his forces to move closer to the Palace: the Second Baltic Fleet Crew, apparently left in their barracks until now, was called up, and machine guns were finally emplaced in the Alexander Garden across the street from the Palace to the west. A mere hundred sailors arrived from Finland and the Kronstadt sailors finally landed to provide a backup force, but they evidently saw little action.

In the wake of Chudnovsky's mission, the ordinary soldiers in the Palace began muttering about abandoning the defense. The officers decided to let the shock battalion leave rather than infect the morale of the rest of the defenders. Great shouts, "Hurrah, they have surrendered," were heard when the shock troops appeared on the Palace Square. About the same time the Cossack foot soldiers in the Palace decided that the government cause was hopeless and sent a man out to negotiate with the Pavlov troops. According to Dzenis, "They wanted to leave but asked us not to disgrace them, and to let them come out with their weapons. We hesitated, not completely believing in the sincerity of the negotiator—we wondered whether they wanted to set up positions in our rear. Nevertheless we decided to let them go. The Cossacks went out onto the embankment. In a nearby alley an armored car was hidden, and as soon as the ranks of Cossacks had passed, it was sent to follow them right to the barracks of the Cossack Regiment, located not far from the Pavlov barracks."

While the garrison of the Winter Palace was melting away between 8 and 9 P.M. a number of the government's harried supporters, mostly moderate socialists, met in the City Duma building on the Nevsky Prospekt to discuss what action they might take. They organized themselves as the Committee for the Salvation of the Country and the Revolution with Avksentiev as chairman, and decided to send a peacemaking delegation to the Palace. By chance the group met Podvoisky, who was driving around to inspect his troops, and he warned them away from the Palace because of the shooting. They went instead to the General Staff building to try to reach the Palace by phone. They succeeded around ten, only to be told that the Palace defenders had repulsed the first assault and had the situation well in hand while they awaited reinforcements from the front.

Podvoisky with his colleague Yeremeyev meanwhile drove over to the Peter-Paul fortress to check on its readiness for battle. He arrived just after Commissar Blagonravov had received the exaggerated report of the government's surrender, based apparently on the abandonment of the Palace by the shock troops and the Cossacks. Blagonravov was on his way out the fortress gate when he met the car and told Podvoisky and Yeremeyev that the Palace had surrendered. They all heard at once back toward the Palace, over the Troitsky Bridge and westward along Millionaya Street. The driver no longer took the precaution of turning the headlights off. They passed units of the Pavlov Regiment along the street, and close to the Palace, where the street crosses a branch of the Moika Canal, they were stopped by the roadblock. They told the unit there that the Palace had fallen, but the soldiers shook their heads in disbelief and warned of danger if they went ahead. Assuming that the Palace must have been taken by the forces moving in from the opposite direction, the commissars drove ahead. They were almost past the arch between the Hermitage and the Winter Palace when the blast of a machine gun from the Palace barricade shattered the darkness ahead of them and bullets whistled around their heads. The driver jammed the car into reverse as Podvoisky and Blagonravov fell to the floor, while Yeremeyev leapt from his seat beside the driver and threw himself on the pavement. In another moment they were back to the bridge and out of danger, but now the soldiers on Millionaya Street thought an enemy vehicle was leading an attack on them. It took a round of shouting by the commissars to persuade the unit that the car was friendly and avert a panicky retreat.

Aware now that the Provisional Government was still far from surrendering, Podvoisky sent Blagonravov back to the Peter-Paul fortress to give the signal for artillery fire as planned. Blagonravov drove back and made his dispositions quickly: the two navy gunners readied the field artillery, the machine gunners prepared to fire across the river from the parapets, and a screen of infantry was stationed along the bank adjacent to the parade ground in case the government forces should somehow or other attempt a landing. The problem of the signal lantern had finally been solved, and at 9:35 P.M. it was hoisted on the flagpole as the signal for the cruiser *Aurora* to open fire and initiate the general bombardment. At 9:40 a great salvo—or perhaps it was just one shot—boomed forth from the *Aurora's* six-inch guns. At any rate the *Aurora* was firing blanks, but they were enough to terrify the remaining defenders of the Winter Palace and to make the *Aurora* a revolutionary legend. The ship has been kept as an historical museum, tied up to a Neva quay, but officially maintained in commission as a unit of the Soviet Navy, like *Old Ironsides* in Boston.

The *Aurora's* noisy outburst was answered by the fieldpieces at the fortress, firing real shells. Altogether some thirty rounds were aimed at the Palace, though the gunners managed to miss their target all but two or three times. Ambassador Buchanan wrote the next day,

> I walked out this afternoon to see the damage that had been done to the Winter Palace by the prolonged bombardment of the previous evening, and to my surprise found that, in spite of the near range, there were on the river side but three marks where the shrapnel had struck. On the town side the walls were riddled with thousands of bullets from machine-guns, but not one shot from a field gun that had been fired from the opposite side of the Palace Square had struck the building.

The Provisional Government was, for the most part, simply frightened to death. "In general up to this time the whole attack on the Palace had a very disorderly character," wrote Antonov, "but the numbers of the defenders of the Provisional Government quickly thinned out." The sound of bursting shells and raining shrapnel was enough to destroy the spirits of the remaining defenders of the Palace, the cadets and the women. To encourage surrenders Chudnovsky undertook a second mission to the Palace, talked with some of the cadets, and reached an agreement to let them leave the Palace with their arms. However, when he reported the agreement to Antonov, the latter rejected the terms. This was another instance when the overcautious soviet forces actually obstructed attempts by the defenders to surrender. But under the artillery fire small groups of cadets began to lay down their arms without any formal agreement, and made their way to the soviet lines.

The besiegers had called on the women's battalion, crouching behind their barricades, to do the same thing, but shouts came back in answer, "We will die, but we won't surrender." The girls had reportedly been told by their officers that a fate worse than death awaited them if they surrendered, a warning not entirely without foundation. Before long the besiegers were surprised to see the women's battalion (actually only about 140 strong) leave their firewood barricades and march out into the square. (According to some reports, they intended to recapture the General Staff building, but this may only have been an excuse for surrendering.) The girls can hardly be blamed for being no more ready to face artillery and machine-gun fire than the Cossacks were. In any case, they were disarmed by the Bolshevik troops without the slightest resistance and sent to various barracks for the night.

At the Pavlov barracks some of the treatment of the female prisoners was scarcely consistent with the Geneva Convention. Rumors spread like wildfire; John Reed cites official reports acknowledging three rapes and one suicide. According to Ambassador Buchanan, "In the evening two officer instructors of the women's battalion came to my wife and beseeched her to try and save the women defenders of the Winter Palace, who, after they had surrendered, had been sent to one of the barracks, where they were being most brutally treated by the soldiers. General Knox at once drove to the Bolshevik headquarters at the Smolny Institute. His demands for their immediate release were at first refused on the ground that they had resisted desperately, fighting to the last with bombs and revolvers. Thanks, however, to his firmness and persistency, the order for their release was eventually signed, and the women were saved from the fate that would inevitably have befallen them had they spent the night in the barracks." It was actually the next day when the girls were marched to the Finland Station to take a train to their suburban barracks; two weeks later they were disbanded.

While the artillery fire was going on some of the besiegers actually reached one side of the Palace, in the narrow passage between the Palace and the Hermitage, and a number of them managed to infiltrate this end of the building. At first most of them were disarmed by the defenders, though they did everything they could to agitate among the cadets and try to persuade them to surrender. Then there was a lull in the firing outside, and a government spokesman told the City Duma delegation when they made phone contact, "The first attack was repulsed at 10 P.M."

*   *   *

All evening there was tremendous tension at the Smolny Institute, as the nearly six hundred delegates to the Congress of Soviets swarmed around impatiently. Lenin held off giving the signal for the Congress to be opened; as Podvoisky described him, "He threw himself around his little room in Smolny like a lion locked in a cage. He needed the Winter Palace no matter what: the Winter Palace was the last barrier on the road to the power of the toilers. Vladimir Ilyich railed and shouted—he was ready to have us shot." At nine o'clock, to stall for time, a meeting was called of the leaders of the various parties among the Congress delegates—the Bolsheviks, with their clear majority; the Left SRs, making up most of the remainder; and the small groups of Menshevik-Internationalists, Right Mensheviks, and Right SRs. Lenin did not appear, and "Trotsky was very agitated." The Mensheviks were indignant about the siege of the Palace; one of them shouted, "These mad men have gone after the Winter Palace. We must immediately go there where blood is being shed." Some of them thereupon left to join the City Duma in its vain effort to send a group of negotiators to the Palace.

It became impossible to delay the Congress any longer, even though the Palace was still holding out. At 10:45 P.M. the full Congress was officially called to order in the Smolny assembly hall by the Menshevik Dan as chairman of the outgoing Central Executive Committee. Trying not to lose his composure in the face of the hostile multitude, Dan declared,

> The Second All-Russian Congress of Soviets meets at an unusual moment and under most extraordinary circumstances. You will understand, therefore, why I consider it untimely to open the Congress with a political speech. You will understand this especially if you know that at this very moment, while I am addressing you, my party comrades who were sent to the Winter Palace to fulfill their duty [the Menshevik ministers] are being bombarded. Without saying anything further I declare the session of the Congress open and propose that we proceed to the election of presiding officers.

A Bolshevik immediately went up to the speakers' platform to propose a prepared list of members for the presidium of the Congress, figured in proportion to party strength—fourteen Bolsheviks, seven SRs (mostly Left), three Mensheviks, and one Menshevik-Internationalist (Martov). The Bolshevik slate included five men who had opposed the armed insurrection—Kamenev, Zinoviev, Rykov, Nogin, and Riazanov —and documented the quick healing, for the time being, of the split that had existed in the Bolshevik ranks. The ten other Bolsheviks included Lenin and Trotsky, naturally (though Lenin had still not made his appearance), along with Antonov, Lunacharsky, Alexandra Kollontai, Krylenko to represent the army, Muralov from Moscow, Skliansky (another military party activist) and Stuchka, a Latvian, to represent the minorities. (Rather conspicuously missing were Stalin and Sverdlov, perhaps because they were too closely identified with the administration of the party as such.) Overwhelmingly confirmed in a noisy vote, the presidium took its seats on the platform and designated Kamenev to chair the Congress. Missing were the Menshevik and Right SR candidates, who refused to serve in protest against the uprising.

Kamenev quickly took over from Dan and announced the agenda that the Bolsheviks wanted the Congress to act on—the organization of a new government, war and peace, and the prospects of the Constituent Assembly. But he gave the floor to Martov to make a special point, just as the dull boom of cannon was heard announcing the resumption of the attack on the Winter Palace.

Martov was so frantic he could hardly shout his words, "What are they doing there, what are they doing there! . . . The civil war is beginning, comrades! The first question must be a peaceful settlement of the crisis. . . . Our brothers are being shot down in the streets! . . . The question of power is being settled by means of a military plot organized by one of the revolutionary parties." At this point he was almost shouted down, but nevertheless he tried to propose a compromise: "A peaceful solution is possible and that solution lies in the formation of a uniformly democratic power [i.e., a government of all the socialist parties but no others]. We should elect a delegation to negotiate with the other socialist parties and organizations for the purpose of putting an end to the strife." Against the background noise of artillery Martov proposed a resolution to this effect. Lunacharsky announced for the Bolsheviks that it was perfectly acceptable, and it passed unanimously. With much lingering sentiment in their ranks against a one-party dictatorship, the Bolsheviks were not yet prepared to repudiate such a gesture of coalition.

It was the Mensheviks, deeply embittered by the assault on the Provisional Government, who took the initiative for a complete rupture between the moderates and the Bolsheviks. The Menshevik army delegate Khinchuk announced that to demonstrate their repudiation of the Bolshevik action, the party was going to quit the Congress. (Sukhanov, a Martov Menshevik-Internationalist, was astounded that the main Menshevik group would take such a stubborn stand just after the passage of Martov's resolution.) Amidst noisy protests, Khinchuk read a declaration on behalf of the Menshevik Party:

> Whereas (1) the military conspiracy was organized and executed by the Bolshevik Party in the name of the soviets and behind the backs of all other parties and groups represented in the soviet,
>
> (2) the seizure of power by the Petrograd Soviet just before the Congress assembled is a distortion and a violation of the principle of soviet organization, tending to undermine the value of the Congress as a plenipotentiary representative of the revolutionary democracy,
>
> (3) the said conspiracy throws the country into civil war, hinders the convocation of the Constituent Assembly, threatens a military catastrophe, and leads to the triumph of a counterrevolution,
>
> (4) the only possible way out of the situation is to begin negotiations with the Provisional Government with the purpose of forming a government that can win the support of the whole democracy. . . .

For all these reasons the party was leaving the Congress and inviting all like-minded groups to join it. Spokesmen for the Right SRs and the Jewish Bund made similar statements, and amid the howls of the revolutionary majority the democratic moderates walked out of the Congress.

At this juncture Martov again made a plea for compromise negotiations. He was answered by Trotsky, cold and uncompromising:

> What has happened is an insurrection, and not a conspiracy. We hardened the revolutionary energy of the Petersburg workers and soldiers. We openly forged the will of the masses for an insurrec-

tion, and not a conspiracy. The masses of the people followed our banner, and our insurrection was victorious. And now we are told: renounce your victory, make concessions, compromise. With whom? I ask: with whom ought we to compromise? With those wretched groups who have left us or who are making this proposal? But after all we've had a full view of them. No one in Russia is with them any longer. . . . No, here no compromise is possible. To those who have left and to those who tell us to do this we must say: you are miserable bankrupts, your role is played out; go where you ought to be: into the dustbin of history.

"Then we'll leave," Martov shouted in rage as he got up and made his way off the platform. Trotsky went right on, reading a resolution which he had composed to exploit the walkout of the opposition parties: "The Second All-Russian Congress of Soviets is bound to state that the departure of the Mensheviks and the Socialist-Revolutionaries is a hopeless and criminal attempt to break up the representative assembly of the workers and soldiers at a moment when the advance guard of the masses is attempting to defend the revolution against the attacks of counterrevolution." The moderates were accused of persistent efforts to compromise with the counterrevolution. "They are now resorting to their last measure and are breaking with the soviets. . . . Their departure, however, does not weaken the soviets. On the contrary, it gives them additional strength by removing from . . . the revolution the counterrevolutionary admixture." From here on, Trotsky would remain of one mind with Lenin, to exploit the cleavages that the insurrection had hardened, and press for rule by the Bolshevik Party alone.

❊   ❊   ❊

About 11 P.M. the attack on the Winter Palace was resumed, after a lull of about an hour while the soviet forces were presumably waiting for more of the defenders to surrender. The artillery began firing again, at some risk of hitting their own men, since crowds of besiegers were now pressing up to the entrances of the Palace and forcing their way inside. Suddenly there were two loud explosions inside the Palace. The ministers were frozen by the thought that the artillery bombardment was beginning to hit home, but it was only some hand grenades that a couple of Bolshevik sailors had managed to toss down a Palace stairwell. Some cadets were lightly wounded by the explosions, and

Governor-General Kishkin, a physician by profession, bandaged them up. A Bolshevik sailor wrote, "Towards eleven, we observed that there were no longer any cadets on the Neva side. Then we broke through the doors and began to enter by different stairways, one by one or in small groups. Reaching the top of the stairs, we were arrested by cadets who disarmed us. But our companions continued to arrive, and we were soon in the majority. Then it was our turn to take away the cadets' arms." "Break-ins by various stairways," Palchinsky wrote in the notes he jotted down in prison the next day. "Personally led engineer cadets in disarming a group of about fifty men who broke in through the Hermitage entrance. Surrender without resistance. Pavlov men downstairs. All doors open. The servants let them in. Slaves. The command too." Even the soviet editor of Palchinsky's notes had to concede that this was one man in the Provisional Government who showed courage and vigor.

With Lieutenant Sinegub, Palchinsky took a platoon of cadets to try to clear the Bolsheviks out of the east wing of the Palace. But the defenders no less than the attackers were as confused as tourists today by the maze of corridors and stairways in the building; they were all new to the building and had no plan to show the proper connecting passageways. Blundering along, Sinegub met other cadets "aimlessly wandering around the Palace." They came to a door from which they had to cross one of the arched entrances to the Palace courtyard, exposed to the square and the sounds of machine-gun fire and whining bullets. They ran across to the door opposite, and no one was hit. Then they began to find some Bolsheviks, "scattered figures of soldiers and sailors, armed to the teeth. . . . With the shout, 'surrender,'" Sinegub recalled, "I headed for the stairway to cut off their retreat that way. The first pair of cadets hurried behind me. . . . The cadets charging with their rifles stunned the group and for a moment confusion reigned." Sinegub shouted as though he were followed by an army, and some dozens of soviet troops allowed themselves to be disarmed. The cadet prisoners they had taken were in turn released, and joined Sinegub's platoon to search for more invaders. Sinegub discovered a Bolshevik soldier with an armload of hand grenades, and commanded, "Empty your hands when an officer speaks to you!" The soldier automatically complied.

Successes like these were the exploits of a few valiant individuals, and they could not stem the overwhelming numbers of the attackers nor the discouragement of most of the defenders. At one point, around midnight, there was something like a real charge, when with a great cry of "hurrah" a crowd of soldiers and Red Guards rushed the firewood barricades on the square side of the Palace around the main entrance. More of the defending cadets surrendered; the others fell back into the Palace. The attackers crowded into the doorway, and forced their entrance, more by literal mob pressure than by gunfire. "Occupied below," Palchinsky wrote. "Defense of stairways and corridors. Enough in numbers present for the defense, if good officers and organization. Too late. No officers, spirit, or provisions. Inform government of course of affairs."

The cabinet still did not want to give the appearance of yielding to the threat of force: "Determined to stay to the end without surrendering," Palchinsky noted. "Rejection of ultimatums." By this time Antonov and Chudnovsky had entered the Palace, and began to search for the government, while their men cleared the building room by room and disarmed the remaining cadets with practically no resistance. In this anticlimactic fashion the last hour of the "seige" ran its course. It had been a curious battle of noise and talk, for the most part, while the attackers hesitated and the defenders lost their resolve. For all the considerable firing, it is not certain that anyone had been killed on the attacking side, and among the defenders there were few if any dead.*

Shortly after Antonov and Chudnovsky pushed into the Palace they found Palchinsky and demanded a complete capitulation. Palchinsky had no choice but to comply; he formally surrendered the Palace on condition that the cadets' lives be spared. But when the Bolsheviks asked the whereabouts of the cabinet in the building, Palchinsky gave them wrong directions, and the mob of attackers pressed off on the false scent. In the meantime he went to the cabinet room himself to urge the ministers to flee.

He found the cabinet listening to a routine report, as though their

---

* Ioffe and Lunacharsky asserted later that no attackers were killed; Antonov reported six fatalities, but there was no ceremonial funeral and no homage to the martyrs that would surely have taken place had Bolshevik lives been lost. The later soviet literature avoids the evidence of how trivial the actual fighting was on October 25. As a military engagement it was completely overshadowed by the events of October 29 and 30.

minutes were not numbered. They were apathetic: "I can die here," murmured Tereshchenko, "but to flee, to flee, I no longer have the strength." The rumbling noise of the Bolshevik crowd approached—they had finally found the way. A cadet from the guard detail went into the cabinet room to tell the ministers that the detail was ready to resist if ordered. There was a profusion of quick replies: "This isn't necessary." "It is pointless. This is clear." "We don't need blood." "We must surrender."

Kishkin, the Governor-General, did not seem to know whether the Palace had actually been occupied. "It is taken," the cadet replied. "They have taken all the entrances. Everyone has surrendered. Only this room is being guarded. What does the Provisional Government order?"

"Tell them," said Kishkin, "that we don't want bloodshed, that we yield to force, that we surrender."

Palchinsky was waiting in the outer room to report the decision to the Bolsheviks. His notes read: "Breakthrough up the stairs. Decision not to fire. Refusal to negotiate. Go out to meet attackers. Antonov now in charge. I am arrested by Antonov and Chudnovsky." The two Bolshevik leaders entered the Malachite Hall alone and demanded that the cadet guards surrender. The cadets handed over their weapons. In the inner room, one of the ministers suggested that they all sit down at the table in a position of official dignity. There they waited helplessly to be arrested.

A moment later, the crowd of attackers with Antonov at its head burst through the door into the cabinet room. Antonov was not the type who would terrify an adversary, and Justice Minister Maliantovich was able to form a careful impression of him: "The little man wore his coat hanging open, and a wide-brimmed hat shoved back onto the back of his neck; he had long reddish hair and glasses, a short trimmed moustache and a small beard. His short upper lip pulled up to his nose when he talked. He had colorless eyes and a tired face. For some reason his shirt-front and collar especially attracted my attention and stuck in my memory. A very high starched folded collar propped his chin up. On his soft shirt-front a long necktie crawled up from his vest to his collar. His collar and shirt and cuffs and hands were those of a very dirty man."

Acting Prime Minister Konovalov calmly addressed Antonov: "This is the Provisional Government. What would you like?"

To Antonov's nearsighted eyes the ministers "merged into one pale-grey trembling spot." He shouted, "In the name of the Military Revolutionary Committee I declare you under arrest."

"The members of the Provisional Government submit to violence and surrender to avoid bloodshed," Konovalov replied, amidst the hoots of the Bolshevik crowd. It was 2:10 A.M. on the morning of Thursday, October 26.

On Antonov's demand, the ministers turned over their pistols and papers. Chudnovsky took the roll of those arrested—the whole cabinet except for Kerensky and Prokopovich. This was the first knowledge the attackers had that the chief prize had eluded their grasp, and in their anger some of the soldiers shouted demands to shoot the rest of the ministers. Antonov appointed a guard of the more reliable sailors to march the prisoners down to the square, designated Chudnovsky as commissar of the Palace, and sent a message to Blagonravov at the Peter-Paul fortress to tell him that the government really had surrendered and to order that prison cells be made ready to receive the Provisional Government. "We were placed under arrest," wrote the Minister of Agriculture, Maslov, "and told that we would be taken to the Peter-Paul fortress. We picked up our coats, but Kishkin's was gone. Someone had stolen it. He was given a soldier's coat. A discussion started between Antonov, the soldiers, and the sailors as to whether the ministers should be taken to their destination in automobiles or on foot. It was decided to make them walk. Each of us was guarded by two men. As we walked through the Palace it seemed as if it were filled with the insurrectionists, some of whom were drunk. When we came out on the street we were surrounded by a mob, shouting, threatening . . . and demanding Kerensky. The mob seemed determined to take the law into its own hands and one of the ministers was jostled a bit." Bolshevik participants admitted that the crowd was "drunk with victory" and threatened to lynch the terrified captives. A detail of fifty sailors and workers was formed to march them to the fortress.

Antonov started to move off with the group, when suddenly some shots rang out from the opposite side of the square. Everyone scattered, and when the group reassembled, five of the ministers were missing. There were more shouts to kill the rest, but Antonov got the detail moving again in an orderly fashion. Once again, near the Troitsky Bridge, they were fired on from an automobile. It was a car full of Bolsheviks who didn't know about the victory. Antonov jumped on the car and shouted his identity; the sailors swore, and the occupants of the car barely escaped a beating. Finally the group reached the gate of the Peter-Paul fortress, where the five missing ministers turned up with their guards in a car. The ministers were locked into the same damp cells that had once held the enemies of the Tsar.

Within the Palace there was near-chaos. Soldiers started looting the imperial furnishings, until a guard of sailors, workers, and "the most conscious soldiers" were posted to stop them. Other soldiers and sailors broke into the imperial wine cellars and began drinking themselves into a wild frenzy. Troops sent in to stop the orgy got drunk in turn. Finally a detachment of sailors fought their way in and dynamited the source of the trouble. Out on the Palace Square the tumult gradually subsided. Commissar Dzenis wrote, "Order was restored. Guards were posted. The Kexholm Regiment was placed on guard. Towards morning the units dispersed to their barracks, the detachments of Red Guards went back to their districts, and the spectators went home. Everyone had one thought: 'The power has been seized, but what will happen next?' "

* * *

The Congress of Soviets was in a brief recess at the moment when the Provisional Government was captured. When the deputies assembled again, Antonov arrived to report in person on the fall of the Palace and the arrest of the cabinet. Then the Congress was presented with a proclamation drafted by Lenin, which it promptly endorsed— claiming the support of "an overwhelming majority of the workers, soldiers, and peasants, and basing itself on the victorious insurrection of the workers and the garrison of Petrograd, the Congress hereby resolves to take governmental power into its own hands." There would be a peace proposal, land to the peasants, democratization of the army, workers' control of industry, bread to the cities and manufactured goods to the villages, self-determination for the national minorities, and the Constituent Assembly for everyone. It was 5 A.M. when the first of the two sittings of the Congress ended, and the deputies dispersed to find some sleep, all wondering, as one deputy recalled, "How will Russia respond to what has happened in Petrograd? Will it give its support or not?" The morning was cold and misty. It was Trotsky's birthday. Soft flakes of snow began to fall.

CHAPTER TEN

The Last Act

S PEEDING south after his car passed the Bolshevik patrols in Petrograd, Kerensky expected momentarily to meet the loyal troops coming in from the front. They were not to be found. At his first stop, the town of Gatchina some twenty-five miles from Petrograd, there were none but pro-Bolshevik forces; Kerensky was almost arrested. He pressed on, looking in vain for his troops until 9 P.M. when he reached Pskov, headquarters of General Cheremisov's Northern Front.

At Pskov a strange and tangled but ultimately decisive drama had begun. General Cheremisov, hearing that the Kadet Welfare Minister Kishkin was appointed Governor-General of Petrograd, concluded—he said—that a plot by the rightists was afoot. For a general, Cheremisov was unusually democratic-minded, and had already been accused of being a Bolshevik. Like Kornilov a hero of the June offensive, he expected to be made Commander in Chief after Kornilov's debacle in August, and evidently nursed a resentment because Kerensky took the post himself. He was impatient with the government's troubles with the Petrograd garrison, but faced a virtual Bolshevik take-over in his own army group. For one or another of these reasons, Cheremisov took a fateful step—he countermanded the orders to the units of his command (the nearest to Petrograd) to move to the relief of the government in the Winter Palace.

This was the first stupefying news that Kerensky heard on meeting Cheremisov. To compound the mystery, Cheremisov kept Kerensky out of communication with the rest of the command, while he wired General Headquarters that Kerensky had decided to appoint him Commander in Chief and instructed him to stop the movement of the troops. Conceivably, Cheremisov was betraying the Provisional Government with the idea of coming to terms with the soviet revolutionaries if they held out. His own explanation was that his troops would refuse to fight for a government headed by Kishkin, but he did not yield when Chief of Staff Dukhonin wired that Kishkin could be replaced. In any case Kerensky managed to find General Krasnov, commander of the Cossack cavalry corps, and set off with him to get this force moving toward the capital and make up for the precious hours that had been lost. Kerensky was endeavoring to restore his power in the same way—and with some of the same men—that General Kornilov had used to try to overthrow him two months before.

*   *   *

The capture of the Winter Palace was not the end of the real struggle but rather its beginning. Decades of bloodshed, labor and suffering lay ahead for the Russian people as their new rulers beat down their actual or presumed enemies and tried to build the perfect society. Time and again the fate of the Communist regime hung by a hair, from the moment, four days after the fall of the Provisional Government, when Kerensky's hastily organized force penetrated to the outskirts of Petrograd, to the moment twenty-four years later when Hitler's legions were pounding on the gates of Moscow. But it was the first lucky episode of the 24th and 25th of October, 1917, that gave Lenin's party its opening to try to rule, and to rule alone.

On Thursday morning, October 26th, the Bolshevik Party paper appeared for the last time as *Rabochi Put*, before publishing again under its real name, *Pravda*. The headline—"All Power to the Soviets of Workers', Soldiers', and Peasants' Deputies! Peace! Bread! Land!" At 2 P.M. the Congress of Soviets was supposed to assemble again to legalize these promises, but it had to be postponed. The first concern of almost everyone was to get some sleep. "At seven o'clock in the morning," Podvoisky wrote, "many of us decided, after two weeks of uninterrupted work, that we could get some sleep, but that we should not leave our headquarters. We fell asleep right there like hibernating bears."

Lenin went with Bonch-Bruevich to the latter's nearby apartment.

Bonch collapsed in exhaustion, then awoke, and saw to his surprise that Lenin still had the light on. Consumed by the nervous energy that was destined to burn him out at the age of fifty-three, Lenin sat at the desk, writing—writing the decrees by which the Congress of Soviets would announce the new revolutionary order to Russia and the world.

Later on in the day the sleepy politicians of all parties gathered in Smolny to argue about the composition of the government that the Congress of Soviets was going to proclaim. At an informal session, the members of the Bolshevik Central Committee hastily outlined the new cabinet, named "Council of People's Commissars" on Trotsky's suggestion. Kamkov and two other Left SRs were invited to join the cabinet, but they were still unhappy about the violent end of the Provisional Government, and held off for the time being in the hope of bringing the Right SRs and Mensheviks into a coalition soviet government.

It was 11 P.M. on the 26th when the Congress of Soviets reassembled to legislate the revolution. It heard and acclaimed Lenin's decree on peace, promising an end to secret diplomacy and immediate negotiations to secure a "democratic peace without annexations and without indemnities." It heard the decree, shrewdly borrowed by Lenin from the program of the SRs, abolishing private property in land and turning the land over to the tillers in the way the peasants had always demanded. Finally it voted Kamenev's resolution, "to establish for the administration of the country up to the convocation of the Constituent Assembly, a provisional workers' and peasants' government which will be called the Council of People's Commissars, responsible to the soviets.

Lenin was Chairman—i.e., Prime Minister, succeeding the deposed Kerensky. Trotsky was Commissar of Foreign Affairs; Lunacharsky, of Education; Rykov, Internal Affairs; Nogin, Trade and Industry; Shlyapnikov, Labor. Other portfolios were: Agriculture—Milyutin; Finance—Skvortsov; Justice—Lomov; Food—Teodorovich; Posts and Telegraphs—Avilov. Military Affairs, to keep them more democratic, were put under a committee consisting of Antonov, Krylenko, and Dybenko. A special post was created to represent the national minorities and assigned to that eminent non-Russian, Joseph Stalin. After approving the cabinet, the Congress elected a new All-Russian Central Executive Committee of 101 members to serve as an interim legislative

body. It had a Bolshevik majority of sixty-two, plus twenty-nine Left
SRs, but ten seats were nevertheless alloted to the Mensheviks and
Right SRs who had quit the Congress. Kamenev was made chairman of
the new Central Executive Committee, with the implied rank of Chief
of State. Then, in the early morning hours of October 27, the Second
Congress of Soviets adjourned its business and passed into history. The
"provisional" label which it affixed to the new government was soon
forgotten.

The new regime was immediately beset by powerful forces of opposition both within and without. The October Revolution had not
disposed of the Bolsheviks' enemies, and the construction of an effective party dictatorship was still many months off. The effect of the
revolution was negative: it removed the most ineffective force on the
political scene—Kerensky's government—and set the stage for a series
of bloody tests between the real contenders for power.

In Petrograd Lenin and his associates had to contend on the one
hand with widespread strikes and slowdowns by government employees, and on the other by insistent demands from their potential and
necessary allies, the Left SRs and the railroad workers' union, that they
bring all the socialist parties into a coalition government. Outside the
city disaster appeared to loom again in the shape of the Cossack regiments that Kerensky had found and ordered in to restore his authority.
The Military Revolutionary Committee moved its operations to the
military district headquarters near the Winter Palace to assume direction of all defensive operations. At 2 A.M. on October 27, in a soaking
rain, Lenin left the Congress of Soviets to join the MRC and prod it
into the quickest possible action.

The truly decisive military aspect of the revolution came not on
October 25 but during the five days following. On October 27 Kerensky was back in Gatchina with a Cossack "division"—in reality, only
about seven hundred men, still moving ahead without resistance. Although GHQ telegraphed furiously to every front for more divisions to
go to Petrograd, the troops would not move, or if they did, workers
sabotaged the trains and Bolsheviks at every station undermined the
men's resolve. The whole Russian army command could not send more
than Krasnov's seven hundred Cossacks to restore the Provisional Government.

The seven hundred might even have sufficed, had their leaders realized the shaky position of the Bolsheviks and moved more vigorously. As the Cossacks approached Petrograd, the supporters of the Provisional Government inside the city were preparing to take direct action against the Bolsheviks. The Menshevik ministers of the Provisional Government, released from the Peter-Paul fortress, immediately began encouraging the strike movement among the civil servants. In the name of the Committee for the Salvation of the Country and the Revolution, the Military Organization of the SRs led by Gotz began to plan a countermove based on the Cossacks in the garrison and the cadets who still remained in the Vladimir, Pavlov, and Engineer schools. To lead the move Gotz picked none other than Kerensky's repudiated commander Colonel Polkovnikov. The presidium of the dispersed Pre-Parliament met and issued an open appeal for the overthrow of the Bolsheviks.

On the 28th, the tension in Petrograd mounted. The new Bolshevik government, using the Military Revolutionary Committee as its organ to mobilize a defense, closed the conservative newspapers and issued frantic appeals to the workers and garrison units to join a last-ditch struggle against the advancing Kerensky-Krasnov force. Some thousands of Red Guards moved out to the suburbs in trucks, "an amazing, inspired mass in thin tattered coats and . . . pinched white faces . . . , a mighty spontaneous *people's army*—men, women, and children," as Louise Bryant depicted them. A few hundred sailors and some of the more revolutionary units of the garrison, including troops from the Pavlov Regiment, joined them. Military command of the force was vested in a regular officer, Lieutenant Colonel Muraviev, whom the Bolsheviks had persuaded to work for them (a pattern that they would frequently follow in the coming civil war). Chudnovsky was assigned as commissar to keep an eye on him, and Trotsky and Dybenko went along to oversee the whole operation.

On the anti-Soviet side, the Committee for the Salvation of the Country and the Revolution organized a headquarters at the building of the City Duma, and the chief military commissar of the Provisional Government, Stankevich, went out to Gatchina to meet Kerensky and plan coordinated action. (Bolshevik control of the city was not tight enough to prevent such movement.) He found that General Krasnov was moving cautiously, with his small force short on ammunition and lacking infantry support. On the 28th Krasnov advanced only ten miles to occupy Tsarskoe Selo, the site of one of the great summer palaces, where the garrison, outnumbering the Cossacks twenty to one, proclaimed its neutrality. Stankevich and Kerensky agreed to delay both the offensive and the uprising.

On the evening of the 28th, one of Polkovnikov's men was captured by the Bolsheviks with some of the plans of the uprising. The Military Revolutionary Committee decided at once to disarm the cadets the next morning. Polkovnikov got word of what had happened and prevailed upon Gotz and Avksentiev to call the move for that very night and forestall the MRC, even though there was no plan or possibility for immediate support by Krasnov's Cossacks.

The cadets began to put their plan into execution in the predawn hours of October 29. On paper it was a far more systematic move than the Bolshevik take-over four days before. The engineer cadets secured the castle near the Field of Mars in which their school was located, and headed across town to the Mikhailov Riding Hall where the Bolsheviks' armored cars were garaged. They seized all the vehicles that were operating (five of them), made for the telephone exchange, and easily captured it in a surprise assault. There was a special prize in the building—co-commissar of War Antonov, who was made a prisoner for the time being. Nevertheless, despite these initial successes, the revolt lost headway. The Cossacks of the garrison, expected to be the main reserve force of the revolt, failed to do any more than they had on the 25th. The MRC proclaimed a state of siege in the city, as Bolshevik sailors stormed back into the telephone building, and thousands of Red Guards surrounded the military schools. The Vladimir School on the Petrograd Side was battered into submission by Bolshevik artillerymen with one field gun, and the Engineer School surrendered when the futility of the revolt became apparent. It was a bloody day, with many more casualties than occurred in the capture of the Winter Palace. Civil war was underway.

While the cadets were going down to defeat, Gotz and Avksentiev escaped and joined Kerensky's force. The Cossacks were confronted only by the motley force of a few thousand Bolsheviks, badly organized and mostly untrained, holding the hills at Pulkovo between

Tsarskoe Selo and the city itself. On the 30th, while the SR leaders tried desperately to locate infantry units that would support Kerensky, Krasnov attacked.

This Battle of Pulkovo was the Valmy of the Russian Revolution. Like the Austrian attack on the French revolutionaries in 1792, the fighting itself was indecisive; the real test was one of morale. Chudnovsky was wounded at the outset, and Krasnov gained ground easily against the Red Guards. However, the Cossacks found themselves in danger of being outflanked by Dybenko's sailors and cut off by the nonbelligerent troops in their rear. The purpose of linking up with the cadets in the city had lost its point, and Krasnov decided to fall back to Gatchina.

By the evening of the 30th Kerensky was justly in despair. Too late, he decreed the dismissal of General Cheremisov, who had repeatedly refused to support the Gatchina campaign. He designated Avksentiev as his own successor and permitted his troops to open negotiations with the Bolsheviks. Co-Commissar of War Dybenko arrived in Gatchina on November 1, ostensibly to conclude an armistice, but actually to persuade the Cossacks to turn Kerensky over to the soviet authorities. Weary of campaigning against such odds for the defunct government, the Cossacks agreed. Betrayed by his own men, Kerensky narrowly escaped capture; he had to flee Gatchina disguised in a sailor's uniform.

With this, the Provisional Government ceased altogether to exist. The former Prime Minister went into hiding and for several months dodged Lenin's police in Moscow and Petrograd just as the Bolshevik chief had done when Kerensky was in power. Finally, in the summer of 1918, Kerensky was spirited by some homeward-bound Yugoslavs to the British-held port of Murmansk, whence he sailed away from his homeland for the first and last time.

* * *

It proved rather more difficult for the Bolsheviks to establish their authority in the rest of Russia than to take over in the capital and its environs. In many important centers the local soviets were pro-Bolshevik, and copied the Petrograd idea of a Military Revolutionary Committee as soon as they heard an uprising was underway. This was especially the case among the Russian city-dwellers in non-Russian parts of the country—Helsingfors, Reval, Minsk, Kharkov, Baku, Tashkent—where local authority was assumed by the soviets within two or three days. Elsewhere the Bolsheviks had to overcome serious opposition within the soviets as well as armed opposition from the military supporters of the Provisional Government or of the Right.

The toughest center of anti-Bolshevik resistance, and the crucial one, was Moscow. The city Bolshevik leaders—Rykov and Nogin—had leaned against insurrection in the first place, and the Moscow Soviet formed its Military Revolutionary Committee only on the 25th of October. The forces of the Right were much more confident and aggressively led. The Right SRs who dominated the City Duma formed a Committee of Public Safety, a conservative counterpart of the MRC, to lead the defense against any effort to establish a soviet power in Moscow. Pro-Bolshevik soldiers held the Kremlin, but the Committee of Public Safety had a strong force of officer cadets at its disposal.

After two days of sparring between the MRC and the Committee of Public Safety, the colonel in command of the cadets launched a well-planned counter-coup. Early in the morning of the 28th cadets seized all the key communication points and demanded that the troops in the Kremlin surrender or face an artillery bombardment. The Kremlin garrison capitulated, only to be machine-gunned by the score when the cadets thought they were being fired on. This was the first great atrocity presaging the coming terror by Whites and Reds alike.

Bitter fighting ensued for the rest of the day and during the 29th, and the superior numbers and artillery of the pro-soviet regiments and Red Guards began to be felt. Then the local Menshevik and Left SR leaders intervened to force a one-day armistice. By the time the truce expired, the anti-Bolshevik forces had the demoralizing news that Kerensky's drive on Petrograd had failed, while the soviet side could count on a steady flow of reinforcements. The cadets were gradually pressed into a tighter circle, and finally on November 2 troops of the soviet stormed back into the Kremlin itself. Recognizing the hopelessness of further fighting, the Committee of Public Safety surrendered to the MRC. Moscow was won for the soviets, but at the cost of civil war in earnest; some five hundred men had been killed on the Bolshevik side alone.

Bolshevik control of most of the country followed swiftly. Operating through the local soviets, sometimes with strong-arm tactics against the socialist opposition in these bodies, the Bolsheviks secured recognition of the new Petrograd regime and beat down isolated resistance by the military authorities. The army command for the most part allowed itself passively to be dismantled, while the troops deserted en masse to return to their villages and join in the seizure of the estates. GHQ at Mogilev was taken over by Co-Commissar of War Krylenko on November 20, and an angry mob lynched the Chief of Staff General Dukhonin.

The major exceptions to the spread of soviet power were the non-Russian minority areas, where the movement for autonomy vis-à-vis the Provisional Government continued to operate against the soviets. Finland declared its independence outright, and the Soviet Government had no choice but to recognize it. In Kiev the Ukrainian nationalists took over, in the first move of a bloody contest for power in southern Russia. In Tiflis, the Georgian Mensheviks easily maintained control. Most significantly, the Russian-speaking Cossack regions, centering on the Don and Kuban rivers between the Ukraine and the Caucasus, for the most part rejected the authority of the soviets. This region provided a refuge for most of the Bolsheviks' military adversaries, from General Kornilov to Colonel Polkovnikov. It was from this base, principally, that the anti-Bolshevik Whites launched their vain series of efforts to overthrow the soviet regime in the three years of civil war that followed.

❋　❋　❋

While the new soviet regime was fending off the first desperate challenges to its power, there remained profound and unresolved issues as to the nature that this power would assume. The power had been won by the Bolsheviks but only as the leaders and spokesmen of the soviets, and the loyalty of the mass of revolutionary soldiers and workers was still to the system of direct democracy that the soviets represented.

Although the Mensheviks and Right SRs had walked out of the Second All-Russian Congress of Soviets in protest against the violent overthrow of the Provisional Government, they still held their minority seats in the Petrograd Soviet, in the new All-Russian Central Executive Committee, and in most of the local soviets around the country. The burning question of the moment was what relation they would have to the new government that had been proclaimed in the name of the soviets. In the propaganda of "All Power to the Soviets" it had usually been assumed that this power would be exercised by a coalition of all the parties represented in the soviets. Lenin had never expressly repudiated this notion, though his more recent confidence in the soviets rested only on the conviction that the Bolsheviks could dominate them. But as soon as the governmental power of the soviets was announced, coalition became the overriding objective of those revolutionaries—the Left SRs and the Zinoviev-Kamenev Bolsheviks—who feared the consequences of one-party rule. Martov's resolution calling for a coalition government was the one step unanimously supported by all the delegates at the Congress of Soviets.

For a few days after the Congress adjourned, the center of the political stage in Petrograd was occupied by the new All-Russian Central Executive Committee, which momentarily functioned as a soviet parliament to supervise the government of the Council of People's Commissars. In the Central Executive Committee sentiment for a coalition cabinet was particularly strong; the Bolshevik delegation was dominant but its leader was Kamenev, who now spoke as strongly for coalition as earlier he had against insurrection. And the Left SR group echoed the sentiment with an eloquent resolution against "the path of bloodshed."

Special force was given to the coalition movement by the intervention of the National Committee of the Railroad Workers' Union (the "Vikzhel"). On October 29, in the midst of the cadet uprising and the Moscow fighting, the Vikzhel presented to the Central Executive Committee in Smolny a demand that all the parties in the soviet meet to negotiate a compromise. Otherwise, the Vikzhel threatened to strike and paralyze all soviet troop and supply movements, at a time when the fate of the regime still hung in the balance both in Petrograd and in Moscow. The Mensheviks and Right SRs agreed to the conference, but certain of the imminent collapse of the Bolsheviks, they made their terms clear: they would enter no coalition government that included Lenin and Trotsky.

Kamenev brought this news to a hastily summoned meeting of the

Bolshevik Central Committee, its first recorded session since October 24. Both Lenin and Trotsky were absent, Lenin at District Headquarters with the MRC directing operations against the cadet uprising, and Trotsky superintending the mobilization of forces against Kerensky on the Pulkovo front. Under the circumstances, the Central Committee saw no alternative except to "recognize the necessity of broadening the base of the government and the possibility of a change in its makeup." On the actual terms of a coalition government, the old cleavage between the anti-insurrectionists and the majority opened up again; Kamenev and his supporters were even willing to talk about a government without Lenin and Trotsky. Oddly, the Central Committee chose only pro-coalition men—Kamenev and Sokolnikov—to represent it at the Vikzhel conference (along with Sverdlov and Riazanov, another coalition advocate, who came representing the Central Executive Committee).

The Vikzhel conference of some thirty political leaders began its deliberations later the same day, the 29th. The Mensheviks and SRs insisted not only on a new cabinet but also on an armistice in the civil strife and on an expansion of the Central Executive Committee almost making it a reincarnation of the Pre-Parliament. The Bolshevik delegation under Kamenev appeared to be going along, though Lenin, moving rapidly to consolidate his new power, had the Council of People's Commissars vote itself the power to rule by decree.

The coalition issue came to a head when the Bolshevik Central Committee met again on November 1, with both Lenin and Trotsky now present, to hear Kamenev and Riazanov report on the Vikzhel negotiations. There were bitter complaints, particularly by Trotsky and Dzerzhinsky, that the Bolshevik negotiators had passively allowed the conference to repudiate the October uprising. Trotsky was adamant about Bolshevik dominance in the new government: "We would have carried out the uprising for nothing if we do not get a majority." Lenin did not hide his impatient cynicism: "The negotiations should have been like the diplomatic cover of military operations. The only correct decision would be to eliminate the vacillation of the vacillators and become decisive." But the Central Committee majority, reverting to its reflexes of September, voted against Lenin's blunt demand to break off the negotiations. It adopted instead Trotsky's compromise—

to send the Bolshevik delegation back for one more negotiating session, "with the aim of finally exposing the lack of substance of this attempt."

Lenin was still furious, and once again sought a forum to attack the majority view. He found it in a session of the Petrograd Bolshevik City Committee, at which he declared his refusal to come to terms with the advocates of coalition: "If you want a split, go ahead. If you have a majority, take power in the Central Executive Committee and carry on. But we will go to the sailors." He was ready to stage the October Revolution all over again, and against his own men, if his aim of ruling alone was thwarted. But in Trotsky he had confidence, and declared, "There has been no better Bolshevik."

On November 2 the CEC voted on the minimum Bolshevik terms, and passed them—that the coalition cabinet include Lenin and Trotsky and allow the Bolsheviks at least half the portfolios. The Bolshevik conciliationists voted even against this—Kamenev, Zinoviev, Riazanov, and almost half of the members of the Council of People's Commissars. Lenin rammed a resolution through the Central Committee by a narrow margin, to condemn the conciliationists for their "criminal vacillation" and "un-Marxist remarks," and he presented the dissidents with an ultimatum to bow to party discipline or leave the Bolshevik ranks.

The response two days later would seem catastrophic for a new revolutionary government. Five members of the Bolshevik Central Committee—Kamenev, Zinoviev, Rykov, Milyutin, and Nogin—submitted their resignations along with a bitter protest against what they regarded as Lenin's sabotage of the coalition: "The leading group in the Central Committee . . . has firmly decided not to allow the formation of a government of the soviet parties but to fight for a purely Bolshevik government however it can and whatever the sacrifices this costs the workers and soldiers. We cannot assume responsibility for this ruinous policy of the Central Committee, carried out against the will of a large part of the proletariat and soldiers." Kamenev quit the chairmanship of the Central Executive Committee and yielded the office to Sverdlov. Rykov, Milyutin, and Nogin resigned their commissariats at the same time, along with Teodorovich and a number of sub-cabinet commissars. They issued a separate statement (endorsed by Shlyapnikov, too), even more bitter: apart from coalition, they warned, "There is only one path: the preservation of a purely Bolshevik government by means of political terror. We cannot and will not accept this." (With the same misgivings, the Left SRs withdrew their members from the Military Revolutionary Committee, where they were no longer effective anyway.)

In reply Lenin accused the men who resigned of "desertion," and tied their action to the "strikebreaking" of Zinoviev and Kamenev before the uprising. The pressure was too much for Zinoviev, and on November 7 he wrote a letter of capitulation: "We remain with the party, we prefer to make mistakes together with the millions of workers and soldiers, to die with them, rather than stand aside at this decisive, historic moment." The same day the coalition conference met for its last aimless session, with the Bolsheviks not even present. They were winning a vote in the Central Executive Committee, 29 to 23, to approve the power of the all-Bolshevik Council of People's Commissars to rule by decree.

Now that he clearly had the upper hand, Lenin was prepared to make concessions to useful allies who would meet his terms. After two more weeks of negotiations with the Left SRs, representing key peasant support, he admitted three of their leaders to the Council of People's Commissars (in the relatively innocuous posts of Agriculture, Justice, and Posts and Telegraphs). This gave Soviet Russia a semblance of coalition government until the Left SRs quit the cabinet in March, 1918, to protest the Brest-Litovsk peace treaty. After the Left SRs joined the government Kamenev and his friends abandoned their opposition and requested reinstatement in the Bolshevik leadership; three months later they were taken back in.

The one remaining hope of the democratic forces of Russia was the Constituent Assembly. The election of delegates had been scheduled by the Provisional Government, while the Bolsheviks, with one of their major pre-revolutionary promises, were committed to seeing that the election took place. This, Russia's first, last, and only universal, free and democratic election was duly held on the 12th of November. The Bolsheviks, with some nine million votes, did not do badly, but they ran a poor second to the SRs, whose continuing appeal among the peasants earned them an absolute majority in the balloting. Lenin had not been happy about allowing the election at all, and he made it clear that he would not tolerate what he called "the discrepancy between the election to the Constituent Assembly and the will of the people." He permitted the Assembly to meet in the Tauride Palace on January 5, 1918, and elect the SR theorist Chernov its chairman—for that one day only. The next day the troops closed the Tauride Palace, and Russia's experiment in constitutionalism collapsed for the last time. Six months later every political party but the Bolsheviks—or Communists, as they would henceforth be known—had been outlawed, terror had commenced, and the new phenomenon of totalitarian dictatorship was beginning to take over the future of Russia.

CHAPTER ELEVEN

The Myth
and the Reality

THE October Revolution did shake the world. In the eyes of its followers and its enemies alike, it announced the final battle between the international proletariat and the worldwide system of capitalism, the fulfillment of Marx's prophecy. The October Revolution promised a new dawn in human history, a new era of liberation and equality. Its spirit and its doctrine became a new faith for millions of people all over the world, who looked to Moscow as the new Jerusalem. Fifty years afterwards, Soviet Russia still professes to embody the ideals of the revolution, though its claim to the revolutionary heritage is disputed by the radical leaders of lands won by the Gospel of October more recently.

It is only natural that an event that has aroused such commitments and antagonisms should be viewed by both its heirs and its enemies alike as the result of deep historical forces or a long-laid master scheme. Since the days of the October uprising itself, it has been difficult for either side to take stock of the extraordinary series of accidents and missteps that accompanied the Bolshevik Revolution and allowed it to succeed. One thing that both victors and vanquished were agreed on, before the smoke had hardly cleared from the Palace Square, was the myth that the insurrection was timed and executed according to a deliberate Bolshevik plan.

The official Communist history of the revolution has held rigidly to an orthodox Marxist interpretation of the event: it was an uprising of thousands upon thousands of workers and peasants, the inevitable consequence of the international class struggle of proletariat against bourgeoisie, brought to a head first in Russia because it was "the weakest link in the chain of capitalism." At the same time it is asserted, though the contradiction is patent, that the revolution could not have succeeded without the ever-present genius leadership of Lenin. This attempt to have it both ways has been ingrained in Communist thinking ever since Lenin himself campaigned in the name of Marx for the "art of insurrection."

Anti-Communist interpretations, however they may deplore the October Revolution, are almost as heavily inclined to view it as the inescapable outcome of overwhelming circumstances or of long and diabolical planning. The impasse of the war was to blame, or Russia's inexperience in democracy, or the feverish laws of revolution. If not these factors, it was Lenin's genius and trickery in propaganda, or the party organization as his trusty and invincible instrument. Of course, all of these considerations played a part, but when they are weighed against the day by day record of the revolution, it is hard to argue that any combination of them made Bolshevik power inevitable or even likely.

The stark truth about the Bolshevik Revolution is that it succeeded against incredible odds in defiance of any rational calculation that could have been made in the fall of 1917. The shrewdest politicians of every political coloration knew that while the Bolsheviks were an undeniable force in Petrograd and Moscow, they had against them the overwhelming majority of the peasants, the army in the field, and the trained personnel without which no government could function. Everyone from the right-wing military to the Zinoviev-Kamenev Bolsheviks judged a military dictatorship to be the most likely alternative if peaceful evolution failed. They all thought—whether they hoped or feared—that a Bolshevik attempt to seize power would only hasten or assure the rightist alternative.

Lenin's revolution, as Zinoviev and Kamenev pointed out, was a wild gamble, with little chance that the Bolsheviks' ill-prepared followers could prevail against all the military force that the government seemed to have, and even less chance that they could keep power even if they managed to seize it temporarily. To Lenin, however, it was a gamble that entailed little risk, because he sensed that in no other way and at no other time would he have any chance at all of coming to power. This is why he demanded so vehemently that the Bolshevik Party seize the moment and hurl all the force it could against the Provisional Government. Certainly the Bolshevik Party had a better overall chance for survival and a future political role if it waited and compromised, as Zinoviev and Kamenev wished. But this would not yield the only kind of political power—exclusive power—that Lenin valued. He was bent on baptizing the revolution in blood, to drive off the fainthearted and compel all who subscribed to the overturn to accept and depend on his own unconditional leadership.

To this extent there is some truth in the contentions, both Soviet and non-Soviet, that Lenin's leadership was decisive. By psychological pressure on his Bolshevik lieutenants and his manipulation of the fear of counterrevolution, he set the stage for the one-party seizure of power. But the facts of the record show that in the crucial days before October 24th Lenin was not making his leadership effective. The party, unable to face up directly to his browbeating, was tacitly violating his instructions and waiting for a multi-party and semi-constitutional revolution by the Congress of Soviets. Lenin had failed to seize the moment, failed to avert the trend to a compromise coalition regime of the soviets, failed to nail down the base for his personal dictatorship—until the government struck on the morning of the 24th of October.

Kerensky's ill-conceived countermove was the decisive accident. Galvanizing all the fears that the revolutionaries had acquired in July and August about a rightist *putsch*, it brought out their utmost— though still clumsy—effort to defend themselves and hold the ground for the coming Congress of Soviets. The Bolsheviks could not calculate, when they called the Red Guards to the bridges and sent commissars to the communications centers, that the forces of the government would apathetically collapse. With undreamed-of ease, and no intention before the fact, they had the city in the palms of their hands, ready to close their grip when their leader reappeared from the underground and able to offer him the Russian capital in expiation of their late faintheartedness.

The role of Trotsky in all this is very peculiar. A year after the revolution Stalin wrote, "All the work of the practical organization of the insurrection proceeded under the immediate direction of the chairman of the Petrograd Soviet, Comrade Trotsky. It can be said with assurance that for the quick shift of the garrison to the side of the soviet and the bold insurrectionary work of the MRC the party is indebted firstly and mainly to Comrade Trotsky." This passage was naturally suppressed during Stalin's heyday, but after the de-Stalinization of 1956 Soviet historians resurrected it—as proof of another of Stalin's errors, overestimating Trotsky! In fact they are right, though the whole party shared Stalin's accolade at the time: Trotsky in October was at the height of his career as the flaming revolutionary tribune, yet he shied away from the outright insurrection that Lenin demanded. Trotsky exemplified the feelings of the main body of the Bolshevik leadership, eager for power yet afraid either to take a military initiative or to face Lenin's wrath. Trotsky talked revolution but waited for the Congress—until the moment of Lenin's return to Smolny. Then, like most of the party leadership, he persuaded himself that he had been carrying out Lenin's instructions all along; any statement he had made about waiting for the Congress became, in retrospect, a political lie "to cover up the game." But in truth there was far more lying about the October Revolution after the event than before.

How important was the matter of waiting for the Congress of Soviets? What difference would it have made if Kerensky had not precipitated the fighting and the Congress had assembled peacefully to vote itself into power? Lenin, for one, believed it made a vast difference, and his view is underscored from the opposite direction by the conduct of the Mensheviks and Right SRs after the uprising. They were bitter and intransigent and unwilling to enter a meaningful coalition where they might have balanced the Bolsheviks. The Bolsheviks—a majority of them, at least—were emboldened by the smell of gunpowder, and ready to fight to the end to preserve the conquests of their impromptu uprising. The same was true of the Left SRs, reluctant though they had been for violence. Many moderates, on the other hand, were so enraged that they were prepared to join hands with the Ultra-Right, if need be, to oust the Bolshevik usurpers. If the Congress had met without insurrection—a large "if"—Russia would have remained for the time being on the course of peaceful political compromise; with prior insurrection a fact, Russia was headed on the path to civil war and dictatorship.

The October Revolution gave the impetus to the whole subsequent development of the Soviet Russian regime and the worldwide Communist movement. If the revolution had not occurred as it did, the basic political cleavage of Bolsheviks and anti-Bolsheviks would not have been so sharp, and it is difficult to imagine what other events might have established a similar opportunity for one-party Bolshevik rule. Given the fact of the party's forcible seizure of power, civil violence and a militarized dictatorship of revolutionary extremism followed with remorseless logic.

This is not to say that every subsequent development in Soviet Russia was entirely predetermined by the violent revolution of October. A host of other circumstances and political events helped shape the Communist regime from this time on—the Civil War, the death of Lenin, the challenge of industrialization, the threat of foreign enemies, and above all the rise to power of Joseph Stalin, who accomplished a new "revolution from above" more far-reaching than the Revolution of 1917. It was in this epoch, the 1930's, that the most enduring fundamentals of the present Soviet system, economically, socially and intellectually, were laid down, in the course of events that were as much a counterrevolution against 1917 as an extension of it.

During the first decade after the revolution the top Communist leadership remained almost unchanged, despite the careening zigzags it had to make in its policies. The relatively cautious consolidation of power in the first few months gave way to the utopian experiments of "War Communism" in 1918, and the latter yielded to the opposite tack of the New Economic Policy in 1921, but still Lenin and the other leading figures of 1917 remained at the helm—Trotsky, Zinoviev, Kamenev, Stalin, Bukharin, Rykov, Dzerzhinsky. There had been, to be sure, a few notable casualties: Uritsky and Volodarsky were assassinated by anti-Communist terrorists after civil war had broken out in 1918. Sverdlov died of typhus in 1919 and left a great gap in the party's organizational work, a gap that Stalin eventually filled. Chudnovsky and Lazimir were killed fighting against the White armies.

Among the lesser Bolshevik leadership of 1917 there had been more turnover, as energetic men from the provinces worked their way up through the party organization and displaced the Petrograd activists of 1917. Podvoisky was one of those who fell by the wayside; after a few months of military work he was relegated to the directorship of the Young Pioneer movement. Others went into literary work: Nevsky was active as an historian in publishing the records of the revolution, and Yeremeyev founded the Soviet humor magazine *Krokodil* shortly before his death in 1930. Many of the figures of 1917 served out their last years in administrative work in industry or the trade unions—Nogin until his death in 1924, Sadovsky until he died in 1927. Lunacharsky held his Commissariat of Education continuously until Bubnov relieved him in 1929; he died in France in 1933 on his way to serve as Soviet Russia's first Ambassador to the Spanish Republic. Dzerzhinsky, after a notorious career as head of the secret police, had become Chairman of the Supreme Economic Council and headed the whole industrial administration when he died in 1926. Lashevich, the lead man in the takeover of October 25, rose to become deputy commissar of war, but was then disgraced and died in an accident in Siberia in 1928.

The fates of the anti-Bolshevik protagonists of 1917 were diverse. Most fled the country between 1918 and 1921—Kerensky, Konovalov, Lvov, Milyukov, and the majority of the provisional cabinet; General Krasnov; most of the moderate socialist leaders—Tsereteli, Dan, Chkheidze, and Martov of the Mensheviks, Avksentiev and Chernov of the SRs, Kamkov of the Left SRs. The Tsar, of course, was executed in 1918. Kornilov was killed in the Civil War. Some Mensheviks and SRs submitted to Soviet rule and remained, only to suffer repeated prosecutions and eventual oblivion during Stalin's purges—the Menshevik Sukhanov, the SR Gotz. Verkhovsky emigrated but returned and became a professor in the Red Army Military Academy. Kishkin and Palchinsky, the defenders of the Winter Palace, also returned to serve under the Soviet regime.

When Lenin fell ill in 1922, the old cleavages and personal rivalries in the Communist leadership opened up again. This time a majority rallied around the bureaucratic cautiousness of Zinoviev and Kamenev, wedded to the pragmatic line of the New Economic Policy. Trotsky tried to challenge them, only to be beaten down in 1923 by the solid party organization that Stalin now directed. One of Trotsky's key men was Antonov, who had become chief political commissar of the Red Army. Thanks to his role in the opposition, he was removed, replaced by Bubnov, and consigned to a series of diplomatic posts (notably the position of Consul General in Barcelona during the Spanish Civil War).

In 1924, shortly after Lenin's death, Trotsky counterattacked and made the history of the revolution a political issue. The 1917 volume of his collected works was being published, and he wrote an introduction to it called "The Lessons of October." The gist of this essay, published also as a separate booklet, was that Soviet Russia was backsliding from the proletarian revolution in both its domestic and foreign policies because it was led by the same men—Zinoviev and Kamenev—who had lost their nerve in October, 1917. Zinoviev and Kamenev, backed by Stalin, Rykov (now chairman of the Council of People's Commissars), and Bukharin (editor of *Pravda*), fired back with denunciations of Trotsky for every conceivable political error throughout his career, and notably his failure to become a Bolshevik until August, 1917. Stalin now toned down his praise of Trotsky's leadership in the revolution: "I am far from denying the undoubtedly important role of Comrade Trotsky in the insurrection. But I must say that Trotsky did not and could not play any special role in the October insurrection, that as chairman of the Petrograd Soviet he was only carrying out the will of the corresponding party authorities that were directing Comrade Trotsky's every step." To make it appear that Trotsky had always been a schismatic opponent of "Leninism," his enemies seized upon the theory of "permanent revolution"—despite its obvious merit in 1917—and made it the cornerstone of their case against Trotsky's alleged heresy. From this point on, the systematic distortion of the history of the Communist Party—before, during, and after the revolution—grew steadily worse, to blacken the memory of every leader who fell afoul of Stalin's ambitions.

In 1925 Zinoviev and Kamenev, followed by Sokolnikov, Lashevich, Smilga and many other "Old Bolsheviks," broke with Stalin and joined Trotsky in opposition. After vainly challenging the party organization in a wide-ranging controversy over the future of the proletarian dictatorship, the opposition leaders were ousted from all their party posts. There was one last protest: on the 7th of November, 1927—the tenth anniversary of the October Revolution—the oppositionists organized demonstrations and speeches in Moscow and Leningrad. These were the last organized public manifestations of opposition in the history of Soviet Russia. The secret police quickly dispersed the demonstrators, and Trotsky, Zinoviev, and Kamenev with all their important followers were forthwith expelled from the Communist Party for committing a "petty bourgeois deviation." Just over a year later, in February, 1929, Trotsky was expelled from the country by the regime he had helped lead to power.

Meanwhile Stalin had turned against his erstwhile allies Bukharin and Rykov, who led the so-called "Right Opposition" in defense of the NEP. To embarrass his opponents, Stalin embarked on a vast new revolution—the collectivization of the peasants and the forced-draft industrialization of the Five-Year Plans. By 1934, despite great cost and cruelties, it seemed that he had succeeded in his program, but the respite of that year was only the calm before a greater storm.

On December 1, 1934, Stalin's popular second-in-command, Sergei Kirov, was assassinated in Leningrad. Suspicion now points to Stalin's hand in the matter, but whether by design or response Stalin took the murder as the occasion to announce sweeping charges of conspiracy against all the politically broken members of the old opposition groups. Thus began the Great Purge. In 1936, in the first of the "Moscow Trials," Zinoviev and Kamenev and a group of their Leningrad friends were convicted of plotting the assassination of the whole Soviet government. They confessed, probably in the hope of a reprieve, but were nonetheless shot. The same fate was met by a group of Trotskyists in 1937. (Radek and Sokolnikov drew prison terms but were never again heard from.) Finally, the Right Opposition, headed by Bukharin and Rykov, was disposed of in the third trial of 1938. Trotsky's own end in 1940, murder by a pickaxe in his Mexican asylum, was almost certainly the work of a Soviet agent. Stalin was literally the gravedigger of the October Revolution. He seemed determined to wipe out physically everyone who represented independent memories of the revolution and the early Soviet years, while he ordered the complete rewriting of Soviet history to make it appear that he himself had always been the chief lieutenant and "comrade in arms" of Lenin.

Even more bizarre was the extension of the purge from the oppositionists into the core of Stalin's most loyal party officials and down through the ranks of the entire Soviet officialdom. Statistically speaking, Stalin was the world's greatest anti-Communist: hundreds of thousands of party members were arrested and shot or tortured to death without trial or even a public announcement. Famous revolutionary records made no difference: all reference to these people was expunged from the newly rewritten history, and their books disappeared from the libraries and bookstores. They became, as George Orwell termed it, "unpersons." This was the fate of Antonov-Ovseyenko, called back from Barcelona and liquidated; of Central Committee members Bubnov, Milyutin, and Smilga; of Shlyapnikov, Nevsky, Lomov, Hanecki, Krylenko, Dybenko, Yurenev and Riazanov. Some, like Podvoisky who died in 1948, survived the purge but were banished from history anyway. Even the archives were purged in places, to destroy records detrimental to Stalin's image. By the 1940's, only ghosts and a few people who had served Stalin unquestioningly— Molotov, Kalinin, Kollontai—were left to populate the pages on the history of the revolution.

The years from the Great Purge to Stalin's death in 1953 were the Dark Age of Soviet history writing, as of every other political and intellectual facet of Soviet life. Then, gingerly at first and much more substantially after Khrushchev's attack on Stalin's record in 1956, the Soviet regime began restoring the old picture of the revolution. In the later 1950's all of Stalin's purge victims, except Trotsky and the people sentenced in the great show trials, were "rehabilitated"—i.e., readmitted to history. Their books were restored to the library shelves and their revolutionary records appeared again in new Soviet publications. Massive documentary publication and extensive archival research by Soviet historians since then have made the new epoch of revolutionary studies especially significant, though the official biases—the Lenin cult and the repudiation of Trotsky and Co.—are still everywhere evident.

The high point, so far, in objective Soviet reflection about 1917 was reached at a conference of historians in Leningrad in 1962. At this meeting and at a follow-up session in Moscow in 1963 the specialists on the history of the October Revolution began to speak like real historians, with serious debates about some of the difficult problems of fact that the revolutionary story presents. A very acute awareness exists in the minds of the historians, steeped as they are in the archives and the old literature, that the history of the revolution—and of the whole Soviet regime—is not altogether as the officially controlled line would still have it.

* * *

Was the October Revolution necessary, not in the sense of historical inevitability, but as a required step to achieve the revolutionaries' program? An affirmative answer to this question is the first principle of Leninism. For the moderate socialists, who shared the theoretical program, the answer was an equally emphatic no. The question itself involves a problematical assumption: did the revolutionary seizure of power in fact achieve the Bolshevik program at all? Actions do not always produce the results intended, and this is particularly true of political violence. What actually happened to the Bolshevik promises of 1917, "All Power to the Soviets," the magic triad "Bread, Land, and Peace," the ideal of "workers' control" and abolition of bureaucracy, self-determination for the peoples of Russia, the doctrine of the dictatorship of the proletariat and international civil war against capitalism? Every one of these points was decreed into law by the Second Congress of Soviets, and together they constituted the program by which the Bolsheviks justified their resistance to a coalition government and their establishment of a one-party dictatorship. But it was not many years before most of the program had been violated by its authors or their heirs.

"All Power to the Soviets" appeared to be a reality on the 26th of October, 1917, but it was mostly power to the Bolsheviks in those soviets. The procedures of parliamentary responsibility—of the cabinet to the Central Executive Committee and of the latter to the Congress of Soviets and the electorate—lasted scarcely six months. By July, 1918, all the parties but the Communists were outlawed, and the locus of decision-making, both centrally and locally, shifted from the soviets to the organization of the Communist Party. Through single-slate elections and Communist Party discipline the whole system of soviets and executive committees was reduced to an administrative and propaganda auxiliary of the party. To this day the official organs of the "Soviet" state are devoid of real power.

The promise of workers' control of industry, the highest hope of the

Bolsheviks' favored constituents, fell by the wayside even sooner than the soviets. Lenin was quick to decide (if he ever had any real illusions on this score) that industry could not be run by untrained committees, and he had no intention of dispensing with the bureaucratic and coercive apparatus of government. Deprived of power in the soviets and in the factories, the Russian proletariat (save for its members who climbed up into the party bureaucracy) found that the triumph of the dictatorship in its name was a very hollow victory.

Peace and the international civil war were intimately linked in Lenin's mind: he waged peace not for its own sake but because he thought the issue would rouse the masses against their governments throughout Europe. When he found himself in power, thanks to the peace issue as much as anything, he had to choose: peace with Germany and the postponement of international revolution or "revolutionary war" by a country in chaos with no army that would fight. Over the agonized cries of many of his most ardent followers, Lenin unhesitatingly chose the former, and concluded the Treaty of Brest-Litovsk with Germany in March, 1918. The priorities were set for good: ever since, international revolution has been subordinated, as an occasional and expendable instrument, to the great-power interests of the Soviet Union.

Self-determination for Russia's national minorities became a quick reality in some cases—Finland, practically independent already and recognized as such by the Soviet government in December, 1917; and Poland and the Baltic provinces, lost under the terms of Brest-Litovsk. Elsewhere—in Belorussia, the Ukraine, the Caucasus—the Communists did not tolerate the dismemberment of the Russian Empire. After the Civil War, in the theoretically federal system of the Soviet Union, they restored the authority of the Russian center.

Bread and land were interdependent by nature, and impossible to deliver simultaneously. Bread symbolized the dislocation and underdevelopment of the whole Russian economy, while the immediate gratification of the peasants' land hunger meant worse shortages in the food delivered to the cities. Russian agriculture was a problem that would tax even the wisest government; it has always been the Soviet regime's greatest difficulty. The first Communist solution was to give the peasant the land, but take the bread from him—the "requisitions" of the

War Communism period. The NEP of 1921–28 left the peasant the land and the free commercial disposal of his bread, while the urban economy barely inched back to the level of tsarism. Stalin found this arrangement a major barrier to the political and economic power that he desired, and forcibly imposed on the whole Russian peasantry the system of collectivized agriculture. The land, as the peasant understood possession of it, was gone as absolutely as it had been under serfdom.

This chronicle of disappointment in the aftermath of revolution is not peculiar to Russia. The high hopes of revolution are always more than offset by the institutionalized violence that revolution begets, and by the subtle return of the hated but deep-seated characteristics of a nation's past. The distinctive thing about the Russian Revolution, compared with the other great revolutions of modern history, was the seizure and consolidation of power by the radical extremists, instead of a counterrevolutionary military or fascistic take-over. It was this unique success of the Left that was responsible for the special appeal of revolutionary Russia as the idealized model both for social renovation in the West and for national regeneration in the East.

The Bolsheviks had a singular role both in Russian and world history, a role they would never have played without the sheer force of Lenin's personality—his determination to seize power no matter what and his unrelenting pressure on the party he had created to make it prepare to seize and hold power in defiance of the historical odds. Lenin could have disappeared from the scene at any one of a number of critical points: he could have been kept out of Russia by a more cautious German policy in April, 1917; he could have been caught crossing the border into Finland in August; he could have been recognized and arrested by the cadet patrol on the night of October 24. There was only one Lenin, and had any one of these contingencies gone the other way, his followers could not have found a substitute.

Nor would they have cared to. Lenin was always ahead of his party, pushing it always into bolder, more violent, more irreversible action than it cared to contemplate. There was an inertia, a mixture of democratic scruple and skin-saving timidity, that caused the party to lag behind whenever Lenin was not physically confronting his lieutenants to commit them to action. (The moderate socialist parties had the same qualities in greater measure and no Lenin to offset them.) In

October the crucial test between the party's inertia and Lenin's drive for power was the question of an insurrection *before* the Congress of Soviets. Had it not occurred, dividing the socialist parties over the issue of violent change, the whole subsequent development of Russian politics could have been different. Here enters the greatest and most ironic contingency of all—Kerensky's desperate decision to attempt what looked like a counter-coup, but instead brought out the Bolsheviks' full forces in a panicky defense, and turned the city of Petrograd into an armed camp surrounding the Winter Palace. By this odd stroke of luck Lenin won what he had been unable to get from his party—a commitment of the revolution to violence that made dictatorship of one sort or another the only alternative.

The spirit of combat embodied in the October Revolution soon permeated most of Russian life; it was heavily reinforced by the grueling experience of the Russian Civil War from 1918 to 1920. All of the noble utopianism that animated Russian society in 1917 soon came to grief between the relentless millstones of grim reality and the Communist determination to hold power at any cost. The manner of the revolution eventually destroyed its spirit.

The drift of Soviet Communism away from the inspiration of the revolution did not, however, prevent it from clinging to the revolutionary story as one of its principal sources of legitimacy. The revolution became and remains in official Soviet history "a revolution opening a new era in human history." The history of the revolution became an official myth, that had to prove and justify certain things—the inevitability of Communist Party rule in Russia; the genius of Lenin without whom the inevitable would never have come about; the iniquity of all Lenin's opponents, Bolshevik as well as non-Bolshevik; the retrospective treacherousness of Lenin's supporters, who later ran afoul of Stalin; the vacillation of Stalin, whose successors could not forego the temptations of rewriting history in turn.

The ironic thing is that none of this revolutionary legend is necessary for the recognition of the substantial achievements of the Soviet regime. These achievements, above all the industrialization of the country and the development of the military potential of a superpower, have little to do with the program of the October Revolution. They were inherent in the resources, human and material, that Russia would have offered to any post-revolutionary government. Little of the actual Soviet future was clear in the minds of the people who made the revolution, only to be devoured by the power they had created. They had forgotten the warning of their number-two prophet, Friedrich Engels, written forty-two years before: "People who boasted that they had made a revolution have always seen the next day that they had no idea what they were doing, that the revolution *made* did not in the least resemble the one they would have liked to make."

ORGANIZATION OF THE BOLSHEVIK PARTY, 1917

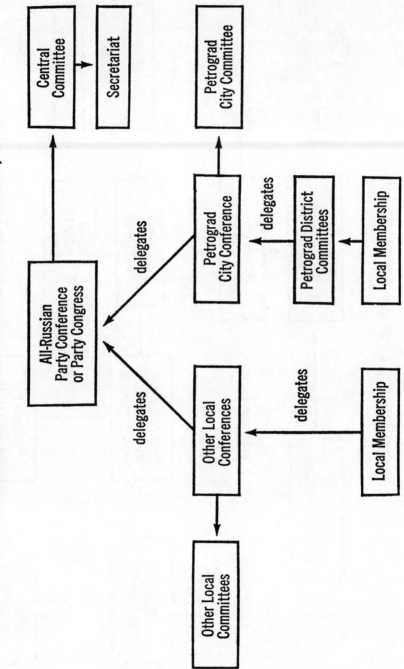

THE SYSTEM OF SOVIETS, 1917

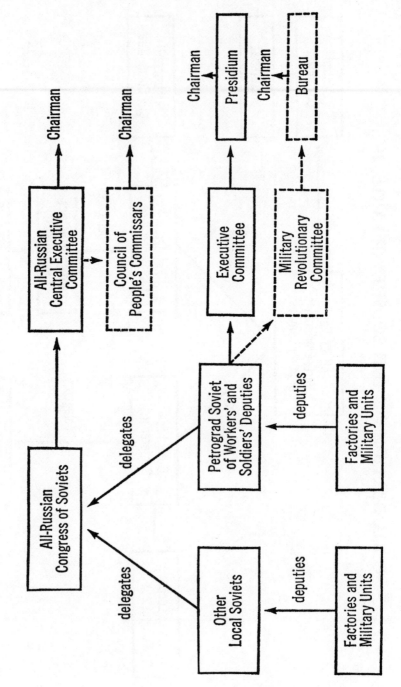

CHRONOLOGY OF EVENTS

Chronology of Events

——OLD STYLE DATES——
(Feb. 27, old style=Mar. 12, new style;
Oct. 25, old style=Nov. 7, new style)

1825–1916

1825	(Dec.)	"Decembrist" uprising; beginning of revolutionary movement
1861	(Feb.)	Emancipation of the peasants by Tsar Alexander II
1870	(Apr.)	Lenin born
1879	(Oct.)	Trotsky born
	(Dec.)	Stalin born
1881	(Mar.)	Assassination of Alexander II by the "People's Will"; Alexander III succeeds to throne
1893	(Sept.)	Lenin joins Marxist circle in St. Petersburg
1894	(Dec.)	Alexander III dies; succeeded by Nikolai II
1895	(Dec.)	Lenin arrested (exiled to Siberia, 1897)
1898	(Mar.)	First Congress of Russian Social Democratic Workers' Party, Minsk
1900	(spring)	Lenin released from Siberia, emigrates to Western Europe
1901		Party of Socialist-Revolutionaries formed
1902	(Mar.)	Lenin publishes *What Is to Be Done?*
1903	(July–Aug.)	Second Congress of RSDWP, Brussels and London; split of Bolsheviks and Mensheviks
1904	(Feb.)	Outbreak of Russo-Japanese War
	(Aug.)	Organizational meeting of Bolshevik faction, Geneva
1905	(Jan.)	Bloody Sunday (beginning of Revolution of 1905)
	(Aug.)	Treaty of Portsmouth ends Russo-Japanese War
	(Oct.)	Constitutional Democratic Party (Kadets) founded
St. Petersburg Soviet and general strike
October Manifesto promises constitution and Duma
	(Dec.)	Moscow uprising; suppression of the Revolution of 1905
1909	(June)	Lenin purges the Bolshevik faction
1912	(Jan.)	Prague Conference: Lenin creates separate Bolshevik Party organization

CHRONOLOGY OF EVENTS

1914 (July–
    Aug.)   Outbreak of World War I; splits in socialist parties
1915 (spring)   Russian defeat in Poland
1916 (Dec.)   Assassination of Rasputin

1917

Feb. 23 (Thurs.)   International Women's Day; demonstrations begin in Petrograd leading to February Revolution
26 (Sun.)   Troops fire on demonstrators; mutiny of garrison begins
27 (Mon.)   Mutiny of the Petrograd garrison and collapse of Tsarist authority
    Formation of Temporary Committee of the Duma
    Formation of Petrograd Soviet
28 (Tue.)   Duma-Soviet negotiations begin
Mar. 1 (Wed.)   Soviet issues "Order Number One" to army
2 (Thurs.)   Provisional Government announced; Prince Lvov Prime Minister
    Evening. Nikolai II abdicates
3 (Fri.)   Grand Duke Mikhail refuses the throne
12 (Sun.)   Stalin and Kamenev reach Petrograd
27 (Mon.—
    April 9,
    new style)   Lenin leaves Switzerland
28 (Tue.)   Bolshevik conference supports national defense
Apr. 3 (Mon.)   Lenin arrives in Petrograd
7 (Fri.)   Lenin's "April Theses" published
15 (Sat.)   Lenin wins majority in Petrograd party conference
18 (Tue.—
    May 1,   May Day
    new style)   Milyukov's note to Allies
20 (Thurs.)   Milyukov note published; April Days demonstrations (Apr. 20 and 21)
24 (Mon.)
to 29 (Sat.)   Bolshevik Party Conference
May 4 (Thurs.)   Trotsky reaches Petrograd
5 (Fri.)   Provisional Government reorganized: first coalition
June 3 (Sat.)   First All-Russian Congress of Soviets opens (to June 24)
8 (Thurs.)   Bolshevik Central Committee votes for armed demonstration on June 10
9 (Fri.)   Bolshevik demonstration called off
18 (Sun.)   Bolsheviks dominate soviet demonstration
    Russian offensive in Galicia
24 (Sat.)   First Congress of Soviets adjourns
July 2 (Sun.)   Kadet ministers resign
3 (Mon.)   "July Days" demonstrations begin (to July 5)
4 (Tue.)   Minister of Justice releases charges that Bolsheviks financed by Germany
5 (Wed.)   Government seizes Bolshevik press; Lenin and Zinoviev go into hiding
6 (Thurs.)   Government seizes Bolshevik headquarters
    German counteroffensive in Galicia

	7 (Fri.)	Arrest of Kamenev, Trotsky, etc.
		Prime Minister Lvov resigns
	8 (Sat.)	Cabinet makes Kerensky Prime Minister
	9 (Sun.)	Lenin and Zinoviev move to Razliv
	18 (Tue.)	Kerensky appoints Kornilov commander in chief
	23 (Sun.)	Kerensky forms second coalition cabinet
	26 (Wed.) to Aug. 3 (Thurs.)	Bolshevik "Sixth" Party Congress
Aug.	9 (Wed.)	Lenin escapes to Finland
	13 (Sun.)	Bolshevik daily paper revived
	21 (Mon.)	Germans occupy Riga
	25 (Fri.) to 30 (Wed.)	Kornilov movement
	31 (Thurs.)	Bolshevik resolution on proletarian-peasant power adopted by Petrograd Soviet
Sept.	1 (Fri.)	Kornilov arrested
		Kerensky forms "Directory"
	1 to 3 (Sun.)	Lenin writes on compromise and peaceful development of revolution (rejects it in postscript of Sept. 3 or 4)
	3 (Sun.)	Central Executive Committee issues call for Democratic Conference. Supported by Bolshevik Central Committee
	4 (Mon.)	Trotsky released from jail
	5 (Tue.)	Bolshevik resolution adopted by Moscow Soviet
	6 (Wed.)	Bolshevik CC discusses preparations for Democratic Conference and Constituent Assembly
	9 (Sat.)	Petrograd Soviet reaffirms Bolshevik vote; Menshevik-SR Executive Committee resigns
		Regional Congress of Soviets opens in Finland with Bolshevik majority
	10 (Sun.)	Bolshevik Petrograd Committee approves participation in Democratic Conference
	12 to 14 (Thurs.)	Lenin writes to Bolshevik CC to call for seizure of power
	14 (Thurs.) to 22 (Fri.)	Democratic Conference
	15 (Fri.)	Bolshevik CC postpones action on Lenin's call for uprising
	17 (Sun.)	Lenin moves from Helsingfors to Vyborg, Finland
	18 (Mon.)	Bolshevik declaration to Democratic Conference warns of danger of counterrevolution
	19 (Tue.)	Democratic Conference decides to convoke a Council of the Republic or "Pre-Parliament"; votes for government without Kadets
		Moscow Workers' Soviet elects a Bolshevik Executive Committee with Nogin as chairman
	20 (Wed.)	Trotsky says Congress of Soviets must decide transfer of power
		Bolshevik CC sets party congress for Oct. 17 (called off Oct. 5)
	21 (Thurs.)	Petrograd Soviet resolves against Democratic Conference and in favor of immediate Congress of Soviets to settle the question of power

Sept. 21 (Thurs.)   Bolshevik CC compromises decisions: (1) not to walk out of Democratic Conference, and (2) to confer with Bolshevik delegation of Democratic Conference, about participating in the Pre-Parliament

Bolshevik Conference decides to participate in Pre-Parliament

22 (Fri.)   Lenin calls for boycott of Pre-Parliament

Democratic Conference closes

23 (Sat.)   Zinoviev resumes participation in Bolshevik CC; CC selects delegation to Pre-Parliament (headed by Trotsky). Delegation issues call for a revolutionary power.

CEC convokes Second Congress of Soviets for Oct. 20

24 (Sun.)   Bolshevik CC and Party Conference urge campaign for transfer of power to soviets

25 (Mon.)   Kerensky forms third coalition cabinet

Petrograd Soviet elects new Executive Committee with Trotsky chairman; condemns Third Coalition as counterrevolutionary

27 (Wed.)   Lenin writes to Smilga on need to take power without waiting for Congress of Soviets

29 (Fri.)   Bolshevik CC plans for elections

Lenin writes article on "treason" of waiting for Congress of Soviets, threatens to resign from CC

Oct. 3 (Tue.)   Bolshevik CC decides to ask Lenin to move back to Petrograd

4 (Wed.)   Provisional Government secretly discusses moving capital to Moscow

5 (Thurs.)   Bolshevik CC reschedules Congress of Soviets of the Northern Region, to be held in Petrograd Oct. 10; decides Bolsheviks should walk out of Pre-Parliament on opening day; calls Party Conference for Oct. 10; calls off Party Congress

Bolshevik Petrograd Committee debates armed uprising

6 (Fri.)   Soldiers' Section of Petrograd Soviet passes Trotsky's resolution protesting plan to move capital

7 (Sat.)   Third Petrograd Bolshevik City Conference opens. Lenin sends letter on plot to surrender Petrograd to Germans, and need to seize power before Congress of Soviets.

Bolshevik delegation to Pre-Parliament, by a narrow margin, accepts Trotsky's call for a walkout

5 P.M. Pre-Parliament opens. Trotsky reads declaration on bourgeois danger to revolution, and Bolsheviks walk out.

Evening. Lenin returns from Vyborg, Finland, to Petrograd hideout on Serdobolskaya Street.

8 (Sun.)   Rodzianko's speech on possibility of surrendering Petrograd published

Lenin writes letters on insurrection as an "art" and on need to start international revolution

9 (Mon.)   Petrograd Headquarters orders part of garrison to move to front

Executive Committee of Petrograd Soviet argues over liaison with Headquarters, adopts Menshevik resolution to organize a "committee of Revolutionary Defense"

Petrograd Soviet (plenary session) rejects the EC resolution and adopts Bolshevik resolution to form the Committee of Defense and arm the workers. Lazimir made chairman of committee to prepare proposal.

10 (Tue.)	Petrograd Bolshevik City Conference calls for a "workers' and peasants' revolutionary government"
10 to 11	Night. Bolshevik CC with Lenin (instead of Party Conference), in Sukhanov's apartment. Lenin argues for seizure of power. CC votes 10 to 2 to "place the armed uprising on the agenda."
[11 to 15	No preserved writings by Lenin]
11 (Wed.)	Zinoviev and Kamenev issue handwritten declaration against seizure of power
	Petrograd Bolshevik Conference hears Lenin's letter of Oct. 7 read; adjourns
	Leaders of the Soldiers' Section of the Petrograd Soviet endorse plan of defense committee and propose a garrison conference
	Congress of Soviets of the Northern Region opens (to Oct. 13); Trotsky calls for transfer of power to soviets, to save Petrograd and the revolution
12 (Thurs.)	Conservative papers report Bolshevik "move" expected on Oct. 20 when Congress of Soviets convenes
	"Congress of Public Men" hints at rightist move
	Kerensky denies plan to evacuate Petrograd
	Conference of district soviets of Petrograd—schedules "Day of the Petrograd Soviet" for Sunday, Oct. 22
	Congress of Soviets of the Northern Region passes resolution calling for transfer of power to soviets, to save the nation
	Executive Committee of Petrograd Soviet votes to set up "Military Revolutionary Committee" to plan defense, and "Department of the Workers' Guard"
13 (Fri.)	Cabinet discusses steps to prevent expected Bolshevik "move"
	Pre-Parliament protests idea of moving the capital; Kerensky denies plan
	Soldiers' Section of Petrograd Soviet sets up a Department of the Workers' Guard, to organize a headquarters and to call a city-wide conference of the Guard later in October
	Congress of Soviets of the Northern Region closes; issues appeal to see that the Congress of Soviets on Oct. 20 not be disrupted
14 (Sat.)	Kadet Party Congress
	Cabinet argues defense plans and release of jailed Bolsheviks; Kerensky leaves for GHQ at Mogilev (returns to Petrograd Oct. 17)
	Central Executive Committee of Soviets debates expected Bolshevik "move"
	Moscow Bolshevik Regional Bureau votes to endorse uprising
15 (Sun.)	All newspapers discuss Bolshevik "move"
	Conference of Bolshevik Petrograd Committee and ward representatives hears doubts about popular readiness for uprising
	Garrison Commander Col. Polkovnikov forbids troops to participate in "irresponsible demonstrations" (repeated each day following)
	Cabinet gets word that Bolsheviks will "move" on the 19th, not the 20th. (Some Oct. 17 papers reported move was coming that evening.)

Oct. 16 (Mon.)	Petrograd Soviet decides to send only observers to conference in Pskov called by General Cheremisov, Commander in Chief of Northern Front; hears Lazimir's report on Military Revolutionary Committee, and approves the idea
	Government starts to deploy troops to meet Bolshevik "move" expected on Oct. 19 or 20. Vice-Premier Konovalov phones Kerensky, who says he will return "if" the "move" begins.
Night of 16–17	Bolshevik CC meets in the Lesnoye district hall. Lenin calls for insurrection. Committee debates readiness, evades setting a date; by vote of 19 to 2 with 4 abstentions, confirms resolution of Oct. 10 and calls for preparation of uprising; selects a "Military-Revolutionary Center" to participate in the projected Military Revolutionary Committee. Kamenev offers to resign from CC in protest.
17 (Tue.)	Gorky's newspaper reports on the Zinoviev declaration against the "move"
	Central Executive Committee postpones Second Congress of Soviets from Oct. 20 to Oct. 25
	First All-Russian Conference of Factory Committees opens (to Oct. 22)
	Conference of the Northern Front in Pskov; Petrograd delegation insists soviet approve troop movements, walks out
	Lenin writes "Letter to Comrades" denouncing Zinoviev and Kamenev
	Evening. Kerensky returns to Petrograd from GHQ, expresses hope Bolsheviks will move
	Evening. Conference of the Bolshevik Petrograd Committee and Military Organization debates insurrection
	Late evening. Leaders of Bolshevik Military Organization (Antonov, Podvoisky, Nevsky) visit Lenin, discuss preparations for uprising. Lenin calls for insurrection before Congress of Soviets; Podvoisky asks for more time.
18 (Wed.)	Note by Kamenev against the uprising published in Gorky's paper
	Lenin sends letter to CC denouncing Zinoviev and Kamenev for "strikebreaking"
	Garrison conference begins sessions, expresses loyalty to soviet, against government
	In Petrograd Soviet, Trotsky questioned about Zinoviev-Kamenev statement; he denies intention of insurrection but threatens counterattack to protect Congress of Soviets
	Bolshevik leaders meet Lenin; Trotsky explains his disavowal of insurrection; they appoint organizational bureau of Military Revolutionary Committee
Night of 18–19	Government plans defense against Bolshevik move
19 (Thurs.)	Bolshevik paper publishes first installment of Lenin's attack on Zinoviev and Kamenev
	Kerensky again expresses readiness to smash Bolsheviks as soon as they move
	Lenin writes to CC to demand expulsion of Kamenev and Zinoviev from party, and to uphold Trotsky's position of Oct. 18.

20 (Fri.)   Bolshevik paper publishes second installment of Lenin's attack, and Zinoviev's rejoinder

Conference of Red Guard opens (to Oct. 23)

Bolshevik CC debates Kamenev-Zinoviev affair (Trotsky vs. Stalin); accepts Kamenev's resignation; decides that Bolshevik military work should be done through Military Revolutionary Committee

First session of Military Revolutionary Committee; report by its organizing bureau

Lenin writes an article on peasants; no preserved writings from this until evening of Oct. 24 (except one note)

Evening. War Minister Verkhovsky demands immediate peace; suspended by cabinet

21 (Sat.)   Bolshevik paper publishes third installment of Lenin's attack on Zinoviev and Kamenev

Bolshevik CC discusses problems of running the Petrograd Soviet and the Congress of Soviets (no further recorded meeting until Oct. 24)

Garrison conference approves creation of the Military Revolutionary Committee and calls on Congress of Soviets to take power

Polkovnikov, fearing a provocation, calls off Cossack parade scheduled for the "Day of the Soviet," the 22nd

Evening. Military Revolutionary Committee sets up a "Bureau" with Lazimir as chairman, Podvoisky as deputy chairman, and Antonov as secretary; begins to appoint commissars to military units. Lazimir leads delegation to Petrograd HQ; Polkovnikov refuses them the right to check on his moves.

22 (Sun.)   Early morning. Military Revolutionary Committee discusses HQ refusal. Special garrison conference called; issues appeal to the troops voiding orders not countersigned by the MRC.

Kerensky instructs Petrograd Chief of Staff General Bagratuni to give the soviet an ultimatum to retract its appeal to the troops; government calls loyal troops from the front

HQ calls conference of garrison representatives; they affirm that orders must be approved by the MRC, and walk out

"Day of the Petrograd Soviet"—demonstrations and speeches; Trotsky speaks on soviet power

MRC debates how to take the Peter-Paul fortress (Antonov vs. Trotsky)

Conference of Petrograd Red Guards

Night of 22–23   Government discusses MRC; Kerensky wants to liquidate it but others call for negotiations and defensive measures; decide to allow more soviet representatives at HQ. HQ invites MRC to send representatives.

22 or 23   Lenin writes to Sverdlov to complain of not being informed of action regarding Zinoviev and Kamenev

23 (Mon.)   Trotsky gets the Peter-Paul fortress to follow MRC

MRC sends representatives to HQ; HQ agrees to accept commissars from Soldiers' Section of the Soviet, but without right to countermand orders. Representatives report back to MRC; MRC makes no reply.

General Cheremisov confers with Kerensky

Oct. 23 (Mon.)   6 P.M. Garrison conference asserts readiness to implement decisions of the Congress of Soviets

Late evening. Antonov reports to session of Petrograd Soviet that MRC has allegiance of the garrison; Trotsky concedes that MRC is "political headquarters for the seizure of power"

General Bagratuni sends ultimatum to MRC to withdraw the Appeal of Oct. 22

Night of   Kerensky decides to arrest MRC and close Bolshevik
23–24   newspapers

24 (Tue.)   3 A.M. MRC accepts HQ ultimatum. Kerensky rejects this as delaying action. HQ begins to call troops from suburbs into Petrograd and orders MRC commissars ousted from all military units.

Early morning. MRC proclamation warns of impending Kornilovite plot against the Congress of Soviets

5:30 A.M. Officer cadets occupy Bolshevik newspaper plant and smash the plates

Morning. MRC sends troops to reopen the newspapers; issues proclamations to warn of Kornilovite offensive, to call for battle readiness, and summon a new meeting of garrison representatives in Smolny; also to bar entry to city by anti-Soviet units. Further preparations to defend Smolny. Bolshevik CC discusses measures of defense, break of relations with Central Executive Committee, assignment of members for liaison, auxiliary headquarters if Smolny falls.

11 A.M. MRC notifies all units to be ready for orders. Bolshevik papers resume publication.

12:30 P.M. Kerensky addresses Pre-Parliament to justify his attack on the Bolsheviks; proclaims state of insurrection and demands extraordinary powers

2 P.M. Meeting of Bolshevik delegates to Congress of Soviets

About 2:30 P.M. HQ orders drawbridges lifted. Cadets raise some, prevented at others.

3 P.M. Smolny phones and electricity cut off

Afternoon. City Council negotiates with MRC; Trotsky threatens counterattack if government moves before Congress of Soviets; Trotsky tells Kronstadt to send men next morning

5 P.M. MRC commissar takes over telegraph office

6 P.M. Pre-Parliament reconvenes, votes to censure Provisional Government

About 6–7 P.M. Lenin hears bridges raised; sends phone message to Smolny requesting permission to come; they refuse; he writes letter to CC to denounce delaying uprising to Oct. 25

7 P.M. Petrograd Soviet hears Trotsky report on plan for Congress of Soviets to assume power

8 P.M. MRC wires to Helsingfors for ships and men to be sent

Evening. MRC denies it is preparing uprising, but only defending Congress of Soviets

Aurora ordered to close Nikolaevsky Bridge

9–10 P.M. MRC commissars take over news wire service and Baltic Station

10 P.M. Cadets attempt to close Bolshevik editorial office

About 10:30 P.M. Lenin leaves for Smolny by streetcar and on foot, arrives around midnight

24 (Tue.) Late evening. Socialist leaders argue with Kerensky over averting uprising; Kerensky threatens to resign

25 (Wed.) **Midnight–1 A.M. Cabinet meeting receives reports on MRC take-overs**
Midnight–4 A.M. Last session of old CEC protests uprising
After 1 A.M. Kerensky transfers command from Polkovnikov to Bagratuni. Officials arrested by Pavlov Regiment.
1–2 A.M. Units of Kexholm Regiment take over telephone exchange, Post Office, railroad stations
3:30 A.M. *Aurora* anchors at Nikolaevsky Bridge; bridge closed
Early morning. Cossacks refuse to defend government
About 9 A.M. Ships finally sail from Helsingfors
After 9 A.M. Lenin writes proclamation declaring Provisional Government overthrown (issued at 10 A.M.); decision to attack the Winter Palace
About 11 A.M. MRC forms "troika" to direct attack on Winter Palace
About 11:30 A.M. Kerensky leaves Petrograd by car to get troops from the front. Cabinet meets in Winter Palace, decides to stay until relieved or captured; appoints Kishkin "Governor-General."
Noon. Pre-Parliament convenes for last time; dispersed by Bolshevik forces
2:35 P.M. Meeting of Petrograd Soviet to endorse uprising; first public appearance of Lenin and Zinoviev since July
About 6:50 P.M. Ultimatum from Peter-Paul fortress delivered to government HQ; cabinet decides to ignore it. Chief of Staff Dukhonin wires that movement of relief troops is being blocked. Appointment of Kishkin reported to General Cheremisov.
About 7:30 P.M. Artillery leaves Winter Palace and is captured. Soviet troops capture HQ building.
About 8 P.M. Chudnovsky mission to Palace to try to negotiate surrender
8–9 P.M. Cossacks and some cadets quit the Palace
About 9 P.M. Kerensky reaches Pskov, clashes with General Cheremisov over dispatch of troops
9:40–10 P.M. Artillery fire on Palace by *Aurora* (blanks) and Peter-Paul fortress
About 10 P.M. Delegation from City Duma prevented from going to Palace
After 10 P.M. Women's battalion surrenders. Bolshevik forces begin to infiltrate Palace.
10:45 P.M. Second Congress of Soviets opened; Kamenev elected chairman; Martov resolution on all-socialist government passed; anti-Bolsheviks walk out
About 11 P.M. Attack on Winter Palace resumed
About midnight. Bolshevik forces rush main entrance of Palace; Antonov enters to look for cabinet

26 (Thurs.) 2:10 A.M. Cabinet, headed by Vice-Premier Konovalov, arrested
About 3 A.M. Congress of Soviets resolves to take power. Recesses at 5 A.M.
Morning. Kerensky and Krasnov start towards Petrograd with Cossacks

Oct. 26 (Thurs.)   Midday. Bolshevik CC plans new cabinet. Left SRs decline to joint it.

11 P.M. Congress of Soviets reconvenes, ratifies Lenin's decrees and Council of People's Commissars (Lenin chairman, Trotsky Commissar of Foreign Affairs)

27 (Fri.)   2 A.M. Lenin assumes command of defense; Congress of Soviets adjourns

Dawn. Kerensky and Cossacks reach Gatchina

Committee for the Salvation of the Country and the Revolution plans uprising

28 (Sat.)   Morning. Anti-Bolshevik attack in Moscow; Kremlin surrenders

Cossacks take Tsarskoe Selo

29 (Sun.)   Early morning. Cadet uprising in Petrograd, put down by soviet troops and Red Guards

Vikzhel convenes conference to negotiate a coalition government; Bolshevik CC votes to participate

Evening. Twenty-four-hour truce in Moscow

30 (Mon.)   Battle of Pulkovo: Cossacks repulsed, Kerensky abandons campaign

Bolsheviks gain as fighting resumed in Moscow

Nov. 1 (Wed.)   Armistice with Cossacks at Gatchina; Kerensky goes into hiding

Bolshevik CC hears Lenin and Trotsky attack negotiations on coalition

2 (Thurs.)   Moscow Bolsheviks take Kremlin; end of anti-Bolshevik resistance

CEC votes Bolshevik terms for coalition; Bolshevik CC condemns conciliationists

4 (Sat.)   Conciliationists resign from Bolshevik CC and Council of People's Commissars

7 (Tue.)   Zinoviev gives in to Lenin

12 (Sun.)   Election of Constituent Assembly (SRs lead, Bolsheviks second)

20 (Mon.)   Bolsheviks take over GHQ in Mogilev; General Dukhonin killed

Nov.–Dec.   Left SRs join coalition government

1918

1918 (Jan.)   Constituent Assembly convened and dissolved

——NEW STYLE DATES——

1918–1956

1918 (Mar.)   Treaty of Brest-Litovsk; Left SRs quit Council of People's Commissars

(May)   Civil War begins

(July)   Left SR uprising; all non-Bolshevik parties outlawed; terror begins

1919 (Mar.)   Death of Sverdlov (replaced as titular chief of state by Kalinin)

Communist International founded

1921 (Mar.)   Beginning of New Economic Policy

1922	(Apr.)	Stalin made General Secretary of the Communist Party
	(May)	Beginning of Lenin's illness
1923	(Dec.)	Beginning of Trotskyist opposition
1924	(Jan.)	Death of Lenin
	(Oct.)	Trotsky denounced for "Lessons of October"; political manipulation of the history of the revolution begins
1925	(fall)	Zinoviev and Kamenev break with Stalin
1927	(Dec.)	Expulsion of Trotsky-Zinoviev-Kamenev opposition from the Communist Party
1928	(summer)	Beginning of Stalin's struggle with the Right opposition; end of the NEP
1934	(Dec.)	Assassination of Kirov
1936	(Aug.)	Trial of Zinoviev, Kamenev, et al.
1937	(Jan.)	Trial of Radek, Sokolnikov, et al.
1938	(Mar.)	Trial of Bukharin, Rykov, et al.
1940	(Aug.)	Trotsky assassinated
1953	(Mar.)	Death of Stalin
1956	(Feb.)	Twentieth Party Congress; "de-Stalinization" and rehabilitation of purge victims

Sources

The nature of the materials available for the study of the October Revolution makes the subject a difficult one. On the one hand there is an abundance of raw material—the newspapers, memoirs, and published documents—so much so that it is almost impossible for one author to take account of the whole mass. On the other hand, there is a serious lack of detailed and objective historical studies of the various aspects of the revolution, although there are a number of good general histories of the year 1917. The best Soviet work on the revolution was done in the 1920's and after 1956; it is better on the collection of documents and the description of special topics than on overall accounts of the revolution, which are severely limited by doctrinal preconceptions. (In citing Russian publications in the Bibliography I have used the Library of Congress system of transliteration.)

Still the best general history of the Russian Revolution, after thirty years, is

William Henry Chamberlin, *The Russian Revolution* (2 vols., New York: Macmillan, 1935)

On the October Revolution itself, one book stands out:

S. P. Melgunov, *Kak bol'sheviki zakhvatili vlast'* (How the Bolsheviks Seized Power, Paris: Editions La Renaissance, 1953)

Other important general books and articles on the revolution, the Bolshevik Party, or its leaders which I have found useful at various points in this book include the following:

David Anin, "The Failure of the February Revolution," *Soviet Studies*, April, 1967
Oskar Anweiler, *Die Rätebewegung in Russland, 1905–1921* (Leiden: Brill, 1958)
S. I. Avvakumov et al., eds., *Oktiabr'skoe vooruzhennoe vosstanie v Petrograde:*

SOURCES

Sbornik statei (The October Armed Uprising in Petrograd: A Collection of Articles, Moscow: Academy of Sciences, 1957)

James Billington, "Six Views of the Russian Revolution," *World Politics,* April, 1966.

Pierre Broué, *Le Parti bolcheviste* (Paris: Editions de Minuit, 1963)

Edward Hallett Carr, *The Bolshevik Revolution* (3 vols., London: Macmillan, 1950–1953)

G. D. H. Cole, *A History of Socialist Thought:* Vol. IV, *Communism and Social Democracy* (London: Macmillan, 1953–1954)

Robert V. Daniels, *The Conscience of the Revolution: Communist Opposition in Soviet Russia* (Cambridge: Harvard Univ. Press, 1960)

"Deiateli oktiabr'skoi revoliutsii" (Active People of the October Revolution), *Entsiklopedicheskii Slovar'* (Encyclopedic Dictionary, Moscow and Leningrad: Granat, supplement to vol. 41, parts 1–3, 1925–1928)

Isaac Deutscher, *The Prophet Armed: Trotsky, 1879–1921* (London: Oxford, 1954)

Marc Ferro, *La Révolution de 1917: La chute du tsarisme et les origines d'octobre* (Paris: Aubier, 1967)

L. S. Gaponenko, *Velikaia oktiabr'skaia sotsialisticheskaia revoliutsiia—istoricheskii ocherk* (The Great October Socialist Revolution—an Historical Sketch, Moscow: Academy of Sciences, 1957)

G. N. Golikov, *Ocherk istorii velikoi oktiabr'skoi sotsialisticheskoi revoliutsii* (Sketch of the History of the Great October Socialist Revolution, Moscow: State Press for Political Literature, 1959)

G. N. Golikov et al., eds., *Velikaia Oktiabr'skaia Sotsialisticheskaia Revoliutsiia: Khronika Sobytii* (The Great October Socialist Revolution: Chronicle of Events, 4 vols., Moscow: Academy of Sciences, 1957–1961)

Maxim Gorky et al., eds., *History of the Civil War* (Moscow: Foreign Languages Publishing House, 1938); also 1947 Russian ed., *Istoriia grazhdanskoi voiny* (Moscow: State Press for Political Literature)

Gorod Velikogo Lenina (The City of the Great Lenin, Leningrad: State Press, 1957)

Georges Haupt and Jean-Jacques Marie, *Les Bolcheviks par eux-mêmes: Les Autobiographies des dirigeants de la revolution d'octobre* (Paris: Maspero, 1967)

A. P. Konstantinov, ed., *Bol'sheviki Petrograda v 1917 gody: Khronika Sobytii* (The Bolsheviks of Petrograd in 1917: Chronicle of Events, Leningrad: Leningrad Press, 1957)

Sofia M. Levidova, *Ot fevralia k oktiabriu—po pamiatnym mestam revoliutsionnykh sobytii 1917 goda v Petrograde* (From February to October—the Memorable Places of the Revolutionary Events of 1917 in Petrograd, Leningrad: Leningrad Press, 1957)

I. I. Mints et al., eds., *Lenin i Oktiabr'skoe Vooruzhennoe Vosstanie v Petrograde: Materialy Vsesoyuznoi Nauchnoi Sessii, sostoiavsheisia 13–16 noiabria 1962 g. v Leningrade* (Lenin and the October Armed Uprising in Petrograd: Materials of the All-Union Scientific Session Held in Leningrad November 13–16, 1962, Moscow: Science Press, 1964)

P. Nikitin et al., *Po Leninskim mestam v Leningrade* (Places where Lenin was in Leningrad, Leningrad: Soviet Artist Press, 1964)

Jean-Paul Ollivier, *Quand fera-t-il jour, camarade? Historie de la révolution d'octobre* (Paris: Robert Laffont, 1967)

S. A. Piontkovsky, *Oktiabr'skaia Revoliutsiia v Rossii—predposylki i khod* (The October Revolution in Russia—its Background and Course, Moscow: State Press, 1924)

248

A. A. Popov, *Oktiabr'skii perevorot—fakty i dokumenty* (The October Coup—Facts and Documents, Petrograd: New Epoch Press, 1918)

Oliver Radkey, *The Agrarian Foes of Bolshevism: Promise and Default of the Russian Socialist Revolutionaries, February to October, 1917* (New York: Columbia Univ. Press, 1958)

Oliver Radkey, *The Sickle under the Hammer: The Russian Socialist Revolutionaries in the Early Months of Soviet Rule* (New York: Columbia Univ. Press, 1963)

Edward A. Ross, *The Russian Bolshevik Revolution* (New York: Century, 1921)

Leonard Schapiro, *The Origins of the Communist Autocracy: Political Opposition in the Soviet State—First Phase, 1917–1922* (London: London School of Economics and Political Science, 1955)

David Shub, *Lenin: a Biography* (Garden City, New York: Doubleday, 1951)

P. N. Sobolev et al., *History of the October Revolution* (Moscow: Progress Publishers, 1966)

Adam B. Ulam, *The Bolsheviks: The Intellectual and Political History of the Triumph of Communism in Russia* (New York: Macmillan, 1965)

Gerard Walter, *Lenine* (Paris: Julliard, 1950)

T. M. Zelenov et al., *Lenin v 1917 g.: Daty zhizni i deiatelnosti* (Lenin in 1917: Dates of his Life and Activity, Moscow: State Press for Political Literature, 1957)

To date the strongest side of the work on the October Revolution, both Soviet and Western, is the publication of documents and memoirs. There are a number of valuable collections of translated materials:

Robert P. Browder and Alexander F. Kerensky, eds., *The Russian Provisional Government, 1917: Documents* (3 vols., Stanford, Calif.: Stanford Univ. Press, 1961)

James Bunyan and H. H. Fisher, eds., *The Bolshevik Revolution, 1917–1918* (Stanford, Calif.: Stanford Univ. Press, 1934)

Gilbert Comte, *La Révolution russe vue par ses témoins* (Paris: La Table Ronde, 1963)

Frank A. Golder, *Documents of Russian History* (New York: Century, 1927)

Manfred Helmann, ed., *Die russische Revolution 1917* (Munich: Deutscher Taschenbuch Verlag, 1964)

Richard Kohn, *La Révolution russe* (Paris: Julliard, 1963)

Serge Oldenbourg, *Le Coup d'état bolcheviste* (Paris: Payot, 1929)

Roger Pethybridge, *Witnesses of the Russian Revolution* (London: Allen & Unwin, 1964)

The documents and memoirs published under Soviet aegis have been sifted with some care, particularly since the 1930's, and access to the Soviet archives on this subject is highly restricted. I was personally shown only a few documents in the Museum of the Revolution in Leningrad; in the Central State Archive of the October Revolution and Soviet Construction in Moscow I saw only the microfilms of the just-published documents of the Military Revolutionary Committee. The most important Soviet papers on the revolution appear to be in the Central Party Archive, which is altogether closed to non-Communist foreigners. It is necessary therefore to rely heavily though carefully on Soviet publications of archive material and on monographs that cite unpublished material.

An indispensable Soviet collection of documents is

G. N. Golikov et al., eds., *Oktiabr'skoe vooruzhennoe vosstanie v Petrograde* (The October Armed Uprising in Petrograd, Moscow: Academy of Sciences, 1957)

Other Soviet documentary publications that I have used repeatedly are

D. A. Chugaev et al., eds., *Petrogradskii voenno-revoliutsionnyi komitet: dokumenty i materialy* (The Petrograd Military Revolutionary Committee: Documents and Materials, 3 vols., Moscow: Science Press, 1966)

A. K. Drezen, ed., *Bolshevizatsiia petrogradskogo garnizona* (The Bolshevization of the Petrograd Garrison, Leningrad: Leningrad Province Press, 1932)

I. I. Mints, ed., *Dokumenty velikoi proletarskoi revoliutsii* (Documents of the Great Proletarian Revolution, Moscow: State Press, 1938)

Pervyi legal'nyi peterburgskii komitet Bol'shevikov (The First Legal Petersburg Committee of the Bolsheviks, Moscow-Leningrad: Bureau of Party History, 1927)

Protokoly Tsentral'nogo Komiteta RSDRP(b), August 1917–Fevral' 1918 (The Minutes of the Central Committee of the RSDWP (B), Aug. 1917–Feb. 1918, Moscow: State Press for Political Literature, 1958)

Along with the basic documents should be included the collected works of the Bolshevik leaders. Of Lenin's collected works, the third Soviet edition is the most reliable and best annotated:

Lenin, *Sochineniia* (Works, 30 vols., Moscow: Marx-Engels-Lenin Institute, 1928–1937)

Volumes 20 and 21 on 1917 were translated into English:

Lenin, *The Revolution of 1917* and *Towards the Seizure of Power* (New York: International Publishers, 1932)

A very few additional items by Lenin from the revolutionary period are contained in:

Lenin, *Polnoe sobranie sochinenii* (Complete Collected Works, vol. 34, Moscow: Institute of Marxism-Leninism, 1962)

Leninskii sbornik (The Lenin Collection, vol. 36, Moscow: Institute of Marxism-Leninism, 1959)

Collections of the 1917 writings of other Bolshevik leaders are

N. I. Bukharin, *Na podstupakh k oktiabre* (On the Approaches to October, Moscow: State Press, 1926)

J. V. Stalin, *Na putiakh k oktiabriu* (On the Way to October, Moscow: State Press, 1925)

L. D. Trotsky, *Sochineniia* (Works, vol. III, Moscow: State Press, 1924)

G. I. Zinoviev, *Sochineniia* (Works, vol. VII, Moscow: State Press, 1925)

The bulk of the available memoir literature on the revolution, both Communist and non-Communist, was published in the 1920's. It is indispensable for a detailed picture of the events, which were often documented in no other way. However, memoir accounts are always limited by errors of observation, recollection, and conjecture, and particularly on this subject they must be critically checked against each other and against other forms of documentation.

The two richest repositories of memoirs on the revolution are the Soviet journals

Krasnaia Letopis' (The Red Chronicle, Leningrad, 1922–1936, especially number 6, 1923; hereafter cited as KL)

Proletar'skaia Revoliutsiia (The Proletarian Revolution, Moscow, 1920–1932, especially number 10, 1922; hereafter cited as PR)

The greatest memoir of the revolution is

N. N. Sukhanov, *Zapiski o revoliutsii* (Notes on the Revolution, 6 vols., Berlin and Petrograd: Grizhebin, 1922–23), translated into English in an abridged edition by Joel Carmichael as *The Russian Revolution, 1917: A Personal Record* (London: Oxford, 1955)

Justly famous for its drama, if not always for its accuracy, is

John Reed, *Ten Days that Shook the World* (New York: Boni and Liveright, 1919)

Two participant histories that should be regarded as memoirs are

Pavel Miliukov, *Istoriia vtoroi russkoi revoliutsii* (History of the Second Russian Revolution, Sofia: Russian-Bulgarian Press, 1921)

Leon Trotsky, *History of the Russian Revolution* (3 vols., New York: Simon and Schuster, 1932–1933)

Other useful works by Trotsky are

Leon Trotsky, *Lenin* (New York: Blue Ribbon Books, 1925)

Leon Trotsky, *My Life: An Attempt at an Autobiography* (New York: Scribner's, 1931)

Leon Trotsky, *Oktiabr'skaia revoliutsiia* (The October Revolution, Moscow: "Kommunist," 1918)

Leon Trotsky, *Stalin: An Appraisal of the Man and his Influence* (New York: Harper, 1946)

Alexander Kerensky has published a series of memoirs, partially overlapping; the most important is

A. F. Kerensky, *The Catastrophe* (New York: Appleton, 1927; includes an abridged translation of his *Izdaleka* [From Afar], Paris: Povolotsky, 1922)

Some additional material is contained in

A. F. Kerensky, *The Crucifixion of Liberty* (London: Barker, 1934)

A. F. Kerensky, *Russia and History's Turning Point* (New York: Duell, Sloan and Pearce, 1965)

SOURCES

Other important first-hand accounts by non-Soviet authors are

Claude Anet, *La Révolution russe* (Paris: Payot, 1918)

Louise Bryant (Mrs. John Reed), *Six Red Months in Russia* (London: Heinemann, 1918)

Sir George Buchanan, *My Mission to Russia* (London: Cassel, 1923)

David R. Francis, *Russia from the American Embassy* (New York: Scribner's, 1922)

Joseph Noulens, *Mon ambassade en Russie sovietique* (Paris: Plon, 1933)

Phillips Price, *My Reminiscences of the Russian Revolution* (London: Allen and Unwyn, 1921)

Jacques Sadoul, *Notes sur la révolution* (Paris: Editions de la Sirène, 1919)

I. Shteinberg, *Ot fevralia po oktiabriu 1917* (From February to October, 1917, Berlin: Skify, 1922)

V. B. Stankevich, *Vospominaniia 1914–1919 gg.* (Recollections of 1914–1919, Berlin: Ladyzhnikov, 1920)

Albert Rhys Williams, *Through the Russian Revolution* (New York: Boni and Liveright, 1921)

Apart from Trotsky's works listed above, the two most important Soviet memoirs are

V. A. Antonov-Ovseenko, *V semnadtsatom godu* (In 1917, Moscow: State Press, 1933)

N. I. Podvoisky, *Krasnaia gvardiia v oktiabr'skie dni* (The Red Guard in the October Days, Moscow: State Press, 1927)

A more recent version of Podvoisky's account is, like many Soviet publications, heavily edited and unreliable:

N. I. Podvoisky, *God 1917* (The Year 1917, Moscow: State Press for Political Literature, 1958)

To a lesser degree this is true of

V. A. Antonov-Ovseenko, *V revoliutsii* (In the Revolution, Moscow: State Press for Political Literature, 1957)

There are innumerable Soviet editions of collected extracts (more or less edited) of the memoirs of the leading participants in the revolution. I have used in particular:

Velikaia Oktiabr'skaia Sotsialisticheskaia Revoliutsiia: Sbornik vospominanii uchastnikov revoliutsii v Petrograde i Moskve (The Great October Socialist Revolution: A Collection of Recollections of Participants of the Revolution in Petrograd and Moscow, Moscow: State Press for Political Literature, 1957)

Vospominaniia o V. I. Lenin (Recollections of V. I. Lenin, 3 vols., Moscow: State Press, 1956–60)

Other Soviet memoir accounts which I have used repeatedly include

G. I. Blagonravov, "Oktiabr'skie dni v petropavlovskoi kreposti" (The October Days in the Peter-Paul Fortress), PR, no. 4, 1922

B. Elov, "Rol' petrogradskogo garnizona v oktiabr'skie dni" (The Role of the Petrograd Garrison in the October Days), KL, no. 6, 1923

M. V. Fofanova, "Poslednee podpol'e V. I. Lenina" (V. I. Lenin's Last Underground), *Istoricheskii Arkhiv*, no. 4, 1956

V. Kaiurov, "Moi vstrechi i rabota s V. I. Leninym: v gody revoliutsii (1917–1921 gg.)" (My meetings and work with V. I. Lenin in the years of the Revolution, 1917–1921), PR, no. 3, 1924

V. Kaiurov, "Oktiabr'skie ocherki" (October Sketches), PR, no. 7, 1925

N. I. Krupskaya, *Vospominaniia o Lenine* (Recollections of Lenin, 2 vols., Moscow: Party Press, 1932)

M. I. Latsis, "Nakanune oktiabr'skikh dnei" (On the Eve of the October Days), *Izvestiia*, Nov. 6, 1918

G. I. Lomov, "V dniakh bur'i i natiski" (In the Days of Storm and Stress), *Izvestiia*, Nov. 6, 1918

N. I. Podvoisky, "Kak proizoshla oktiabr'skaia revoliutsiia" (How the October Revolution Originated), *Izvestiia*, Nov. 6, 1918

N. I. Podvoisky, "Voennaia organizatsiia TsK-RSDRP(b) i voenno-revoliutsionnyi komitet 1917 g." (The Military Organization of the CC of the RSDWP(B) and the Military Revolutionary Committee in 1917), KL, nos. 6 and 8, 1923

E. Rakhia, "Poslednoe podpol'e V. I. Lenina" (The Last Underground of V. I. Lenin), KL, no. 1, 1934

Alexander Shliapnikov, "K oktiabriu" (Towards October), PR, no. 10, 1922

A. V. Shotman, *Kak iz iskry vozgorelos plamia* (How the Flame Sprang up from the Spark, Leningrad: Young Guard Press, 1935)

N. Sveshnikov, "Iz epokhi oktiabria 1917 g." (From the Epoch of October, 1917), KL, no. 6, 1923

"Vospominaniia ob oktiabr'skom perevorote" (Recollections of the October Coup), PR, no. 10, 1922 (contributions by P. A. Kozmin, L. D. Trotsky, Kozlovsky, V. D. Bonch-Bruevich, A. Sadovsky, and N. I. Podvoisky)

SOURCES

The following is a list of other works directly utilized, chapter by chapter.

CHAPTER ONE

F. Drabkina, "Priezd tov. Lenina" (The Arrival of Comrade Lenin), PR, no. 4, 1927
George Katkov, *Russia, 1917: the February Revolution* (London: Longmans, 1967)
I. S. Lukash, *Pavlovtsy* (The Pavlov Men, Petrograd: Temporary Committee of the Duma, 1917)
F. F. Raskolnikov, "Zasedanie pervogo legalnogo Peka" (The Session of the First Legal Petrograd Committee), PR, no. 8, 1922
Alexander Shliapnikov, *Semnadtsadtyi God* (The Year 1917, Moscow: State Press, 1927)

CHAPTER TWO

Robert V. Daniels, "Intellectuals and the Russian Revolution," *The American Slavic and East European Review*, Apr., 1961
Robert V. Daniels, "Lenin and the Russian Revolutionary Tradition," *Harvard Slavic Studies*, IV (1957)
Leopold Haimson, *The Russian Marxists and the Origins of Bolshevism* (Cambridge: Harvard Univ. Press, 1955)
J. L. H. Keep, *The Rise of Social Democracy in Russia* (Oxford: Clarendon, 1964)
"The March, 1917, Party Conference," in Leon Trotsky, *The Stalin School of Falsification* (New York: Pioneer, 1937)
Alfred Meyer, *Leninism* (Cambridge: Harvard Univ. Press, 1957)
Shliapnikov, *op. cit.*
Leon Trotsky, *Our Revolution* (New York: Holt, 1918)
Bertram Wolfe, *Three Who Made a Revolution* (New York: Dial Press, 1948)
I. Yurenev, "Mezhraionka, 1911–1917" (The Interdistrict Committee), PR, nos. 1–2, 1924

CHAPTER THREE

F. Drabkina, *loc. cit.*
Merle Fainsod, *International Socialism and the World War* (Cambridge: Harvard Univ. Press, 1935)
Michael Futrell, *Northern Underground* (London: Faber and Faber, 1963)
George Kennan, "The Sisson Documents," *Journal of Modern History*, June, 1956
Richard Lorenz, "Zur Industriepolitik der Provisorischen Regierung," *Jahrbücher für Geschichte Osteuropas*, Sept., 1966

W. E. Odom, "Sverdlov—Bolshevik Party Organizer," *Slavonic and East European Review*, July, 1966

M. N. Pokrovsky, ed., *Ocherki po istorii oktiabr'skoi revoliutsii* (Essays on the History of the October Revolution, Moscow: Bureau of Party History, 1926)

Stefan Possony, *Lenin: The Compulsive Revolutionary* (Chicago: Regnery, 1964)

F. F. Raskolnikov, "Priezd tov. Lenina v Rossiyu" (Comrade Lenin's Arrival in Russia), PR, no. 1, 1923

F. F. Raskolnikov, "V tiur'me Kerenskogo" (In Kerensky's Prison), PR, no. 10, 1923

RSDWP(B), *Sedmaia (Aprel'skaia) Konferentsiia: Protokoly* (The Seventh [April] Conference: Minutes, Moscow: Marx-Engels-Lenin Institute, 1934)

RSDWP(B), *Shestoi Sezd: Protokoly* (The Sixth Congress: Minutes, Moscow: Marx-Engels-Lenin Institute, 1934)

A. V. Shotman, "Tov. Lenin v podpol'i" (Comrad Lenin in the Underground), *Pravda*, Nov. 6–7, 1921

V. V. Vladimirova, *Revoliutsiia 1917 g.: Khronika sobytii* (The Revolution of 1917: Chronicle of Events, vol. 3, Moscow: Bureau of Party History, 1923)

Z. A. B. Zeman, *Germany and the Revolution in Russia* (London: Oxford Univ. Press, 1958)

CHAPTER FOUR

Fyodor Dan, "K istorii poslednikh dnei Vremennogo Pravitel'stva" (On the History of the Last Days of the Provisional Government), *Letopis Revoliutsii*, vol. 1, 1923

"Iz rechi tov. Bukharina na vechere vospominanii v 1921 g." (From the Speech of Comrade Bukharin at an Evening of Reminiscences in 1921), PR, no. 10, 1922

A. S. Smirnov, "Ob otnoshenii bolshevikov k levym eseram v period podgotovki oktiabr'skoi revoliutsii" (On the Relation of the Bolsheviks to the Left SRs in the Period of the Preparation of the October Revolution), *Voprosy Istorii KPSS*, no. 2, 1966

CHAPTER FIVE

M. V. Fofanova, "O date vozvrashcheniia V. I. Lenina iz Finliandii v Petrograd v 1917 g." (On the Date of V. I. Lenin's Return from Finland to Petrograd in 1917), *Istoricheskii Arkhiv*, no. 2, 1958

CHAPTER SIX

M. V. Fofanova, "Iz vospominanii 1917 g." (From Recollections of 1917), *Pravda*, Jan. 22, 1928

SOURCES

V. Maksakov, "Moskovskoe oblastnoe biuro pered oktiabr'skimi dniami" (The Moscow Regional Bureau Before the October Days), PR, no. 10, 1922

V. I. Nevsky, "Dve vstrechi" (Two Meetings), KL, no. 4, 1922

V. I. Nevsky, "Istoricheskoe zasedanie petrogradskogo komiteta RSDRP(b) nakanune oktiabr'skogo vosstaniia" (An Historic Session of the Petrograd Committee of the RSDWP(B) on the Eve of the October Uprising), KL, nos. 2–3, 1922

"O voennoi deiatelnosti V. I. Lenina—iz vospominanii N. I. Podvoiskogo" (On the Military Activity of V. I. Lenin—from the Recollections of N. I. Podvoisky), *Kommunist*, no. 1, 1957

S. Poles'ev, "Odin ugolok Leningrada" (One Little Corner of Leningrad), *Leningradskaia Pravda*, Oct. 19, 1966

CHAPTER SEVEN

R. R. Abramovich, *The Soviet Revolution, 1917–1939* (New York: International Universities Press, 1962)

I. G. Dykov, "Petrogradskii voenno-revoliutsionnyi komitet" (The Petrograd Military Revolutionary Committee), *Voprosy Istorii*, no. 7, 1957

M. M. Lashevich, "Oktiabr'skie dni v Petrograde (vospominaniia)" (The October Days in Petrograd—Recollections), *Politrabotnik Sibiri*, no. 11, 1922

K. A. Mekhanoshin, "K vospominaniiam tov. Trotskogo" (On the Recollections of Comrade Trotsky), PR, no. 10, 1922

I. A. Peskovoi, "Nakanune oktiabr'skogo perevorota" (On the Eve of the October Coup), KL, no. 6, 1923

S. Poles'ev, *loc. cit.*

V. I. Startsev, *Ocherki po istorii petrogradskoi krasnoi gvardii i rabochei militsii* (Essays on the History of the Petrograd Red Guard and Workers' Militia, Moscow: Science Press, 1965)

CHAPTER EIGHT

Dan, *loc. cit.*

O. Dzenis, "Kak my brali 25 oktiabria Zimnii Dvorets" (How We Took the Winter Palace on October 25), *Pravda*, Nov. 6–7, 1921

E. F. Erykalov, "Osveshchenie oktiabr'skogo vooruzhennogo vosstaniia v Petrograde v istoriko-partiinoi literature 1956–1966 gg." (The Illumination of the October Armed Uprising in Petrograd in the Literature on the History of the Party, 1956–1966), *Voprosy Istorii KPSS*, no. 5, 1966

I. P. Flerovsky, "Kronshtadt v oktiabr'skoi revoliutsii" (Kronstadt in the October Revolution), PR, no. 10, 1922

G. N. Golikov, "Oktiabr'skoe Vooruzhennoe Vosstaniye v Petrograde" (The October Armed Uprising in Petrograd), *Istoriia SSSR*, no. 4, 1957

E. N. Gorodetsky, "Iz istorii oktiabr'skogo vooruzhennogo vosstaniia" (From the History of the October Armed Uprising), *Voprosy Istorii*, no. 10, 1957

A. Ignat'ev, "V noch' na 25 oktiabria 1917 g." (On the Night of October 25, 1917), KL, no. 6, 1923

A. Kelzon, "Padenie Vremenogo Pravitel'stva" (The Fall of the Provisional Government), *Byloe*, no. 6, 1925

"Knizhnik" [pseud.], "Oktiabr'skaya Revoliutsiia v dome pisatelei" (The October Revolution at the House of Writers), KL, no. 6, 1923

Lashevich, *loc. cit.*

P. I. Palchinsky, notes, in M. Levin, "Poslednie chasy Vremennogo Pravitel'-stva v 1917 g." (The Last Hours of the Provisional Government in 1917), *Krasnyi Arkhiv*, no. 56, 1933

S. Pestkovsky, "Ob oktiabr'skikh dniakh v Pitere" (On the October Days in "Peter"), PR, no. 10, 1922

"Petrograd 24–25 oktiabria 1917 g. Khronika dvukh dnei" (Petrograd on the 24–25 of October, 1917: A Chronicle of Two Days), *Novyi Mir*, no. 11, 1957

A. Zakharov, "Iz dnei oktiabria" (From the Days of October), KL, nos. 5–6, 1931

M. Zhakov, Letter to Vasilchenko, Oct. 25, 1917, PR, no. 10, 1922

Archive of the Museum of the Revolution, Leningrad

CHAPTER NINE

K. Akashev, "Kak ushla artilleriia iz Zimnego Dvortsa" (How the Artillery Left the Winter Palace), *Byloe*, nos. 27–28, 1925

V. A. Antonov-Ovseenko, "Oktiabr'skaia Buria" (The October Storm), *Izvestiia*, Nov. 6, 1922

V. A. Antonov-Ovseenko, "Vziatie Zimnego dvortsa" (The Capture of the Winter Palace), PR, no. 10, 1922

Arsenev, "Iz vospominanii uchastnika oktiabr'skikh dnei v Petrograde" (From the Recollections of a Participant of the October Days in Petrograd), PR, no. 10, 1922

J. W. Bienstock, *La Révolution russe, le coup d'état et le regime maximaliste* (Paris: Bureau de l'Action Nationale, 1918)

V. D. Bonch-Bruevich, "Ot iiulia k oktiabrie" (From July to October), PR, no. 10, 1922

F. I. Chaliapin, *Maska i Dusha* (The Mask and the Soul, Paris: *Sovremennye Zapiski*, 1932)

G. I. Chudnovsky, "O vziatii zimnego dvortsa" (On the Capture of the Winter Palace), *Istoricheskii Arkhiv*, no. 56, 1933

Dzenis, *loc. cit.*

A. A. Ioffe, "V noch' na 25 oktiabria" (On the Night of October 24), *Krasnoarmeets*, no. 78, Nov. 1925

George Kennan, *Russia Leaves the War* (Princeton: Princeton Univ. Press, 1956)

"Knizhnik," *loc. cit.*

A. V. Liverovsky, "Poslednie chasy Vremennogo Pravitelstva" (The Last Hours of the Provisional Government), *Istoricheskii Arkhiv*, no. 6, 1960

A. V. Lunacharsky, "7-oi noiabria–neskol'ko vospominaniia ob oktiabr'skoi revoliutsii" (The 7th of November—Some Recollections of the October Revolution), *Ogonek*, no. 46, 1924

P. N. Maliantovich, "V zimnem dvortse 25–26 oktiabria 1917 g." (In the Winter Palace, October 25–26, 1917), *Byloe*, no. 12, 1918

Palchinsky, *loc. cit.*

"Petrograd on the 24–25 of October," 1917, *loc. cit*

Alexander Sinegub, "Zashchita Zimnego dvortsa" (The Defense of the Winter Palace), *Archiv Russkoi Revoliutssi*, vol. IV, 1922

V. I. Startsev, "Begstvo Kerenskogo" (The Flight of Kerensky), *Vechernyi Leningrad*, Oct. 12, 1966

"Stavka 25–26 oktiabria 1917 g." (Headquarters on October 25–26, 1917), *Arkhiv Russkoi Revoliutsii*, vol. 7, 1922

S. Uralov, "Stranichka Oktiabria" (A Little Page of October), PR, no. 10, 1924

CHAPTER TEN

V. D. Bonch-Bruevich, *Vospominaniia o Lenine* (Recollections of Lenin, Moscow: Science Press, 1965)

CHAPTER ELEVEN

Robert V. Daniels, "Soviet Historians Prepare for the Fiftieth," *The Slavic Review*, March 1967

Martin Dewhurst, "L'Historiographie sovietique recente et l'histoire de la révolution, *Cahiers du monde russe et sovietique*, Oct.-Dec. 1964

G. N. Golikov, "K izucheniyu istorii velikogo oktiabria" (On the Study of the History of Great October), *Voprosy Istorii*, no. 11, 1962

Leon Trotsky, *The Lessons of October* (New York: Pioneer, 1937)

INDEX

Index

ILLUSTRATION ACKNOWLEDGMENTS

Bettmann Archive: 46, 49, 56

Brown Brothers: 5, 13, 18, 22, 28, 54

Robert V. Daniels: 19, 36, 38

Keystone Press: 2, 15, 30, 34, 43

Radio Times Hulton Picture Library: 3, 23, 44, 48, 52

Sovfoto: 1, 10 (Novosti), 16, 20, 21 (Novosti), 24 (Tass), 25 (Tass), 27 (Tass), 29 (Novosti), 33 (Tass), 35, 37, 40 (Tass), 42, 45, 47 (Soviet Life), 55

UPI Photos: 4, 7, 8, 9, 14, 17, 31, 32, 39, 41, 50, 51, 57

Roger Viollet: 6, 11, 12, 26, 53

1. Winter Palace
2. Palace Square & Alexander Column
3. General Staff
4. District Headquarters
5. Hermitage
6. Admiralty
7. Ministry of War
8. Marinsky Palace
9. City Duma
10. Engineer School
11. Pavlov Barracks
12. Bolshevik Military Organization
13. Bolshevik Secretariat, Fall 1917
14. Bolshevik Printing Plant
15. Telephone Exchange
16. State Bank
17. Mikhailov Riding Hall
18. Central Post Office
19. News Wire Service
20. Central Telegraph Office
21. Kexholm Barracks
22. Baltic Crew Barracks
23. Technological Institute (Soviet of 1905)
24. Menshikov Palace (First Congress of Soviets)
25. Location of *Aurora*, Oct. 25
26. Ksheshinskaya Mansion
27. Circus Modern
28. Sukhanov's Apartment (Bolshevik Central Committee, Oct. 10)
29. Bolshevik Editorial Office
30. Mikhailovsky Artillery School
31. Site of Sixth Party Congress
32. Vyborg District Bolshevik Headquarters
33. Fofanova's Apartment (Lenin's Hideout)
34. Lesnoye-Udelnaya District Council
35. Pavlov Military School
36. Vladimir Military School
37. Arsenal
38. Peter-Paul Fortress
39. Finland Station
40. University
41. Tauride Palace
42. Smolny Institute
43. Litovsky Barracks
44. Nikolaevsky (Moscow) Station
45. Vitebsk Station
46. Franco-Russian Shipyard
47. Baltic Station
48. Warsaw Station
49. Putilov Factory

VASILEV

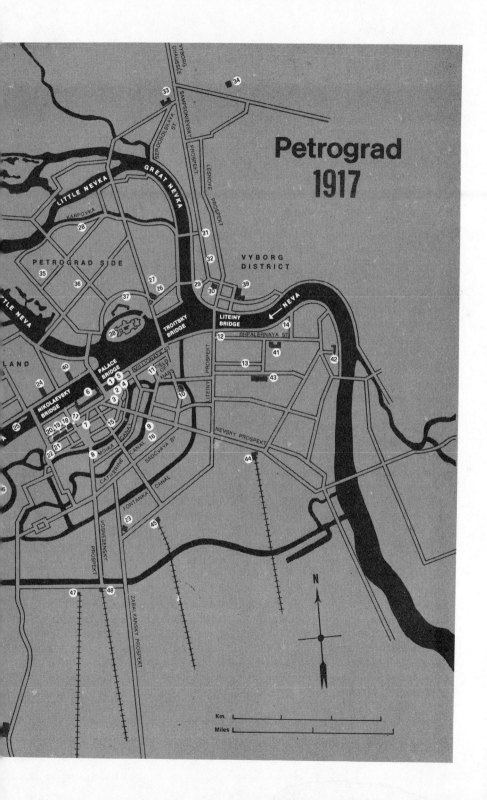